№ 89

ARMS AND THE WOMAN

BORIS UXKULL 1793–1870

BORIS UXKULL

Arms and the Woman

The Intimate Journal of a Baltic
Nobleman in the Napoleonic Wars

WITH HISTORICAL NOTES, FOREWORD

AND EPILOGUE BY DETLEV VON UEXKÜLL

TRANSLATED BY JOEL CARMICHAEL

THE MACMILLAN COMPANY, NEW YORK

First published in England 1966 by
Martin Secker & Warburg Limited
14 Carlisle Street, Soho Square, W.1

Copyright © 1965 by Rowohlt Verlag GmbH
Reinbek bei Hamburg

English translation copyright © 1966 by
Martin Secker & Warburg Limited and
The Macmillan Company, New York

Library of Congress Catalog Card Number: 66–26093

The Macmillan Company, New York
Collier-Macmillan Canada Ltd., Toronto, Ontario

Printed in the United States of America

CONTENTS

PLATES

MAPS AND SKETCHES

FOREWORD

THE MILITARY diary of my great-great-great-uncle, Baron Berend-Johann (called Boris) Uxkull, is one of the very few constituents of the Uexküll* family archives that have survived the turmoil of the wars and revolutions of the past sixty years. It is a book bound in grey cardboard, bearing the title *Journal militaire et stratégique des années 1812, 1813, 1814, 1815*, and is written in German, French, and Russian.

Neither the military diary nor the other writings of Boris Uxkull, such as his travel diary of 1818–1819, were ever destined for any "reading circle" other than the writer himself and perhaps some of his intimate friends. Since Boris's death in 1870, they had rested well preserved in the family archives of Fickel Castle in Estonia; very few members of the family had any notion of their existence. During the revolution of 1905 Fickel Castle went up in flames; the bulk of the library was consumed. Of Boris Uxkull's writings only the military diary, his travel diaries, and many original letters were salvaged. My father, Berend (1879–1963), brought the writings of his great-great-uncle from Fickel to Germany, and finally from occupied Berlin to Hamburg. He translated the French and Russian parts, but hesitated a long time before giving these extremely private notes of his ancestor to the public. Shortly before his death he decided to do so in the conviction that, uncoloured by any official historiography and

---

* The various ways of spelling the family name "Uexküll" are attempts to give a phonetically accurate reproduction of the old Livonian place-name "Üxküll", on the Dvina, in a number of languages: Uexküll (German), Uxkull (French), Yxkull (Swedish). The original name of the family was "von Bardewies". The change to "von Uexküll" came about after a von Bardewies was invested with the Üxküll castle and locality by the Bishop of Riga around the year 1300. The Baron used the French spelling in his journals.

written directly from the point of view of someone concerned, they shed light on the political and military events of the period. They simply report how a young Russian officer of German origin lived through some years of the Napoleonic War and what took place on the periphery of that war.

Boris was born on 7 August 1793 at Fickel Castle. He was the eldest of six brothers and three sisters. His father, Berend-Johann, master of the entailed estate of Fickel, was appointed Russian Councillor and Senator and for a time was Governor of Estonia. The Order of Knights of German Noblemen in Estonia twice elected him Captain of Knighthood. His mother, Elizabeth, Countess Sievers, was the daughter of Jakob-Johann Count Sievers, a statesman decorated with high honours by Empress Catherine the Great.

While still in the cradle Boris received as a "godfather's gift" from his maternal grandfather the title of Polish Royal Court Councillor. He attended St. Peter's School in St. Petersburg, and in 1809, at the age of sixteen, he entered the Imperial Russian Cavalry Guards Regiment (*Garde à Cheval*) as an ensign. He took part in seventeen battles, was decorated eleven times, and in the space of three years (1812–1815) was promoted to captain. In 1819, at the age of twenty-six, he left the army. His years of study took him to Heidelberg, Göttingen, Tübingen, Berlin, Paris, and Munich, where he was in contact with important philosophers such as Hegel, Friedrich von Schelling, and Franz Xaver von Baader. He made numerous trips, visiting Italy, Spain, England, Greece, and Turkey.

In Estonia he followed his father's example and attended to the needs of the peasants of the Fickel estate in a manner that for his time was exemplary. He translated songs and chorales into Estonian for school use and established at Fickel the first old people's homes and clinics in Estonia. He died at Fickel Castle, at the age of seventy-seven.

In his book *Niegeschaute Welten* (Worlds Never Seen), the biologist Jakob von Uexküll writes as follows about his great-uncle Boris:

Boris's life was full of romantic adventures, and since he had great musical gifts he succeeded in turning many women's heads. This Don Juan was engaged twelve times, until his thirteenth fiancée forced him to marry her. [This was the twenty-two-year-old minister's daughter, Klara Walter, who married Boris when he was fifty years old. They had no children.]

Boris entered the Masonic Order and soon became a Lodge Master. As such he had the impudence to have himself accepted into the Jesuit College in Rome. When suspicion was aroused and this situation became dangerous, he fled to Ancona. As a Lutheran and a Mason he was in those days not qualified to enter a Jesuit college. He managed to escape aboard a ship sailing for Greece, but on the ship he found a man who seemed suspect. He invited him into his cabin, set a purse and a pistol on the table in front of him, and asked him to make his choice. The stranger chose the money, disembarked at the next harbour, and abandoned the pursuit.

Jakob von Uexküll goes on to relate:

Now and again the events of [Boris's] previous life played a part in his marriage too. At a visit to St. Peter's in Rome the married couple had sat down on a bench where a heavily veiled lady, completely dressed in black, was already sitting. The unknown woman, who was in deep meditation, looked up fleetingly and with a cry fell swooning to the ground. My aunt helped her into the sacristy, where she gradually came to herself. When asked what had occasioned her sudden fright the unknown woman answered, still quivering, "I saw a ghost next to you!" "By no means," replied my aunt, "that was my husband."

"What—he's really still alive? Oh, how happy I am that I no longer have a murder on my conscience!" And now the stranger told her story, of being a Greek from Constantinople who had made Boris's acquaintance in her youth and become engaged to him. But she had soon observed that he was on the trail of her younger sister. Inflamed by jealousy, she had set a poisoned dish before him at breakfast one day and then had left the city. She had later heard that he had been brought to a hospital very ill, and had died there.

My uncle had indeed been close to death. When he recovered

he spread the news of his own death in order to avoid any further difficulties.

This adventurer who led such a tumultuous life was at the same time filled with intellectual interests. Earlier than others he had recognized the importance of the young Hegel; he became one of his early pupils, and, indeed, all his life remained a zealous champion of his great teacher. Hegel's flight of thought enabled Boris to give his adventurous universe a loftier note; he attempted to give the course of his life some justification by linking it to the most exalted problems.

Was the life of this Baltic nobleman typical of his class and age? Yes and no. Not typical were his restlessness, his love of travel and adventure, his wavering between religious and philosophical meditations, and his unbridled, sybaritic joy in living. Typical, on the other hand, were his fidelity to the Russian tsar and his love of homeland, especially Estonia, but also the great Russian Empire. Typical, too, were his European style of living and his lively interest in every innovation in science and literature. Whatever important books appeared in London, Weimar, or Berlin came with only a slight delay to the Baltic estates, to St. Petersburg, and to Moscow to be read and discussed. At this time the Russian upper classes were cosmopolitan and European, and in these upper classes the Germans from the Baltic played a leading role socially, politically—in some ministries there were more Germans than Russians—and militarily. The officers' corps, too, up to and including commanding generals, had a strong German imprint.

Boris was eighteen years old when he went to war against Napoleon. His diary begins on 30 March 1812, or, on Russian reckoning, 17 March. All of his entries retain the dates according to the Russian (Julian) calendar which, in the nineteenth century, was twelve days behind the Western European (Gregorian) calendar.

Hamburg, July 1965   DETLEV UEXKÜLL

PART ONE

ARMS:

*The Napoleonic War
1812–1815*

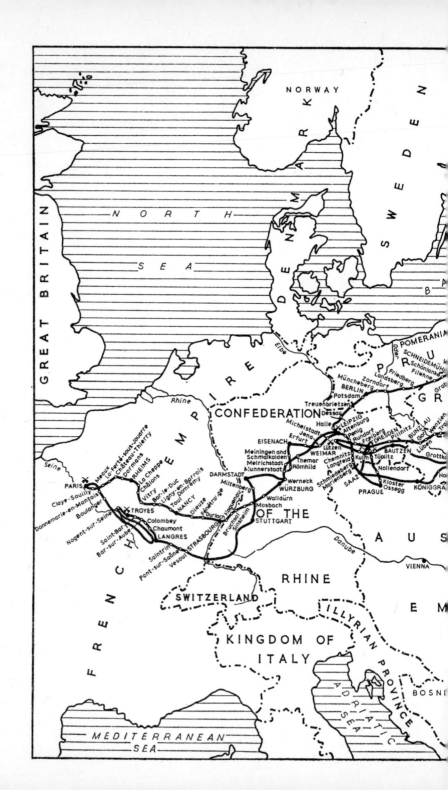

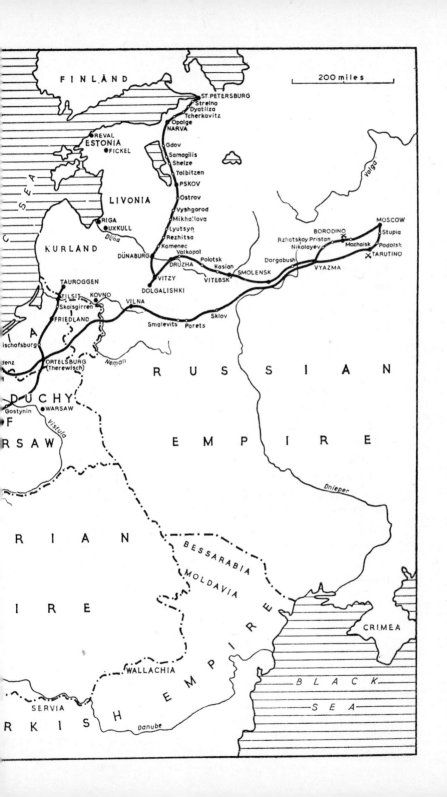

A NOTE ON THE TEXT

The Foreword, Epilogue, Introductions to Chapters and other connective material were added by Dr. Detlev von Uexküll, a descendant of Baron Boris Uxkull, to fill in pertinent personal and historical background. With the exception of the Foreword and the Epilogue, all added material has been set in different type.

The section dealing with the Napoleonic War—*Arms*—was translated from the original diary, written mostly in French and German. The original of the second section—*and the Woman*—was lost along with many of the letters of Boris Uxkull at the end of the war in 1945. However, this diary—written mostly in German—had been accurately transcribed some years earlier by Berend von Uexküll, the father of Dr. Detlev von Uexküll, and it is this manuscript from which the translator worked. In addition to French and German, some portions of the diaries were written in Russian, and Mr. Carmichael's translation was made from these three languages.

Chapter I

BETWEEN PEACE AND WAR

On 24 February 1812, the King of Prussia and the Emperor of France concluded an alliance that "also touched on the undertakings against Russia". It guaranteed reciprocal holdings and strengthened the blockade against England. Free passage was accorded the French and Allied troops, and the King of Prussia was obligated to participate in the undertaking against Russia with a contingent of 14,000 infantry troops, 4,000 cavalry troops, 2,000 artillery troops, and 60 cannon. In the event of a happy outcome in the war against Russia, Prussia was to be compensated with land.

On 24 March Russia and Sweden concluded an alliance in St. Petersburg, in which Sweden "was assured that Norway would shortly be given it", and was to respond with a promise of 30,000 men in the struggle against Napoleon.

On 25 March an alliance between Austria and France was ratified in Vienna. Both powers mutually guaranteed the integrity of their holdings and renewed the prohibition of any trade with England. Austria bound itself to maintain 30,000 men and an artillery pool of 60 cannon in a state of complete preparedness for war. If the war against Russia turned out well, Austria's territory was to be enlarged.

On 27 March (15 March in the Julian calendar) the setting up of a reserve army was announced in St. Petersburg.

17 March, Strelna

Our regiment, after being passed in review by the Tsar, left St. Petersburg at noon; it was nine o'clock by the time we arrived here. A great many people from the city were present when we left, and a big crowd on foot and in carriages accompanied our troops. The farewells of so many soldiers to their families were quite merry in one way, but very sad in another. I was delighted to leave St. Petersburg. In brilliant colours my imagination traced out the future camp life waiting for me on the fields of honour in the far-off countries I was burning to explore. I regretted only the loss of the company of Mademoiselle W., who had become so dear to me and so interesting in so many ways.

After arriving in Strelna, we rushed off, some other officers and I, to the inn for dinner, since we were rather fatigued from the march and needed proper restoration. We spent the evening chatting and making plans for the future. Now, for the first time, we were going to sleep on straw in barns.

18 March, Dyatliza, a village near Kypeni

In Robsha, which we passed through, we had a splendid breakfast. The march was rather fatiguing and we did not arrive here until five o'clock. A good dinner was waiting for us, spiced by my comrades' sallies. Afterwards I had nothing better to do than consign myself to the care of Morpheus, protector of the soldier and of the human race, especially those whose good conscience has made them worthy of his benevolence.

19 March, Tcherkovitz

I was sleeping this morning like a king; suddenly I heard the sound of a trumpet and the horses whinnying, and saw my servant Fyodor approaching my modest bed. He had not dared awaken me, but seeing that I was awake he tried to read in my eyes whether he was disturbing me. I got up; in an instant my broadsword was buckled to and my prancing horse was stamping his hoofs impatiently on the shaky steps of my hut. I swung myself upon him and a military fury took hold of me; I vowed I would conduct a good fight one day and never leave the cavalry.

So here I am again in the midst of my comrades, playing and jesting; I have nothing to confide to my Diary except that I sometimes think with regret of Mlle W., that I live only for the future, and that the present has but little of interest to offer me.

20 March, Opolge

It's unbelievably cold. I've done nothing but run about on foot. The Grand Duke* has joined us here.

21 March, Narva

I have been refused a fortnight's leave. I've just lost 400 rubles. Saw the cataract of the Narva River. Magnificent! I've never seen anything so beautiful.

22 March

A day of rest. I've been ordered ahead to requisition fodder for the regiment. A fine assignment—I don't know the first thing about it.

23 March, Gdov

Here I am, finally arrived, stiff with cold, soaked to the marrow, and cursing the innkeepers and postilions who understand nothing but blows or money. After handing out a number of blows with the flat of my sword, after paying through the nose, shouting a lot, eating little, I've received as the reward for my pains lodgings worthy of being inhabited by those animals so despised by the sect of the Arabian Prophet.

Here I am, shut up in a filthy room so small I can scarcely take three or four steps in it and filled with those infernal insects that are such a torment to their victims. On top of it all my landlady had nothing to satisfy my appetite but a little milk and some eggs that I snatched up with such greed that I think it must have thrown into a fright all the hens of St. Petersburg Province.

24 March

My sweet Akulina amuses me with her good nature and her chatter; we get along very well—as though we had

* Constantine, commanding officer of the regiment (Ed.).

known each other for two years. I had a fine day today. My amiable rustic nymph from Gdof came over and sat down in a most friendly way on my knees; I regarded her with a blissful face; her own was radiant too. You have to learn to amuse yourself wherever and whenever you can, I said to myself. I asked her to describe the best of her wedding days; the description interested me a great deal, and the conversation grew so ardent that I was scarcely aware of the entrance of my servant, who seemed to be holding back a smile. It was really comical to see my Akulina abruptly leave her place, and I myself come back from the heights to the depths.

By degrees I lost myself in philosophical syllogisms that made me forget both my hostess and our amusements. All is vanity in the world! I cried. Scarcely does a man touch pleasure when it is suddenly snatched away from him. Imagination, that lovely faculty of our soul sung of so well by Delibes, made a few bold leaps; then I returned to my chilly philosophy. I thought of my youth and of my present condition. What changes I saw in my person! The past unfolded before my eyes. I thought of my happy childhood, when I gazed at all things with laughing eyes, when imagination took pleasure in adding an inexpressible charm to every little event that interested me. But now! What a difference! To be sure, my soul and my character have not taken on a sombre and melancholy tint; yet sometimes I feel a despondency, an indifference towards everything surrounding me; this gives me pain. There are moments when my heart feels free and I would like to embrace the whole world; when my imagination is sweetly agitated and I create a new world. But these moments are fleeting and vanish like melting snow, which disappears at the approach of the warming rays of a springtime sun. But a truce to these romantic notions.

25 March

I've just seen my dear [brother] Jacques again. What joy,

what satisfaction to see again the people dear to us! He's going back from leave to rejoin his regiment; he's leaving right now. I've just finished my business. The regiment is leaving tomorrow.

26 March, morning

Jacques and the horse guards have left; I'm staying on alone in this accursed hut, near my amiable princess, abandoned to boredom and solitude. Yet sometimes I love the solitude which makes a man turn back to himself. I might call it good medicine, because moments spent in ripe and authentic reflection are as beneficial to a man distracted and dependent on the objects surrounding him as an infusion.

26 March, evening, Samagitis

After arranging and finishing my business affairs and having sent forward my command, I sat down in my *kibitka*;* the coachman, who seemed to have measured with his lips the quality and quantity of the contents of a bottle, sent his troika flying along. There was fine moonlight; it covered the ground with a sweet and magical clarity. Lake Peipus stretched out on the right; a dark forest rose up at the left. All together enchanted me, and I fell to dreaming, until my coachman's vapours and a huge stone upset my carriage and me, and dissipated my exaltation. But we soon recovered from our accident, and towards nine o'clock I arrived here, bones aching and cursing all brandy, stones, and coachmen.

27 March

Day of rest. Filthy weather; only the company of my friends cheers me up sometimes.

28 March, Shelze

I'm marching again with the regiment. I think of my family very often; it's my dearest occupation.

29 March

A miserable day today. Not only was the march extremely

* A covered troika (Ed.).

long and painful, but the Devil tempted me to play cards after having drunk a glass of punch. I lost all my money. In vain do I breathe out my lamentations onto this paper, a sad comforter since it doesn't speak. What am I going to do now without money? Accursed be the rascal who invented cards; they've worked me much mischief. To think they were invented for a poor madman and now make so many men unhappy.

30 March, Tolbitsin

Fine weather; the march was very cheerful. I've begun consoling myself for my losses, and I've promised myself never to play a game of chance again. The peasants around here are very poor.

31 March, Pskov, and 1 April

A day of rest. Spring, coming closer with rapid strides, makes man and nature born again. Our entry was solemn; no one had ever seen the Imperial Guard before; everyone looked at us with big eyes. The town is small, badly built, and old. Took a stroll yesterday evening to investigate things. The people here talk a rather peculiar jargon. The women wear pretty bonnets. I had the pleasure of finding a piano at an apothecary's, where I passed the time until six o'clock; then I went to a so-called concert by a sad collection of six Gypsies who knew more Greek, I believe, than music. We dined with the Governor, Prince Shakhovskoy, who entertained us to perfection.

2 April

From Pskov to Ostrov I noticed a great many beggars along the highway imploring the compassion of the passers-by. Their government is the cause of it; in fact, most of them were robust and healthy. Can this be the industry and activity of Russia so lauded in the descriptions of the country? Can a whole nation be judged when only a part of it is known? In these countries the peasant is very poor. He can scarcely cover himself in rags against the rigours of the season. Luckily he is too backward for even the seed of an awakening spirit (attempts are made to stifle that at the source) to make him aware of the wrongs inflicted on him.

3 April, Ostrov

This morning we crossed a river, the Velikaya [Great River], on whose shores the town is built. I went to visit the estate of Mme K.; there was an air of ease and simplicity all over. At six o'clock in the evening I was back in my quarters. We spend the evenings playing boston or chatting. What would military life be like without the company of one's comrades?

4 April, Vyshgorod

We were marching today along the sides of the highway; our march was very short. The colonel and I went off for a stroll after dinner. Each of us invented military manœuvres. We took turns on the offensive and defensive. The terrain was cut across; nevertheless we made good use of our batteries (in our imaginations, that is). Some peasants who passed took us for madmen and crossed themselves. Off to bed on my straw pallet.

5 April

Today's march was very pleasant. Birds' singing announced the imminent return of spring, though the countryside is still covered with snow. We're in a village called Vyshgorod, which is very well situated. One of the high hills surrounding it was climbed by our officers and myself, though the melting snow made riding impossible. Once on the summit we had a lovely vantage point. The valley and its distant surroundings, which were charming, heightened our spirits so much that we were an hour late returning; dinner was already cold.

Nevertheless, what a sad life I should be leading if my equable character and lively temperament did not sometimes make me look at things from a cheerful point of view! For instance, we are three officers and five servants in one little room hardly big enough for the family already living in the house. I amuse myself by observing the various groups here, which look as though they stepped straight out of a Hogarth. Weeping here, ill temper there, uproarious laughter, much making of faces. A naughty child is beaten; someone is baking bread. One is washing, another eating, a third drinking, a fourth is making his toilette. An unbelievable mix-up! An old woman with a wobbly head and myself are the only inactive spectators. Heavens, a dozen pipes are lit—ugh! what dense fumes! Just look at that soldier softly slipping a pancake out of the oven. He eats it, or rather swallows it, with such rapidity that the beginning seems scarcely followed by the end! But what the Devil is he doing there, that rascal Fyodor?—heavens, he's twisting the neck of a poor hen that doesn't even have the chance to scream bloody murder.

How to sleep or rest in this crowd? And on top of all other misfortunes, these insects that are created to torture the human race—these lice, these bedbugs, these cockroaches; who will defend me against their countless attacks? Nevertheless I'll try to sleep; perhaps slumber will take pity on my torments. Farewell, charming objects that fill my exalted imagination with laughing scenes! Farewell, vast and splendid castle which is threatening to crumble! Farewell then—or accursed be this hut that has more the look of a vestibule of hell!

6 April

We're making a stop. The weather is bad. This morning I thought about the true object of military service; since it's a sad necessity, I gave myself the task of defining it and of searching in vain for the trifle of utility this condition brings to the human race. As people cannot exist without war, being divided into numerous nations of which each has its own interest, the military condition must exist everywhere. But in peacetime? It's a way of maintaining order and stability, you say. Yes, but isn't it sad in time of war to slaughter one's fellowmen and to take all possible pains to disrupt the happiness, fortune, and peace of men—and to do nothing, or vegetate, in time of peace? And then, is the right cause always served? Aren't we the tools of a capricious will and of unjust undertakings and plans? The intrigues of cabinets, the personal quarrels of a monarch with his neighbour, are not they often the cause of the goriest wars? Wasn't one of the chief causes of the Seven Years' War that witticism of Frederick the Great at the expense of his splendid neighbours, Catherine the Great and Maria Theresa? The wars of the Spanish Succession and of the Bavarian Succession are similar examples which prove that we poor lowly ones are always the executors of the sanguinary will of our elevated people. Then the sacred words Faith, Honour, Fatherland, are used to cover various individual and self-interested intentions with a veil, religious or other, that is beautiful to look at but that hides a hideous and repellent spectacle.

Why don't they slaughter each other, these great people who think themselves earthly gods and for whose sake we are obliged to sacrifice everything—our happiness, our lives—and for what reason? To serve their base interest! It's true there have been wars that were more or less excusable from a philosophic point of view and whose aim was nobler, as I hope this one will be. But that is rare, and who is going to vouch for the motives behind this campaign? But what is the use of entrusting even to paper these ideas; it is merely criminal, in this empire where no one dares think freely; it is swimming against the tide of men's superstitions!

8 April, Mikhailova

The breaking up of the ice on the Düna [Dvina] is holding up our march; we shall be obliged to stay on several days in this village; a fatal delay. It's neither the quarters nor the weather to wish for, nor the season nor the countryside to make it more endurable. This morning I amused myself by strolling about on foot and climbing a fairly high mountain. Ever since childhood I've had a taste for that. What can it mean? Is it that my spirit, as well as my eyes, loves to

have its horizon magnified? Shall I too with time attain a
certain degree of human eminence? Who knows! For the
moment I had to overcome great difficulties to arrive at
my goal. The melting snow and a little brook I had to cross
held me up for some time; but finally I reached the fore-
summit; and my curiosity as well as my efforts were rewarded
by a splendid vantage point that I was delighted by and
from which I could see a vast stretch of country. I sat down
on a stone and abandoned myself to the pleasure of seeing a
great deal all at once and to reflections on "obstacles" in
general. They give that salt, that savour, to the different
pleasures of men that makes them still more agreeable;
pleasures are very imperfect (experience proves it) when
there are no obstacles to make them still more desirable.
A child, for instance, will have no particular concern for
the pretty toys he has in his hands the moment something
attracts him which is perched on a cupboard he has difficulty
climbing up in order to reach. Would love be so violent if
the rules of respectability, the coquetries on both sides, or
even the separation and enforced silence were not obstacles,
barriers that are hard to surmount? And why, finally, do
men, even old men, rush after the grandeur offered by their
ambition? Is it because the difficulties they overcome to
arrive at a certain degree of elevation seem to be just so
many triumphs they deserve, merely pleasures to be enjoyed?
This feeling of loving (in secret) and even the tendency of
seeking out obstacles is inherent in man; it was for a very
wise reason implanted within us.

But I had completely forgotten the hundred steps I still
had to take to reach the topmost summit of the mountain.
I soon reached it—a vast horizon, covered with distant
woods, presented itself to my view at first; objects in the
valley, actually big, seemed small to me. That's how everything is in the world. There is nothing that cannot be
diminished by something still bigger. The course of my
thoughts finally came to rest on human pride. Is man not a
miserable creature the moment he draws a parallel between

himself and the perfected majesties offered by nature for his contemplation? Yet he believes himself master of the universe.

And why, after all, does he imagine himself to be such a masterpiece favoured by the Good Lord? Might He not have given existence to far more accomplished individuals inhabiting the distant globes scarcely seen by our eyes? Man is a very small mite, nothing at all physically, but surely *something* because of the qualities of his soul and spirit; but are these really as remarkable as we believe or as our pride represents them? I think not. But these good qualities that remain to us and seem very great on the horizon of our intellectual faculties, why are they *so often stifled* by egoism, this pride that depraves and debases man? A single hour spent in contemplation on this mountain would make man blush for his pettiness in the face of grandiose nature, which alone is capable of suppressing his vanity and his presumptions. The more man believes himself elevated beyond all else, the more he finds himself a degree below moral perfection.

I meditated on all these interesting points on my way back to the house. While walking along and passing on human pride I had forgotten my own! Oh vanity of vanities!

9 April

Thanks to the kindness of one of my comrades who has loaned me some books, I spend my leisure hours reading. At present I'm devouring *Delphine*,* by Mme de Staël. What style! What thought! What character! The preface is a masterpiece; a pity it's too romantic, too sentimental, but that's not a great shortcoming; romance becomes a virtue, an additional quality, the moment the sentiment is true and not affected. The splendid character of the heroine of this work! Might it not be, by accident, her autobiography she wanted to write? But let that be—does it concern us? I find something in the character of Mathilda that is a little

* An epistolary novel published in 1802, in which Germaine de Staël tried to demonstrate that a "a man ought to oppose public opinion, and a woman submit to it" (Ed.).

too lightminded, and there is far too much oddity in the situations! But the work is charming; this de Staël is a female Rousseau, but a different kind, from a different point of view.

The province of Vitebsk, which we are crossing now, is more cultivated than the others we have passed through. You see Jews everywhere. The Jewesses are pretty. I've seen several with very interesting faces. A pity they're not clean.

10 April

Bad weather. There's nothing as horrible as the roads in this part of the country. Our poor horses could hardly walk; the mud and mire came up to their knees. How I pity the poor infantry and my poor brother Jacques, who's an under-officer. The way we lead life on the march is very monotonous. I was filled with the most passionate feelings this evening, reading about Leonie and Delphine.

11 April, Lyutsyn

This name is very difficult to write in French; it resembles the name of the town that witnessed the exploits and the tragic death of Gustavus Adolphus, the hero of the North. It doesn't do any good for this town to bear the name, since it is very small and very ugly, though prettily situated. After making a march of forty versts* we came to our quarters, soaked to the marrow and numb with cold. I had nothing better to do than to go to bed after a very frugal meal that was, however, seasoned by the excellent company of my comrades.

12 April, Rezhitsa

A little place, like Lyutsyn, but in a perfect location. The countryside around here is very mountainous. I don't know what attracts me to everything that is *irregularly* beautiful; in particular, I'm very drawn to everything that is picturesque and big. We're lodging with a forest inspector, who entertained us very nicely. His niece appeared after

---

* One verst equals 1·066 kilometres, or 0·663 miles (English miles not Russian; one Russian mile equals seven versts) (Ed.).

dinner; she played the piano and sang prettily. She did the lyrical song *"Parle moi de ce que j'adore"* with a great deal of verve. How a sweet feminine voice moves a man! The simpler it is the more charm it has! Content with the course of my day, I went to bed, inviting my dreams to carry me off to the arms of my family, who may be thinking of me and have no news of their son who loves them and who prays ardently to the Good Lord to preserve every member and for the happiness of a brother, another son, of the best of all parents. They may be giving themselves worry and pain without cause, especially my sweet mother, the tender friend and guardian angel of her Boris.

13 April, Rezhitsa

Day of rest. This morning while getting up I saw something interesting. The sun was illuminating a tableau that was as touching as it was beautiful. An old man, with a long white beard and the noblest of faces one can imagine, was propping up his venerable head, furrowed by age, on the knees of a charming peasant girl who was suckling a lovely child and seemed to look at the old man's face with a great deal of tenderness. A boy about fifteen was standing behind the peasant girl's bench holding the hands of a girl the same age and looking at her passionately, though she seemed to be avoiding the infatuated looks of the young man. A tableau worthy of a Correggio or a Vernet! I rubbed my eyes; I could scarcely believe myself in a Russian hut; the tableau took me back to antiquity—it bore the Roman or Greek stamp. My enthusiasm and the illusion I was under vanished as I looked about me and caught sight of my Fyodor snoring on a pallet filled with armour, boots, and helmets; nevertheless the beauty of this group seemed to me just as rare as it was beautiful, especially from a Russian hut.

The countryside around here is very friendly. Today I strolled about a great deal. The air is getting milder; you can sniff the beginning of spring. The province is inhabited by Jews and the *Raskolniki*, a numerous sect little liked in

Russia.* They differ in many nuances and in some cere-
monies from the dominant religion, with usages of their
own. Drink is prohibited them, as well as tobacco. I've been
assured that they choose their wives by touch, in the darkness; something as strange as it is comical. A menstruating
girl and a pregnant woman never venture to eat together
with the family, but alone. Many of these bizarre customs
demonstrate this sect's stupidity and their preposterous
prejudices, which are apparently maintained by their
leaders in the latter's own interest.

In my moments of solitude I sometimes think of a young
person in St. Petersburg who had interested me a great deal.
To her personal charms she added those of a well-born
and noble soul, and to a cultivated mind, lively, tender, and
naïve feelings. Several times I thought I was in love with
her. But I am persuaded of the contrary, because I have
formed a completely different idea, a more energetic notion
of this supernatural leaning, that ardent passion we call
Love. I was accustomed to seeing her every day; her qualities enchanted me. All this drew me toward her, though
without feeling the emotions one should when one is really
in love. Without allowing myself any illusions and without
going too deeply into my feelings about this, I came to
various ideas and reflections on Platonic and physical love
in general.

After meditating for a long time on the possibility of a
love that is pure and quite free of the senses, I was obliged
to deny it completely for the following reasons. I believe
there could never have been a woman of fifty who could
inspire a young man of twenty-five with a passion that is
strong, enduring, and *pure,* or the contrary. If, between two
people of such different ages, a tender and strong union were
established, it would be either the result of perfect esteem
or of aroused senses. Perfect love, that pure and celestial
love that Plato described and whose grandeur, strength,
and nobility he preached, is nothing but friendship, which

* A sect refusing to comply with Russian-Orthodox rituals (Ed.).

cannot really exist except between people of the same sex.

It will be said, But there have been so many people who loved each other without having done anything against virtue and decency. Very well. Yet there was always that sensual passion, though more refined, that was satisfied by an embrace, a kiss, a coming together of some kind by means of the language of the eyes, the sound of the voice, etc., etc. People like to deceive themselves on this point; they believe they love each other with complete purity; but that is nothing but refined sensuality. Could you, young man, fall head over heels in love with a woman who had a hump and no teeth but combined all the good qualities of the soul and the mind? Would you, young beauty, lose your heart to a man of fifty-five who had a potato nose and a belly like a keg of beer but was nevertheless the most estimable of men in his virtues and his mind? Surely not. Then why imagine that Platonic love can exist? Why not let the senses have their due and the mind what it demands?

14 April

We had a short march today. By noon we were already quartered. The weather was fine; a comrade suggested that we hunt or go to visit a gentleman in the vicinity in order to pass off the boredom that tormented us and also vexed our hosts, on whom we played all sorts of tricks. The idea had scarcely occurred to us when it was put into effect. We had a couple of peasant horses saddled; taking the gun and the hunting dog of a Mr. S., a lieutenant in our squadron, we prepared to set off. But we could scarcely get out of the stable. At every thrust of the spurs our horses lifted their heads and let out a little cry, looking at us as though wondering what it all meant. Finally we got them moving and came to the nearest village. There we heard that a *Pan* (Polish gentleman) lived some four versts off. "That's enough," said Mr. S. to me, "for us to pay him a visit, but how can we get in to see him?"

"That's my business," I said.

While speaking we were crossing a little brook; my horse calmly went down on his knees to drink. Expecting nothing, I slid, saddle and all, over his head, only to bury my own in the mud with my legs in the air. Luckily I'd taken my feet out of the stirrups, otherwise I might have hurt myself. Getting to my feet I look around furiously for that cursed horse, which after watering was slowly moving off toward the stable. Through the water and the mud that covered me I saw my companion-in-arms—Oh rage! Oh fury!—laughing, but laughing his lungs out; it was useless to get angry. I had to put a good face on a bad bargain; joining voices we laughed heartily for a quarter of an hour. A peasant who had witnessed the scene and our little duet helped us catch the horse. The question was whether we should give up our plans for a visit or not; but people of character like ourselves don't abandon so easily an idea once taken up, especially when they've begun putting it into effect. My friend, having complimented me on the way I had conducted my botanical researches at the bottom of the brook, congratulated me on the new acquisitions that I had apparently made on behalf of natural history that would surely not fail to become known very soon throughout the world. I bit my lip, not daring to reply; he would have made some further critical remarks about my appearance and clothing, all of which looked a great deal like that of the Knight of the Sad Countenance, just as my mare resembled the latter's splendid Rosinante. We soon went into a forest; two paths were before us; like Hercules, each of us began to ponder as to which one to choose. Finally we took the path to the left, making our horses gallop as best we could; but there was no way out at all; it was already beginning to grow dark. The sun had set; the road had left us, or rather, we had lost it. *Ssss!* A rifle shot; the bullet whistled by! A man ran up to us and apologized for having frightened us; shooting his gun, he had just missed killing one of us. He led us out of the woods and invited us to stop by his house; when he told us his name we found him to be the *Pan* in question.

He was charming, and entertained us as best he could. His family was very affable, especially a young orphan girl who was staying in his house. After having eaten well and drunk well, we went back home, where we were to have a good sleep.

15 April

Vitebsk Province differs from the others in the splendour of its cities and the prosperity of its inhabitants. It has a great many varieties of landscape—one sees mountains, lakes, fertile fields—all in an agreeable ensemble. A pity there are so few forests. The soil is good; one sees one village next to another.

16 April, Kamenez

There's no more snow to be seen, but the road is very muddy. Spring is heralded everywhere. Larks enliven the fields, which are still deprived of their springtime finery.

17 April, Dünaburg

We had scarcely arrived when the Grand Duke started the regiment manœuvring. The inhabitants gathered from all over to watch us. We went through our paces very well. But I'm so tired I can't budge. I've found a good restaurant —what else is needed to refresh one's body and soul?

18 April

Day of rest.

Dünaburg is a very small town, located on the banks of the Düna, whose tides lap a fortress that's being rebuilt, though not very quickly. I spent the morning going around the neighbouring country, which isn't very pretty, shopping, and paying my respects to the wife of General Hohmann, an old acquaintance from St. Petersburg. Her husband, who is commander of a division, had left. Madame received me very amiably; I spent the day there extremely pleasantly. She has a fine soul and principles that do honour to her sex. We amused ourselves in the evening racing with the cossacks,

who are very skilful. The Jews in this part of the country
are very rich. I visited one who had gold and silver worth
half a million. *Delphine*, by Mme de Staël, which I'm reading
just now, interests me a great deal. It has a charming style.

19 April

We crossed the Düna this morning, not without danger,
because the pontoons were bad. We had a very long march;
now we're in Mikhailova, a very dirty little place.

20 April, Vitzy

From what is said, it was the decision of our superiors
to stay in this district for several weeks. Our squadron, under
the command of Colonel Leontiev, has been stationed in a
village called Shorukzhik, five versts from the city of Vitzy.
The countryside is radiant. We're four officers quartered
together in the house of a butcher who seems to be a splendid
chap. I have a little room to myself, and I expect to be very
comfortable here.

21 April

Easter. The weather is magnificent. Everything is beginning to blossom and grow. At ten o'clock we went to see the
Grand Duke to congratulate him; he received us very
graciously. The city of Vitzy is small, but rather gay.
It has a huge number of Jews, who are rather dirty but are
so comical and funny, in the way Jews are, that even the
most serious-minded man would be forced to laugh looking
at them. The way they twist themselves into knots the
moment they accidentally meet some colonels or generals,
or especially the Grand Duke, has to be seen.

They are a very peculiar class of people, these Jews. Their
customs, their manners, their religion, are so different from
others. Centuries have not been enough to change them. I
went to visit their synagogue. The way they behave with the
Good Lord is rather curious and comical. One thing that
has struck me is that little Jews of ten to twelve are already

married. One ten-year-old who had his little wife of thirteen at his side amused me with his naïve answers.

We dined with Colonel Andreyevsky, who did his best to entertain us. We were all very merry. A concert given by several Jews, which demanded considerable indulgence, ended up making us so gay that a number of officers started dancing. The Jews' favourite instrument is the *zimbali*, a sort of reclining semi-clavichord without keys; it is played by striking the strings with a little stick. Among the Jewish and Polish women here there are some very pretty faces. One of them in particular struck me by her beauty and her polished manners. The centre for lovers of punch, cards, and strong spirits to assemble is apparently going to be the Hotel de Vilna, managed by a Monsieur Bondanelli, who has a very nice little daughter. We left at seven in the evening.

22 April

I accompanied Mr. S. hunting; he's a great amateur. I find nothing about it in the least agreeable. It's a cruel pleasure and a waste of time. Passing by one of the meadows that are beginning to be covered with that tender greenery that is so enchanting to the eye of even the most indifferent, I saw on the branch of a birch tree two birds celebrating the return of spring and at the same time, love; I sat down on the grass. Involuntarily I thought of Mlle W. How dear she is to me still! The evening was very beautiful. I didn't go home until the rays of the moon began appearing. I thought of *Ossian*,* which I'm reading just now.

23 April

We went into town very early to parade; Leontiev gave us a dinner today; it was excessively boring. There was a great deal of gambling. I slipped off very quickly in order to write back to Reval [Tallinn], which I hadn't done for a long time.

* *The Lays of Ossian*, a literary hoax by Macpherson (1760), ascribed to an ancient Irish bard (Ed.).

24, 25 April

My superior officer's confidence in me gave me the opportunity for a little trip to the outskirts of Vitzy. The object of it was to look for supplies and fodder for our regiment. I had a great deal of difficulty finding any because it had been hidden. Yet I did find enough. A number of Polish *Pans*, who undoubtedly did not look at me with too indulgent eyes, were inconvenienced by myself and my men. But I took leave of everyone on good terms, especially the ladies, who were very happy with me since I paid court to them all.

26 April

Here I am, back again; the weather is foul.

27 April

I'm beginning to get bored. My comrades, though very decent chaps, are not always the best company. They sleep a lot, which I can't do.

28 April

Coming back this morning from an excursion on horseback I received mail from Reval. What a joy to hear from so far away! I sprained my arm; it hurts abominably.

29 April

I rose very early this morning. After I climbed a mountain three versts away from us, my horizon, which had been small, grew vastly larger, and I found myself looking at a radiant landscape. The sun, barely risen and hidden in light clouds, was spreading its sweet light over the forests, the fields, and the valleys, which were reawakening from their winter sleep. A brisk but pleasant wind stirred up the glittering surfaces of three lakes stretching out at my right and left. The villages scattered about here and there were still shrouded in a deep silence; in short, everything I could see of the charms, the creations, and the majesty of nature was, as it were, spread out in front of my enchanted eyes.

It was difficult for me to leave this Mountain of Reflections (that's what I always shall call it); I was sure I would soon come back to it.

30 April

Today is far from as lovely as it was yesterday; it has started raining a number of times. We amused ourselves by making plans for the future and by playing the fool; a fine occupation for Guards officers. But what one won't do to overcome boredom! We go to bed early, we get up early, we dine at one o'clock, we sup at eight o'clock. The hours are well split up with us. That's how we spend our time—drinking, eating, sleeping, and being bored.

1 May

There is a Polish gentleman by the name of Grinzevitch living four versts from our cottage; we go to see him from time to time. He's a very decent fellow who likes chatting about politics and economics; he has a niece who's very nice, who often sings to us to the accompaniment of her guitar, which she plays rather well. We paid him a visit today, M. Sakavnin and myself. He, a devotee of the fair sex, and I, myself no despiser of it, paid court to Mlle Marie, who, however, preferred him, since he's a handsome fellow. I could scarcely master my irritation; I was in a bad mood all day. They began to make fun of me. A man is capable of enduring anything up to a point, but the moment he is mocked he can rarely master himself. Thus I was so furious I no longer recognized myself. Drily wishing everyone good-night, I flung myself on my horse and, spurring him on, distanced myself from the lovely Marie's fateful dwelling. Passing by the forest that still separated me from our house I thought of man's vanity. In this life, that is what causes us so much pain and so many unpleasant feelings the moment it is wounded. Instead of wishing his fellows prosperity and all good things, a man gets angry because others don't see in him the qualities he mistakenly flatters himself he has.

Completely aware of my injustice to S. and M., and of the absurdity of my pretensions, I promised never to give in to this fault again. It is nine o'clock, and time to go to bed.

2, 3 May

Yesterday I stood guard at Vitzy. The Grand Duke was in bad temper. I spent the day today at our Colonel Leontiev's, who is staying with an Italian émigré who has a rather pretty estate and an excellent table. We went boating.

4 May

Splendid weather today. How beautiful nature is in its full form. It is the book of books, in which everything that is grand and noble can be found, and everything to do with all the sciences.

Leaving behind the foolishness and absurdities of a society that is sometimes very boring and insipid, I sought solitude as an escape. This evening I went to the little birchwood behind the hill; the star of the day, having illumined the surface of our terrestrial globe, was beginning to yield its place to the stars of the night. The air was delicious, balmy with scents. A sweet darkness enwrapped nature; the light was vanishing by degrees, but still letting the charming contours of the objects surrounding me be seen. Apollo, to speak mythologically, was hurling himself into the arms of his moist lover in order to allow Diana the time to speak with her beloved Endymion. The dull and confused noise of a toiling and tumultuous world was insensibly slipping away. The inhabitants of the wood were already falling silent so that their queen, the tender Philomel, might sing. A fresh but gentle wind, agitating now and then the budding leaves, joined in unison with a neighbouring spring which, having escaped from the bosom of the earth, was watering the sheen of a youthful sward and spreading its silken aroma; harmony struck the ear attentive to the slightest sound. The gilded horizon toward the setting sun was covered by a mingling of lovely colours in vain imitated by even the most beautiful picture. The moon, just escaping from the clouds and nestling in one after another of the light and frivolous mists of the atmosphere, was spreading its bluish, quivering clarity over the forests, the valleys, the lakes, and the fields; the villages were enshrouded in slumber and bleak silence.

I was ecstatic; I turned my thoughts to bygone times. My imagination outlined the pleasures of a happy love, instead of my thinking, as I should have in contemplating nature, of its Creator. How feeble man is, the slave of his passions! Just then I saw a figure covered with a white veil coming out from behind a tree. The moon, hidden in a cloud, was still keeping from me the traits of its countenance; a little more exaltation and I would have thought myself living in the fabled times of mythology and seeing a hamadryad or an oread before me. But tempted by lust and having been dreaming of the happy days passed in the company of the amiable W., the Serpent and Eve's apple tempted me. I rushed at this object; I clutched it; I even dared squeeze it and grope after its charms—when the moon suddenly appeared and let me see a Shrew at least seventy years old. My amorous fury changed into rage; I thrust her back, and, though she had been quiet as a mouse a moment before, she emitted a shrill cry and fell over backwards. What a situation! I was transformed into a statue, watching this octogenarian spectre struggling to pick herself up, flinging out her dried-up limbs now to the north, now to the south. Finally I came to myself and recognized her as my host's old cook, who had been looking for me to call me to supper. We soon made peace, and for a long time afterwards laughed about it.

5 May
No one dares go out today; it's pouring rain. I've been thinking a great deal of my adventure of yesterday.

6, 7 May
I was away two days. The colonel had sent me to search

for fodder that has been bought for the regiment. I went to see two Polish *Pans*, who were extremely polite. There are three things here I dislike: the dinner always has too much salt meat, the fair sex is too familiar, and there are too many bugs crawling about.

8 May

What joy! I've just found a piano, or rather a poor harpsichord, so that I can express myself as I should. Aside from this treasure, I've just unearthed others, which are still finer—two young ladies, and charming! Rather well-bred and very gay. I'm speaking of the two daughters of my neighbour Lopatinsky, who has a small property quite close to where I'm staying and whose acquaintance I had previously not made. He's a very good-natured chap; his wife is a bit of a grumbler, but their daughters are all the more amiable for that. Svelte figures, pretty eyes, reserved bearing, though a little gauche; their conversation is very naïve, but quite witty; their education has been neglected, but they have a few little talents, and both of them are astonishingly kind. I propose to frequent their house a good deal.

I'm delighted with the way I spent my time today. I came back on my horse; it was a splendid evening; I sat down again in front of my door to enjoy nature, which was all abloom.

9 May

I had a great desire to go see the Mlles Lapatinsky again, but was afraid of imposing on them; I didn't budge from my place. The somewhat noisy but rather interesting company of my comrades; my pipe, my horses, and an old novel—that was what had to make up for my self-sacrifice.

10 May

Not a single visit in the neighbourhood today. I was obliged to go to Vitzy on duty. I went to see the work being done on our military headquarters, which is in a rather bad state.

11 May

I've seen them again! But I shall be asked, Which one do you prefer? The choice is too difficult. Yet my feelings lean towards the older one, who is livelier. What joy! A harpsichord, charming persons, and, as the height of satisfaction, parents who dislike getting in the young people's way. The old papa, whom I'm winning over with my poised manner and discussions of economics, often leaves us to see to his Turkish horse and his Smyrna apple trees. Mama, with her apelike eyebrows, likes to talk about the first days of her passion and of her marriage: I know that, and so, with the help of my imagination, I transplant myself back a quarter of a century and talk with her about a time when I wasn't yet in existence. She leaves us often to look after her animals and household. That's when I'm in my element. Especially when my friend S. accompanies me and pays court to the younger one, freeing me to do the same to the older.

12 May

The Grand Duke has been putting the regiment through manœuvres. I couldn't attend because of an indisposition that seized me yesterday on my return. S., who was keeping me company, had some very bizarre and comical notions today. He was afflicted by boredom, so he started pinching the cat and shooting off his pistol, filled with salt, at all the barnyard animals and fowl. It was nothing but constant outcries and uproar. Then he presented himself to Madame Winsch, our landlady, in his undershirt; scandalized, she fled into the barn. All the people in the house were baptized by him, and the chairs, benches, and tables in our rooms more than once represented the destruction of Sodom and Gomorrah. The evening was calmer.

13 May

I dislike our inactivity very much. We'll soon have been in this part of the country for four weeks. It's said that the

French army is getting closer to our borders. Why don't we go to meet them? Why? Because there are men, our chiefs in Russia, who have more brains than I have, and who have less vanity than I, but are also men who don't love their country as I do, and who are sacrificing the public interest to their private interest. This is true, but since it can't be remedied it's better to have patience. Which the Good Lord will give us.

14 May

I love to think of the past winter. Interesting ideas follow each other and memories too dear to be forgotten take the place of everything in my solitude. A little inclination I had for a young person in the same house where I lived in St. Petersburg still holds my heart. And this doesn't surprise me at all. Even though my character is a little frivolous and I have an element of lasciviousness, I like to let myself go along with such a feeling, which will never harm the morality of a young man and which, on the contrary, will very often restrain him from some unpardonable follies. A lock of her hair, and her profile, which is rather striking, take the place of her person now. Yet they are a feeble substitute. It is not without emotion that I recall that charming face on which the Graces had bestowed an irresistible charm. She was not beautiful, but her lively, irregular little face was enchanting—especially the moment she began speaking. Her features grew animated, and her pretty blue eyes sparkled with a seductively fiery expression. She had read a great deal—indeed, too much. Though a spoiled child and at the same time of bold temperament and somewhat capricious, she joined to these qualities a matchless kindness of heart. A natural wit, some talents, and a coquettishness less refined than badly disguised—the combination made her even more interesting and was enough to trouble my heart. Though I didn't lose the serenity of my heart, I suffered a great deal in leaving her, especially knowing that she was far from indifferent to being separated from me. Time and distractions will wear away this inclination, which for that matter, far from tormenting me, adds to my present happiness.

A saddle-horse I was very fond of has just died. What a pity!

15 May

With no money, with no things, a man is worth nothing, it is said. But that is a little too strong; for I find myself in just that condition and I am worth something—I hope! But this proverb really has some weight, especially to the vulgar who can esteem and judge a man only according to the splendour surrounding him, the clothes he wears, or his pecuniary merits.

But, my dear friend, let us come back to myself. I am really ashamed of our inactivity. I am especially ashamed of my Diary, which contains so little of interest. So many sheets of paper smudged, so many quills used, so many half hours lost! What is the use of it all? Yet it is hard to write down every day what one eats, what one drinks, and how one bores oneself. No, really . . . but how can this boredom that obsesses you be chased away, this languor that oppresses you, this discontent that crushes you? Patience, my dear Boris, you must have patience. . . .

16 May

Splendid weather today. I gave all my horses a run around the ring. Their capers amused us all a lot. In the afternoon we made up a boating party in a half-rotten boat. Everyone got drenched.

17, 18 May

Two days lost. You don't gain much time by spending twenty-four hours on guard and then twelve recuperating from exhaustion. But now I'll be through with it for a long time.

19 May

Spent the morning meditating on my future and on my past, which occupies my imagination a lot. At five o'clock I had my old grey saddled; he's as fiery as he is docile. After racing through the valley and the woods, and up the big hill near by at a gallop, I came to the house of Baron R., who was quartering one of our married officers, Baron Tiesenhausen. I must see this household, I had said to myself; no sooner said than done. I arrived: my eyes ran over the house, the garden, the courtyard, the surroundings; everything seemed radiant. I was announced. A certain flattering harmony prejudiced me at once in favour of the owners of this property. I went inside. There I found some people I knew. The host and hostess looked well. A conversation was going on about economic affairs, which quite lost me. Finally the sound of a carriage was heard, and I was moved at seeing the Mlles Lopatinsky come in with their parents. Everything turned gay among us at once. A piano in the corner of a room gave us some pleasure, and after tea we set out to accompany the guests to their house. The two barons exchanged partners and I approached the demoiselles. The older people followed us, and that was how we went to the Lopatinskys'. At ten o'clock I took my regretful leave; the rays of the moon, which had already made some progress, kept me company all the way home.

20 May

Today I couldn't resist the desire to go back to see my lovely brunettes, who were, to be sure, already waiting for me, since I had promised them to come the next day. But I had to disclose my attachment for one of them and declare myself, since paying court *seriously* to two sisters is impossible. My heart, which by now was already inclined to the older one, made me devise a little strategem. It was the prettiest evening in the world. I had a great desire to stroll with Mlle Clare. But how could I get rid of the younger one? I immediately set about begging her to copy me out a mazurka of which she was very fond. She finally agreed, but casting a mistrustful look at both of us she asked me with a naïve air, "Just what will both of you do tête-à-tête?" "We'll take a walk," I said. Mlle Clare readily gave me her pretty arm; we went down to the garden—there we were! There was a fine wood growing quite close to the garden, but separated from it by a ditch. "Would you like to wager, Mademoiselle, that I can cross it in one leap?" "But it's nothing," she answered—and there she was, already on the other side. In a flash I followed her example. Myself—*Psst* . . . Listen, it's a nightingale. She—Let's get closer to it. Myself— Gladly. But the nearer we came to the source of its sweet warbling, the more it seemed to recede from us. There was something magical about it. Exhausted finally, we were going to sit down to rest on an old tree trunk when Mlle Clare, uttering a piercing cry, fell over backwards. Though quite frightened by this unforeseen accident, I still had enough sangfroid to see at once what its real cause was. She had been frightened by a lizard that had slipped in underneath her dress. I did everything I could to free her from this little monster of cruelty and to console her to the best of my ability; I ended up with a declaration of love which was accepted very graciously. Lovers, you will all understand what such a moment means! And those of you who have not yet fallen in love, just put yourselves in my place and dare to say you would not be moved! The scene that had begun on such a burlesque note ended all the more interestingly. The evening was calm, serene, and velvety. The springtime air, the dense woods, the scents of the young birch and the flowers in the lovely fields, the twittering of the birds, and, finally, the rays and the dying light of a setting sun that spread an inexpressible charm over our voluptuous disarray—the whole of this lovely ensemble made us forget the hour and the passage of time. It rocked us into such a sweet delirium that I came to myself lying at my lover's feet, but unable to recognize her features as it had already grown so dark. The far-off murmuring of the garden waterfall served as guide, and that is how we found our way back to the house, where everyone had been upset by our lengthy walk. A flush came into my lovely's cheeks as she left me, and after taking leave of everyone I cried aloud, galloping along at my hardest:

> A year in all the abysses of Tartary,
> A prey of the frightful torments of the Furies,
> Would not be enough to ransom
> A single hour in the arms of charming Clare.

What a day! And you're unhappy with your stay here— ingrate!

21 May, Vitzy

A great celebration, on the occasion of his Highness's name day. After congratulating his Highness, the officers' corps entertained him with a magnificent banquet. The pavilion built for this purpose looked, from the outside, like a Chinese building; inside there were places for a hundred guests. The soldiers were served in the great square, and we sat down to eat at three o'clock. The champagne flowed in torrents. The Grand Duke was in a good mood. Three different orchestras contributed to the general atmosphere of gaiety. Toasts were given, to the jubilation of the entire regiment; the "Hurrahs" resounded to the skies. At five o'clock we mounted up and took the Grand Duke back. The day ended with fireworks and an illumination, which was, however, quite mediocre. The crowd was prodigious. I was reminded of the celebration at Peterhoff. The local nobility were assembled. The old-fashioned costume of the Poles diverted us enormously.

22 May

Today the Grand Duke put the regiment through manœuvres. The word is out that he is going to Vilna. The heat is oppressive. Everyone is asleep or resting.

Chapter II

QUARTERED IN VITZY

On 23 May the Tsar of Russia put forth an ukaze for drafting two recruits from every 500 members of the population. The recruitment was to be accomplished within a month's time. The ukaze reads in part as follows:

The present situation in Europe calls for resolute and firm measures, tireless watchfulness, and a powerful army, which must be capable of guarding our great realm in a sure and reliable manner against all enemy action. From of old our powerful and courageous Russian nation, mindful of its own peace and the peace of others, has always sought to live in peace and harmony with neighbouring peoples; but when the tempestuous upheaval of an enemy has obliged it to take to the sword in defence of religion and of the Fatherland, there has never been a time in which the zeal of the true sons of Russia, of every rank and estate, has not been displayed in all its might.*

The following men were designated commanders of the various Russian armies: Barclay de Tolly, First Army of the West; Prince Bagration, Second Army of the West; Kutuzov, Army of the Danube; and Tormasov, Galician Army.

The King of Westphalia, Jérôme Bonaparte, left Kassel to take over the supreme command of the French troops assembled in Poland.

23 May, Vitzy
   What a lovely sight, to see all nature blossoming! This

* This and other quotations in the connective sections were taken from *Synchronistischen Handbuch der Neuesten Zeitgeschichte*, by F. W. E. Menck, 1826 and 1834.

morning I took a rather long walk. The apple and cherry trees were blooming; in fact, everything was. In the spring-time of our lives we fly from one pleasure to another, yet sometimes one must think of the autumn and winter. Thoughts involuntarily came to mind; I began thinking of the yearly renewal of nature, and of our mysterious existence beyond the tomb. What is that like? Does man begin to exist only with his birth, or has he already existed before? If he has, as seems to me probable, then his soul must be immortal. But if the opposite is true, can he expect immor-tality? For something that has no end cannot have had a beginning either. What a labyrinth! We must follow the impulse of our hearts, which would have us only *believe* and *hope*. Before glimpsing the dawn of pure and eternal life, before feeling the celestial bliss promised us by the idea of immortality, let us be men, in the true sense of the word, without losing ourselves in the abyss of vice and shame, without trying to penetrate mysteries and climb heights that are not made for our terrestrial existence; let us go along the path indicated to us by nature, which alone holds the key to every problem.

24 May

Vitzy has a sulphur bath, used for reasons of health, located only three versts from the city. The spring was discovered last summer. A number of doctors have a very high opinion of it since the sulphurous water cleanses the blood and strengthens the nerves; it is drinkable as well. Having nothing better to do, I've begun taking these baths. Several of my comrades are doing the same! This evening I paid court to my charming brunette. Exquisite moments!

25 May

I'm beginning to loathe Vitzy. Every day the same thing. At seven in the morning I hear my grey outside the small door which, like the whole of our landlord's tiny house, is close to collapsing. A brisk trot or a more comfortable gallop takes me to Lake Pisani and to Trepchuni with its

manor house. Immediately afterwards the so-called city of
Vitzy comes into view. The sentry presents arms as you
ride in. There are Jews and Jewesses teeming everywhere;
they dart about with a businesslike haste I find amusing.
Finally the big square comes into view. Though it resembles
a barnyard more than a marketplace, it is intended for the
parading and promenading of the great lords who live
around it. At the left, I see the guardroom where I've often
nearly died of boredom while on duty, suffering headaches
and heartaches. They had turned a Jewish tavern into this
guardroom; the filth is unendurable. Finally I come to the
Hotel de Vilna, which is supposed to be a proper hotel, the
most fashionable one. Well, it certainly is the most in
demand—it's the only one. Though the food and drink are
bad, it's very expensive; and the innkeeper's sister-in-law,
Mlle Agnes, who is rather pretty and very lively, is the
attraction for all the young people. She carries her virtue
in her mouth and her fine principles in the pockets of her
apron, but apart from these little weaknesses she's a sweet
child. Beyond the hotel is the church, the meeting-place
for most people. To the left is the school, where the children
learn nothing but stealing and lying. Finally I come to the
end of the city, on the road to Vilna. I move toward the
country house of Count Vavretsky, whose wife is as amiable
as she is witty. Finally the baths, which are restoring my
somewhat weakened health. This is the road I take three
times a week. All very healthful, except for my poor horses,
who have something to complain about.

26 May

I've had myself shown around a flour mill driven by oxen.
A very simple and useful invention, since you don't have to
depend on wind and water to get the mill moving.

27 May

The Grand Duke invited us to a great banquet in return
for the last celebration we gave him. Everyone was merry,
the Grand Duke very affable.

28 May

Surely the study of himself is the most difficult and most important of all studies for a man who wants to make his way in the world. I started the day by meditating on myself, and I instantly caught in myself a defect. After breakfast I was strolling along the shore of Lake Pisani. A few beggars who were bothering me received an "Away with you!" as their only alms; afterwards, as I was sitting in the inn with a number of officers, one of these unfortunates started begging from me again. This time I gave him a silver half ruble. Not out of compassion, but out of vanity. In recalling this I determined to behave the same whether in front of no one or thousands of people. Vanity and self-love—the greatest enemies of my heart and spirit; when shall I be able to say I've overcome them?

29 May

Mlle Lopatinsky, who seems to be very fond of my company, is brightening up from day to day. She's very beautiful and to some extent enables me to forget the princess of my heart!

30 May

No money—but credit! And it's a Jew who's given it to me. What a miracle! I'm tempted to think that my face is very promising if even someone like that believes in it. There is talk that we're soon going to leave our quarters, since the enemy is advancing by leaps and bounds. May God grant it! Nevertheless I shall be obliged to leave half my heart for a time in pawn with Clare, though she would be vexed to know what I've just been thinking and writing.

The sulphur baths are doing me good.

On 31 May the following note was sent by Tsar Alexander to the President of the Imperial Council, Count Soltikov:

The French troops have moved across the borders of our realm;

a treacherous attack is the reward for the strict observance of our alliance. I have exhausted all means consonant with the dignity of the Throne and the interest of my people. All my efforts have been in vain. Emperor Napoleon has determined to crush Russia to earth. The sudden attack has demonstrated in an unmistakable manner the falsity of his promises of peace. . . . There is accordingly nothing left for me but to take to arms and apply all means in my power to drive out force by force, nor will I lay down those arms as long as one enemy warrior is left in my Empire.

31 May and 1 June

I shall never forget what happened to me yesterday. At eight o'clock in the evening the fancy took me to visit Baron R. I was there in twenty minutes. I'd hardly arrived when a storm broke out, the like of which I've scarcely ever seen; thunder rumbled, lightning lit up the skies, and rain came down in torrents. Then it grew dark; there was no way of getting home. I was finally offered hospitality, and the punch soon made us forget what was going on around us.

We went to bed at eleven o'clock. Morpheus had already enveloped my hosts in his beneficent gentleness, my eyelids were already sinking heavily, when—heavens!—I felt—what? I dare not say—I felt a hand slipping, very softly, underneath my blanket. The fright, or rather a sort of curiosity, stupefied me with amazement; the grotesqueness of such a situation is bound to cause anyone consternation, even a very circumspect man. The words "Are you asleep?", softly whispered in a woman's voice, made me close my mouth, which was on the point of issuing a curse.

Finally I found my voice again, and, very softly, I asked, "Who's that?" "It's me!" was the answer. Unafraid of discovery, and risking the danger of embracing some old hag, I answered, "Come, my dear." At once a body, glowing like a coal, stretched out alongside me. The altogether noble fifth and last sense, like a good general, ordered its adjutants, the hands, to reconnoitre the terrain. "Very good, Excellency," was the report. "A round, plump arm," was the despatch from the first hand. "A firm and well-shaped throat," came from the second. Very well, boys. We accepted the battle. Soon the armies were grappling with each other the artillery firing as best it could. My "guest", who seemed pleased with this nocturnal scene, didn't say a word.

Suddenly, in the adjoining room I heard a soft sound; a ray of light penetrated through the opening of the door. Horrors! A man's footsteps were approaching! My amiable unknown seemed disturbed, alarmed by this discovery. I myself was, a hundred times more. Another half minute and I would have had something to be afraid of! But my presence of mind saved me at the last minute. At the very moment the door opened I leaped out of bed and seized the man by the throat, knocking the candle into his face. He fell over backwards; I quickly went back to my room. "Out, at once," I said to my companion through thick and thin. The mistake could be corrected only by swift flight. Half dead with fear, she nevertheless had the strength to make off with the speed of lightning while the man with the candle, coming out of his faint, began shouting at the top of his lungs, "Thieves, robbers!" And I, far from stupid, also began roaring, trying to outshout him. Soon a servant in shirt and underpants, with a candle in his hand, arrived, followed by a number of servant girls and the cook; the cook was dressed so comically that at the sight of her I could hardly hold back a burst of laughter. In her alarm the poor thing had put some underpants around her neck instead of a kerchief, and they were hanging down below her stomach.

Soon the whole household was assembled in the room, and people were standing around in comical and grotesque little groups. But no one had the courage to come close to me or to look behind the screen, where they thought they would find at least a horde of robbers. Finally I took the initiative; I went over to a servant, who looked at me as though I were a ghost, and took the light out of his hand in order to illuminate the back of the room and to see who my opponent was. And—who would believe it?—it was the poor host himself, my dear Baron R., holding in his hand the leg of a tea-table, thinking it was the thief.

I nearly laughed in his face, but I pulled myself together at once, lifted him up, and made a thousand apologies for the (pretended) mistake of having thought him a thief. He began looking at me stupidly; then he scratched his head and finally pardoned me with a good grace, calling himself a great donkey. Whether or not he had any reason to call himself that I have no idea. But I asked him, "What were you doing here in the middle of the night, with the candle? I was so frightened I leaped out of bed and pounced on you." "Yes," he said, with the most pitiable expression in the world, "I was looking for my wife. I'd been waiting for her for more than an hour." Now I'm in the clear, I said to myself. "But why the Devil, sir, were you looking for her in *my* room?" To this he had no reply; he wished me good-night and vanished sulking. I'm still curious to learn the end of this little story!

This is how the puzzle was explained: the Baroness, who had been gossiping and chatting for a long time with her neighbour, Mme de T., till past midnight, was being awaited by her husband; I was occupying the bedroom of her husband, who, being a little tipsy, instead of looking for her at Mme de T.'s, came straight to my room, forgetting it was no longer his. But the only thing that seemed to me ambiguous was that the Baroness, who wasn't at all drunk, lost herself in my room, knowing I was there. The mistake, if it was one, was extremely pardonable—and I pardon it with all my heart.

Over coffee in the morning I passed all the various faces there in review: no one felt entirely at ease. The Baroness especially seemed rosier than usual. What a group!

2 June

Back home again I laughed heartily. What extraordinary things happen! I paid a visit to my lovely Clare; she would have been *much less* amiable, I'm sure, if she'd had any knowledge of the trick the neighbourhood had played on her.

3 June

The word is that we are going to leave in a few days. At last the time is approaching when to the strident note of the war trumpet we shall charge the enemy squadrons. May the Almighty grant us luck and glory!

4 June

The news of our departure had scarcely spread when one fine morning Mr. Strumensky, our landlord, came into our bedroom, which he had never dared do before. We all looked at him very gravely; with uncertain steps, his gaze lowered, he came forward, walking in such enormous boots that I could have set up a whole shop of boots and shoes in them; he muttered some incomprehensible words, taking with two fingers a pinch of tobacco out of his pocket. "What d'you want?" "Very little indeed, gentlemen. It's just that this bill must be settled," he answered, showing us a piece of paper that was scribbled on from top to bottom. I snatched it at once, but having the feeling that I was looking at Chinese gave it back for him to explain. Finally we heard the itemized details of the bill, which declared open warfare on our purses. It was terrible; we felt as if we were dealing with a Jew. On top of everything, no one had any money. What was there to do? How could we cope with it? To revenge this outrageous fraud and to extricate ourselves, S. and I conceived a trick that amused us a great deal. With a straight face we treated our guest with a great deal of politeness, inviting him to take a stroll with us, which he agreed to with alacrity. When we arrived at the lake we asked him to go bathing with us. After making a lot of excuses he finally steeled himself to go into the water. He was hardly in when S., who is very strong, seized him by the legs, and I by the head; we pulled him into the lake and acted as though we meant to drown him while joking. He began struggling, but it was no use; we kept too firm a hold on him. Finally, after giving him a good soaking, we let up for a moment, begging him very humbly to write on a piece of paper, with a pencil that was found as though by accident on the bank, *that he had been paid.* He grew angry and categorically rejected our request. The "joking" began all over again and was repeated until the poor devil, who could no longer either breathe or speak, agreed with a nod of his head to do what we wanted.

And so our "social contract" was signed. We paid no attention to the noise he made while dressing; going back we held him forcefully under the arms, lavishly caressing and embracing him, and thus we arrived at the threshold of the house, where we made him deep bows. Next time, I hope, he'll devote some proper thought to the bills he makes up.

Everything is packed; tomorrow, dear Vitzy, witness of our pranks and adventures, adieu!

We're being brought black armour. It's pretty, but very heavy. My chest is going to suffer a great deal.

5 June

Oh! One disagreeable thing after another!

I woke up very early to get ready for the march, but everyone was still asleep, which astonished me very much. I woke up Fyodor, my servant, and scolded him for not having risen earlier. He answered calmly, "We've received a counter-order. The non-commissioned officer who brought the orders has just gone out. Thank God we're staying!" I could restrain my irritation only with difficulty. S., who had also gotten up, banished the clouds of tedium and concern from my brow. He said that we were now at peace with the Turks. But what I thought more interesting were the faces of our hosts, who would have been delighted to get rid of us.

Jumping out of bed, S. congratulated everyone; he embraced the innkeeper and his wife as though he had gone mad. Drawing me to one side, he said, "Let's repeat yesterday's

picturesque scene, with a few variations!" I didn't know
what he meant, but I let him have his way, and went off
for a short stroll. When I came back I found the entire
household, from the cook to the master, in our bedroom,
collected around a large water barrel; next to it stood a
table set with a number of dishes and bottles. In answer to
my question about what it all meant, I was told that today
was a holiday for all Russians in honour of a saint who had
drowned himself in order to save the Tsar's life. What
nonsense, I thought, and these people believe it with all
their heart. After a good breakfast had been eaten, S. had
the door shut and announced that the ceremony would
begin. Now everyone began getting mistrustful, but imagine
what I felt when he signalled the two servants, who seized
the old cook. Taking up a big soup spoon, he began pouring
water on the poor woman's head, assuring her it was for her
own good and for her happiness on earth. She screamed for
all she was worth, but it was no use. The others, who would
gladly have fled to safety, were forced to remain. One after
another was baptized, and this frightful ceremony ended
with a flood of water that soaked everyone. I'd had enough.
My amusement mingled with a sort of compassion for these
people, and I signalled S. to stop. That's how this moving
scene came to an end. No one had escaped this celestial dew
but ourselves, who had the most innocent air in the world!

6 June

I don't know why, but everyone has a sort of reverence
for us. A complaint to the colonel made the baptismal
ceremony of yesterday well known, but nothing happened.

There's some genuine camomile growing here in the fields,
but no one knows how to cultivate it or to turn it into a
business.

The most disagreeable things in this part of the country
are those swarms of gnats that exist only in order to torment
the human race.

A tender tête-à-tête with Mlle Clare has compensated for the boredom I went through all day long.

7 June

The heat is so stifling that you almost collapse even in a shirt; but every cloud has a silver lining. Even summer, that marvellous season, has its advantages. Nature, which at the same time as creating great afflictions for us like insects, storms, heat, has produced and displayed so many treasures. Winter, which in the beginning seems to bring only boredom, compensates us by making people more sociable and so develops relationships we are unacquainted with in summer. Thus everything here on earth mingles pleasure and bitterness. Every thing, every age, every class, every fate has good and bad aspects, since only a negative change can give something value. Misfortune would not be at all so difficult to endure if one thought it would be followed by fortune. If one resigns oneself to all the situations in life in the knowledge that Good and Bad are weighed in the hands of an Almighty Power that is Justice itself, one consoles oneself more easily; for together with Diderot's Jacques the Fatalist, one should say: "Everything is written down in the Great Book above; and everything works out for the best in this world, come what may."

After this philosophical dissertation I thought it would be better to stop getting annoyed about the heat; and going quite pathetically up into our loft, I got into an empty barrel, where I slept in until eight o'clock in the evening.

8 June, midnight

I don't recall ever having seen a more splendid sight than the one this evening. Towards seven o'clock the sky was covered with thick black clouds which, like savage, overhanging boulders, threatened to swallow up and bury the valley of Vitzy. A powerful whirlwind—forerunner of a still more powerful tempest—forming columns of dust and trembling the trees in the forest, made the storm break out.

The clouds seemed aflame. Lightning ploughed them up with zigzags that crossed each other, followed by thunderclaps that repeatedly came back, echoing far off in the mountains. I am thrilled by such spectacles. My soul rose up to its Creator, admiring His violence, fearsome yet beneficent in its results. A thunderclap that outdid all the ones before made our windows tremble as well as all the people in the house, who kept crossing themselves. I was very amused at the superstitious fear on the faces of my hosts, though I was a little frightened myself. Little by little the storm died down, and at ten o'clock the moon slipped out of the clouds, which seemed to flee the sweet brightness of its rays.

Chapter III

THE MASSACRE OF BORODINO

*On 10 June Napoleon issued the following proclamation from his headquarters in Vilkovsky on the Nyemen:**

The second Polish war is beginning! The first was ended at Friedland, and at Tilsit Russia vowed to France an eternal alliance and to England war. It has now broken its vows and refuses to give any explanation of its strange behaviour until the French eagles have withdrawn beyond the Rhine and our allies are left to its discretion. Russia must now submit to its fate.

Are we thought to have degenerated? Are we no longer the soldiers of Austerlitz? It has left us only the choice between dishonour and war. There can be no doubt which.

Then forward! Let us at this moment march on across the Nyemen and move the war into its own territory. The second Polish war will end for the French armies more gloriously than the first, but the peace we shall attain through it will grant a sure guarantee and put an end to the pernicious influence Russia has been exercising in European affairs for the past fifty years.

On the same day Tsar Alexander, in his headquarters at Vilna, signed the peace treaty between Russia and Turkey concluded on 15 May. In the evening he took part in a ball arranged in his honour by General von Bennigsen in the latter's Zakrett Castle, a half hour's distance from Vilna. It was at this ball that the news of Napoleon's crossing the Nyemen reached him.

The combined French army (without the troops that were to arrive during the campaign) disposed of 477,000 combatants, of which 80,000 were cavalry, under the following commanding officers:

* Russian spelling for the Neman River (Ed.).

First Corps	Marshal Davout, Prince d'Eckmühl
Second Corps	Marshal Oudinot, Duke of Reggio
Third Corps	Marshal Ney, Duke of Elchingen
Fourth Corps	Prince Eugène de Beauharnais, Viceroy of Italy
Fifth Corps	Prince Poniatowski
Sixth Corps	Lieutenant-General Marquis Saint-Cyr (the Fourth and Sixth Corps consisted mostly of Bavarians and Italians).
Seventh Corps (Saxony)	Lieutenant-General Count Régnier, Duke of Massa
Eighth Corps (Westphalia)	Lieutenant-General Count Vandamme
Ninth Corps	Marshal Victor, Duke of Belluno
Tenth Corps	Marshal MacDonald, Duke of Taranto (with the Prussian Auxiliary Corps under General York)
Austrian Corps	Prince Schwarzenberg; this included four reserve cavalry corps under Lieutenant-Generals Count de Nansouty, Montbrun, Marquis de Grouchy, and Latour-Maubourg.

With the troops that arrived during the campaign, as well as the heavy artillery, the engineers, and special army units, there were on Russian soil since the beginning of the campaign 610,058 men, of which 270,000 were allied troops.

Napoleon was confronted by three armies: the First Army of the West under the command of Barclay de Tolly and the generals under him: Prince Wittgenstein, Bagavout, Tuchkov, Count Shuvalov, Grand Duke Constantine, Doktorov, Uvarov, Baron Korff, and Count Pahlen; the Second Army of the West under the command of Prince Bagration and the generals under him: Rayevsky, Borozdin, Count Vorontsov, Baron Knorring, Sievers, Vasilchikov, Count Platov; the Reserve Army under the command of Tormasov and the generals under him: Markov, Komenskoy, and Lambert. Altogether these totalled 241,000 men without the fortress troops of Riga and Dünaburg.

Generals Pfuhl, Armfeld, Bennigsen, and Prince Volkonski constituted the War Council under Tsar Alexander.

The disposition was as follows: Napoleon was with Davout, Oudinot, Ney, Beauharnais, and Murat opposite Kovno; on the right flank there were Poniatowski, Régnier, and Jérôme Bonaparte opposite Grodno; on the left flank MacDonald with the Prussians under York at Tilsit; Prince Schwarzenberg along the Bug River in the Slonym region.

The Russians under Barclay de Tolly, Wittgenstein, Bagavout, Tuchkov, and Shuvalov were along the Nyemen at Grodno; the Russians under Bagration, Doktorov, and Pahlen between Grodno and Slonym; Platov at Bialystok; Tsar Alexander with the Guards at Vilna.

9, 10, 11, 12 June

There is a very cogent reason for my not continuing my Diary; on the 9th I had sentry duty; the 10th, 11th, and 12th I was under arrest! Fate played me an evil trick on the evening of the 9th. After ordering Retreat I had my men present themselves for some brandy, but unfortunately failed to notice that one of my privates was drinking too much. He had hardly relieved the guard on the Grand Duke's balcony when he started cursing and making such noise that his Imperial Majesty, who had not yet gone to bed, came out to ask him what he had said. The soldier, who told him some mixed-up rubbish by way of an answer, ended by making some foolish remarks to the Grand Duke, who took him by the collar and brought him directly to me in the guardhouse. This unexpected apparition frightened me all the more since I had taken off my helmet and my scarf in order to lie down. After giving me a regular sermon, which upset me since I had never before received any reproaches, he put me under arrest. I had already been in jail two days when the orders suddenly came to leave quarters immediately to meet the enemy, who had crossed the border. Delighted at seeing my punishment end in this way, I returned to my squadron to finish up my little affairs. I said good-bye to everyone I knew in the vicinity. One person seemed to me a little sad, but the others seemed rather pleased that we were leaving them.

13 June, Dolgalishki

We set off marching at six in the morning, and we're bivouacking here. I'm seeing a camp for the first time in my life.

14 June

It was a very cold night; I looked around and found a little space in a hut, where I am now; it's not very gay but I thought it was better to be snug and dry under a roof of straw than drenched to the bone under the roof of a sky that is pouring down torrents of rain. But it's so boring; there's nothing to do but stretch out.

15 June

What joy! I've just seen my brother Jacques again! How agreeable, how joyful it is to meet someone you love in situations like this! We spent the day in the most pleasant way possible. What a good chap he is—always cheerful.

16 June

Big review of the Guards. Svintsiani, a little town thirty versts from our camp, is having its meadows filled by the thousands of soldiers constantly arriving from all over in order to enlarge our corps—25,000 of them have been counted already.

17, 18 June, Vitzy

A trick by the colonel, who's got a grudge against me, has forced me to go back to Vitzy to have some bread baked there for the regiment. One must know how to obey if one hopes to have a command some day. I dragged along a whole day going from Svintsiani to Dolgalishki and another to Vitzy. Both horses, at the end of their powers, died, and my non-commissioned officer and I finished the trip on foot. The mud was frightful, the weather awful. Exhausted to the ultimate degree and tormented by hunger and weariness, I collapsed three times. Finally an artillery unit going by put me on a cannon, and that's how I got here, more dead than alive. The enemy, who's performing miracles of speed, is six miles from here. Our army is falling back to look for a good position. I see whole families passing by on foot and on horseback who know the horrors of a bloody war will soon break out in all its fury.

19 June, Vitzy

What has become of this city, once so lively and bustling? Every place is empty; you can scarcely see more than a few Jews, looking very shy, or a few greybeards leaning on their sticks, or some abandoned child crying for his parents, moving about the deserted streets that used to be so animated. A sad spectacle, which has really moved me. The Tsar and the General Staff have just arrived; I've carried out my mission, and this evening I'm going back to rejoin my regiment.

20 June

We are bivouacking. For the first time I hear cannon from afar; what a funny feeling! When shall we hear it closer?

21 June

Our camp is outside Vitzy. Jacques is with me. The French army is at Svintsiani.

22 June

There was an alarm this morning at seven. The opposing outposts have clashed. The army, which is almost 100,000 strong, is deploying itself from the side of the Düna. What a sight, as novel as it is impressive, to see so many soldiers assembled, carrying out the decision of one person, governed by discipline, and inspired by the same unanimous courage and by the same feeling.

The bearing of my men is admirable; the infantry, especially, is magnificent. Very soon, perhaps, a battle will decide our destinies and the destinies of the two most powerful empires, and the lives of several thousand men will be at stake. May the Almighty grant us the victory, for the right is on our side! May the courageous patriotism of the Russians be shown in all its vigour, so that we need never blush at the recollection of our actions as we had to, after all, during the war in Prussia and in Austria!

If fate has decided that I am to meet my death in one of the fields covering the Russian land, and if this Diary comes into the hands of my parents one day, I beg them to grant me the following requests: Take care of my two servants, Fyodor and Petrushka; Keep my grey horse until it dies; and Pay my debts, which consist of 18,000 rubles, according to a list that's among my papers.

But this sounds like a Will, and I have no desire to make one, since I'd much rather go on living.

23 June

It's inconceivable! Why are we always being made to fall back without giving battle? Yet our army is so big. We've marched fifty versts; our quarters are in one of the villages that belong to Count Manuzzi; it has a very pretty location. The count, who has his residence two versts from here, has received the Tsar. His chateau, very beautiful architecturally, is situated on a hill on the shores of a splendid lake, surrounded by woods and mountains which act as a fine amphitheatre. The English garden has some lovely parts. In sum, everything together makes this a dwelling worthy of a king. It will all soon be the prey of the flames, for according to all one hears, the French mark their advance by the most atrocious cruelties—pillaging, ravaging, and burning everything they come across. It's so sad to see the

the peasants and their families leaving the places where they came into the world. But what shocks me most is that the fields, full of wheat and the fruits of nature, are trampled by the hoofs of the cavalry. There's no longer any order among us concerning supplies and fodder; everyone grabs what he finds. This ruination of the peasants and the gentry afflicts me a great deal, even though the latter deserve it, because their tyranny is well known.

24 June

The heat is excessive. Jacques came to see me; the good fellow would share his last crumb with his brother Boris, who is so fond of him! We talked about bygone times and the times to come. He's only just left me. I would like to benefit by this day of rest to gain strength for the future.

25 June

What a night! We left this village at midnight; a tremendous storm pursued us for thirty-five versts. I'm drenched to the bone; I'll have to change my underclothes. After recovering a little, I made a comparison between the present situation and the past, in Vitzy, which I called unendurable. God knows, man is never satisfied. He hopes for everything from the future and is very often punished for his greed. These four days, for instance, were more painful than the whole march from St. Petersburg to Vitzy; and who had desired with greater ardour than I this wanderer's life? How I long to know what's going on at the front and to have news from Reval and W., whom I love so tenderly. But I realize that's impossible, since communications have been cut. Minsk province is prettier than the others we've passed through. But the destitution of the peasants makes me despondent.

26 June, Druzha

Our camp is very close to this city. I am writing these lines at the end of a barn that is quite dark, by the light of a lamp.

Surrounded by shadows and interrupted only by the snoring of the people sleeping round about, I surrender to my reflections. The camp fires scattered around the fields, the singing of the soldiers, the whinnying of the horses make a rather striking background. This morning the general told us of the heroic action of a squadron of uhlans that had been cut off. They forced their way through two French regiments, making mincemeat of them. Platov has arrived with 18,000 cossacks!

27 June, Valkopol

A little town on the banks of the Düna. What bliss to be able to bathe when you're really hot! The word is that we're going to stay on here for a while. So all this retreating is over. The army has taken up a position eight versts from here; its rearguard is just ahead of us. This position is so impressive that the enemy will try to force it in vain. I've already grown accustomed to living in a hut with a thatched roof of straw or leaves called a *shalash* in Russian. It's true that it's difficult to sit up on your knees or to stretch out comfortably, but I sleep well anyhow.

28 June

The sight of such a large army collected together at one point and the splendid spectacle of a camp that is just as magnificent because of its order as because of its various splendid troops are too beautiful to describe properly.

29 June

Jacques comes to see me very often. What are my dear ones doing in Reval? There's no news at all; I feel quite desperate. The harmony between the officers and the cheerfulness of the soldiers, who hardly even have bread to eat, are altogether admirable. Retreat is celebrated very ceremoniously; it's the time of day when the officers of all the regiments gather together around musicians to see each other, talk to each other, or play cards. I always go to bed at nine o'clock after eating my rice soup, which seems delicious to me though it is often very thin and without any meat. Tea is a real benefactor for us; it is nourishing and warming.

30 June

Today for the first time I saw some French prisoners; how proud they are! They do not deign even to answer our questions. It's the cossacks who always capture a great many. A number of Polish noblemen have been severely punished for having had contact with the enemy army. The Prince of Oldenburg, who has said he's quite willing to take a letter to Reval for me, received me very graciously. The enemy has split in two in order to flank us on both sides.

1, 2, 3, 4 July

I don't know what to write in my Diary, since all I do is eat, drink, and sleep.

On 4 July Commander of the First Army of the West, Barclay de Tolly, issued the following proclamation from his camp at Drissa to the French outposts on the Düna:

Remember, Comrades, that you are 400 leagues [1,000 miles] away from your reinforcements. Do not let yourselves be deceived by our initial movements; you know the Russians too well to believe that they are fleeing. They will take up the battle in good time, and then your retreat will be very difficult. We call upon you as comrades: go back *en masse*! Give no faith to the deceitful talk that you are fighting for peace: you are fighting for the insatiable ambition of a ruler who wishes no peace and who is toying with the blood of his best men.

The commander addressed this appeal to the Germans in Napoleon's army:

Germans! While many of superior social station among your people have forgotten their duties to their Fatherland, still the great majority of your people is stalwart, courageous, and impatient with the yoke of tyranny. Faithful to God and the Fatherland, follow the call of the Fatherland and of honour, enjoy the reward of your courage and your sacrifice, and shake off the fetters of the Corsican tyrant; if you bend further beneath the yoke of oppression that weighs upon you, you will go down in shame, misery, and degradation, the mockery of other nations and the curse of posterity!

Shortly thereafter Barclay de Tolly and his whole army suddenly abandoned the entrenched camp at Drissa, which had been built up for years.

5 July

We've just crossed the Düna. Prince Hohenlohe has been captured. L. has taken up service with us. The French wanted to cross the Düna, but their efforts were futile. So Bonaparte is pushing on towards Polotsk in order to cross the river there, but we're getting there ahead of him. The nights are so cold here that a fur coat is very useful to keep out the damp.

6 July

Today in a lovely monastery we found refuge from the wind, which is blowing with all its lungs. We are camping beneath the walls. I've sent my Fyodor off to Kasian to warn my uncle* to leave his estate very soon. We're making long marches.

7 July, Polotsk

We marched all night; it was so lovely. But I was overcome by a desire to sleep so suddenly that I slumped over beneath a tree, holding my horse by the reins. I slept three hours; then I followed after the rearguard until I caught up with the regiment. The Emperor has left for Moscow. Jacques is with me.

* Count Sievers (Ed.).

8 July

Day of rest. The city is rather pretty. There are lots of Jews. Supplies have been laid in. What else is needed for utter contentment? Bagration is said to have attacked the French.

9 July

We left Polotsk yesterday to join forces with Bagration. By moving along the right bank of the Düna we'll soon be able to join up with him. Fyodor has come back; my uncle isn't at Kasian at all. I've been sent some fruit and money.

10 July, Kasian

The colonel, who despatched me to look for the regimental supply train, gave me no indication of the hour or day I was to return. So taking advantage of this, I went straight off to Kasian after collecting some information about the supply train. I was received en route by a number of gentlemen who knew my uncle and who were preparing to receive the French. I reached Kasian in the evening. My uncle wasn't there any longer, but Jacques, who had arrived before me, came out to meet me. All the household people, a little frightened at first by my abrupt arrival since they were afraid of some levies, were delighted when they heard my name. I found my poor cousin ill and abandoned. I pity him from the bottom of my heart. He has been handed over to all the horrors of war!

11 July

It had been a long time since I'd slept in a good bed. It's a real joy after lying about in damp bivouacs for so long. We've looked over the gardens and the surroundings of Kasian; everything there is surely going to go up in flames before long. What's going to happen to poor Fedinka? We did our best to cheer the people up; they were completely despondent. Tomorrow morning at six we're going to look for the army again, in Vitebsk.

12 July, Vitebsk

A pretty city. Everyone here is excited; we scarcely had time to eat lunch. We're supposed to move forward against the enemy. Jacques seemed upset when we said good-bye. The horses have been saddled already.

13 July

I'm lying under my tent. You can hear sustained cannon fire from the distance. The French are already showing themselves on the other side of the Düna. Are we finally going to come to the point of measuring arms with them?

(Eight o'clock in the evening)

We're bivouacking six versts on the other side of Vitebsk. The sight of the wounded, who are being moved into Vitebsk, is so sad! Some of them, without arms or legs, were swimming in their own blood; others, slashed to pieces by sabre strokes, were hiding their pains and agonies while trying to look brave. The Hussar Guards are said to have acquitted themselves well. Seventeen versts from Vitebsk we called a halt in order to take up battle formation. The number of wounded and captured kept growing. Thus the night fell.

14 July

After marching a few versts forward, a few versts back and to the side, at six in the evening we found ourselves in the same position we had occupied yesterday. The cannon fire, which had lasted till noon and then died down for a while, broke out with redoubled strength. The army withdrew. You could see spurts of flame from the cannon. Soon the battle broke out at all points. We were placed on a height in order to attack the enemy columns that were constantly pressing forward. The defensive fire from the woods was very lively. The cannon were being fired successfully; the whistling of the shells, the shouts of fighting men, and the commands of the officers produced a general effect that was very marked and impressive. This whole spectacle took place right at our feet. The broad expanse of the field was specked with troops. It began to grow dark, so that every cannon shot, scattering death, was all the more visible. The engagement ended, to our disadvantage, at ten o'clock. The French set up their camp fires opposite us, with sang-froid and an air of security that astounded us. Even from a distance you could make out their voices and hear what they were saying! We were quite still, for our hearts were as heavy as the shadows that surrounded us. The complaints of the wounded, who were being trampled by our horses, added to our despondency. A number of them wanted to drag along after us in order not to fall into the hands of our pursuers, but being too feeble, they fell time after time. So that's the glory of the soldier! I cried, seeing a chasseur who had lost both his legs to a cannon shell rolling in the dust and full of regret—not at having been mutilated but at being taken captive. Oh! Arrogant tyrants of the earth—what will your consciences say one day! You will have spilt the blood of your subjects without rhyme or reason! But thank God this is a just and true war! Every Russian soul that quits its mortal coil to go off to purer regions will be rewarded and will pray for the welfare of his monarch, who thinks only of the cause of the fatherland, and not of his own interest.

15 July

Long live the Russian arms! Bonaparte, who had ordered Vitebsk to be taken by storm, was vigorously repulsed. But we have fallen back anyway, to ten versts behind the city.

16 July

We left our camp at six in the morning, and after marching until ten in the evening (sixty versts), everyone was so tired that we could hardly look for the fodder to feed the horses.

17 July

Who would have believed that we would fall back again.

Fifty versts today! I can't stand any more; the heat is so intense that the horses are collapsing under the soldiers from fatigue and agony. My throat is sore. The nights are cold, the days hot. Our bed is straw, our roof the universe. Strong drink, which is very unhealthful when one is resting, has become a necessity during the damp nights of Poland.

18 July, Smolensk

In Smolensk at last, having done 180 versts in four days. I already feel like stopping my Diary, since it is so inconvenient for me—but perseverance in all things is a virtue I should like to try to acquire!

19 July

I was in the town. It has beautiful churches, and the fort, though old, represents the frontier of Russia and is quite formidable. The location of the city is magnificent; the outlying parts of town are large and the population numbers 20,000. How hungry one grows after being deprived for a a time of what one needs! The cafés and the sweet shops are in full swing. My stomach is going to have enough for a whole week. The Grand Duke has just arrived. Bagration has joined up with our corps.

20 July

What a joy it is to see once again one's close relatives after a long time, especially in such a situation. Brömsen and his sister, Mme Sebenkov, received me as amiably as possible. They are as alike as two drops of water.

21 July

The Dnieper, which sends out its torrents around Smolensk, is a rather nice river. We shall bathe in it often, S. and I. The weather is wonderful. There is plenty of punch; the camp is teeming with hens and roast turkeys. What else is needed to be gay and happy?

22 July

We went off to town on horseback, S. and I. After an excellent lunch, we took a walk. The schools, the monasteries, and the ladies of pleasure were the objects of our humble visit. The first were in good order, the second very old, and the third were horrible.

23 July

Colonel H., whom I ran into by accident, entertained me very well today; he wanted to sound me out because of my inclination for his sister, but I evaded any kind of explanation. We spend the evenings chatting and smoking and drinking; most of our officers get together in order to gamble, but that's not for me.

24, 25, 26, 27 July

After camping a week in the same place without doing anything, we left Smolensk to look for and defeat an enemy corps that had got lost. We stopped at Kamnishky. Barclay inspected our corps.

28 July

Our plan has failed, the enemy corps escaped us, and tomorrow morning we are going back to our old camping ground near Smolensk.

29 July

Last night at 11.30 one of Barclay's aides-de-camp arrived to tell us to be ready to leave. At midnight the trumpet sounded for the march. The weather, which had been fine, began to turn bad. A chilly rain soon started coming down on us and grew heavier by the minute. The roads began to deteriorate, and the cannon, which were just barely dragging along, blocked our way. The shadows had become as dark as possible, and moving along behind my troops, I could hardly make out the cuirassier's horse directly in front of me. The storm grew increasingly violent; we passed through woods and rapid streams swollen by water flowing in torrents. Drenched to the bone, stiff with cold, we finally arrived at our camp. A splendid forest located on the right side of the highway gave us some protection against the furies of the frightful storm. Luckily my servant had taken possession of an enormous oak that had been hollowed by age; I slept there, soaked to my undershirt and tormented by fatigue and hunger.

If only the braggarts, blowhards, and do-nothings of our capital could find themselves in our position! They would soon have a sound idea of the military life and its drawbacks and would have more veneration for it—or much less for themselves.

30 July

What a sight tonight! Imagine a dense forest that had taken in two cavalry divisions beneath its majestic, bushy roof! The camp fires, now gleaming brightly, now dying down, could be seen burning through the foliage their heat kept agitating; at every moment they revealed to astounded eyes groups of men sitting, standing, and lying down around them. The confused noise of the horses and the axe strokes that were cutting away to feed the fires, all this added to the blackest night I've ever seen in my life—created, in fact, an effect that was as novel as it was bizarre; it resembled a magic tableau. I thought involuntarily of Schiller's *Robbers* and of mankind's primitive life in the forest.

31 July

I've been transferred to Barclay as an aide-de-camp. A number of acquaintances attached to Headquarters have told me some interesting news. Some papers belonging to a French staff officer were taken which prove that the enemy army is in admirable order and numbers some half million men. What a mass of people! The French General Staff has complete knowledge of the terrain of our provinces. It is plain that Bonaparte wants to force our army to fight, but we are only on the defensive. Counts P. and B., as well as a number of other officers, have been obliged to leave the army, since they are mistrusted. Barclay sent me later to the Grand Duke with some important papers. I spent the night at M.'s.

1 August

Jacques and I spent the day together at P.'s regiment with B. It was very pleasant. I got a little drunk in the evening. That's pardonable. But it shouldn't go any further. Katenin charmed me with his wit.

2 August

Here we are again beneath the walls of Smolensk.

3 August

What a march! And at night-time! We did thirty-five versts. What a frightful situation, to want to sleep and be prevented. I can hardly write these lines.

4 August

I was awakened this morning by cannon fire; we were stationed on a great height, from which we could see everything. The city was besieged; the fighting was bloody. Nightfall put an end to the scenes of horror, but the moment dawn comes we shall see once again the furies of war.

5 August

The French mounted an assault five times, but were energetically repulsed. Bonaparte himself commanded. Nevgrovsky distinguished himself. The fighting is still going on. While thousands are about to sacrifice their lives for their country, we're here grilling chickens! What contradictions!

6 August

The engagement has resumed. Our batteries are having great success and our sharpshooters are performing miracles.

The French, dead drunk, scrambled up the walls and, falling back, became ladders for the men following. The ditches are filled with corpses.

7 August

My birthday, a day as memorable for Russia as it was disastrous. At eight in the morning the fighting was engaged with an intensity that was just as cruel on the part of the French as it was gallant on our part.

Our central battery was seized at nine. The Elite Grenadiers mounted the ramparts. Small fire could already be heard in the outer parts of the city. Our cannon, taken, were soon turned against us. Bombs fell and battered first the sides of the buildings, then our gallant troops, who defended every inch of territory. Fire broke out everywhere. The outer parts of the city were burning. Fighting continued in the city itself until nine in the evening; it was then that a sight as fearsome as it was beautiful presented itself to my eyes. I was standing on the mountain; the carnage was taking place at my very feet. Shadows heightened the brilliant sheen from the fire and the shooting. The bombs, which displayed their luminous traces, destroyed everything in their path. The cries of the wounded, the Hurrahs! of the men still fighting, the dull confused sound of the rocks that were falling and breaking up—it all made my hair stand on end. I shall never forget this night! For who could imagine all the horrors I've just seen without having been present! The poor city has become a heap of stones; it's a considerable loss! This encounter is going to have important consequences for us.

8 August

We are on the highway to Moscow and Dorgabush; the French, who hold Smolensk, are pursuing us with as much speed as success. We don't have even the time to rest. We often have to abandon our dinner in order to flee. What a situation!

9 August, Dorgabush

We're running away like hares. Panic has seized everyone. Our courage is crushed; our march looks like a funeral procession. My heart is heavy. We are abandoning all our rich and fruitful land to the fury of an enemy who spares nothing his cruelty, it is said. This lovely season is displaying all its fruits, which will be the prey of flames and bandits.

10 August

It is impossible to imagine the horrors the French are said to be committing. One hears that they're burning and desecrating the churches, that the weaker sex—or rather any individuals who fall into their frantic hands—are sacrificed to their brutality and the satisfaction of their infernal lusts. Children, greybeards—it's all the same to them—all perish beneath their blows. These rumours are producing a sensation among the peasants, who with the greatest sangfroid in the world set their huts on fire so as not to abandon them to the enemy. I see nothing but consternation, sadness, and misery. This evening we went to sleep by the light of a number of such fires.

11 August

We constantly change position to deceive the enemy, who evidently want to bypass us. I've just seen and spoken to the English general called Wilson. He's taken part in campaigns all over the world—he's even been to India and Egypt! Just now he's with Headquarters. He predicts that this war will be one of the bloodiest and the longest in history.

12 August

Grand Duke Constantine has been sent back to St. Petersburg by Barclay. It's a relief for us; he won't torture us any more with his exercises and orders. But everyone is even more annoyed with Barclay because they think he's a traitor and is falling back on purpose in order to give the enemy free play. Yet I think he's a man of probity.

13 August

En route I paid attention to the various elements that give a well-organized army corps its vigour. Every moment passes like a game of chess. The greatest manœuvres are conceived in the head of a single individual. An idea has scarcely formed in the head of the commander-in-chief when the aides-de-camp, like rays of the sun leaving its centre, rush in all directions to announce the decision of a single person. But the execution is still more admirable. Battalions and squadrons that a moment before had seemed like immovable, inanimate heaps begin to move; lines stretch out, advance, and place themselves in battle order. The shouts of the commanders join with the dull, confused sounds of the rolling weapons and the advance of the cavalry. Soon the signal is given. The cannon thunder, the sharp-shooters slip into their positions in the gaps. Then you can see, sometimes on a wing, sometimes in the centre, columns of infantry aiming and firing, then advancing and over-running everything in their path. Smoke envelops the bloody scene, which sees to it that coffins will be ready everywhere for the human race! Suddenly the noise stops! What is it? A cavalry unit is attacking! The clatter of the sabres, the whirling dust, and the shouts of the combatants lend a new aspect to the total picture. Soon the infantry charges; the firing resumes again. Then a retreat ends everything. What a difference from the armies of old, which did not have fire-arms!

My old Fyodor has got frightfully drunk; the pranks he plays are very funny. He's surrounded himself with a number of soldiers to whom he tells hair-raising stories that border on the magical. But to bed!

14 August

Albrecht, of the Dragoons, has just arrived from Polotsk. Wittgenstein has beaten Macdonald; it's said the victory is total. Today was a day of rest.

15 August

We're passing through the most radiant landscape. The fields, laden with the various gifts of Ceres, are being trampled beneath the feet of our warriors, who are destroying the good things of their brothers and compatriots. The peasants leave their dwellings, abandoning them to the flames and violation. A cruel sight! I wouldn't want to be commander-in-chief for anything in the world. He must regard himself as the chief culprit for all this destruction. Every soul plunged into pain, every foot of territory abandoned to the frantic hands of the pirates of Europe, every victim, every single thing produced with such innocent consecration is his responsibility! And if he commits a serious error, his conscience will be tormented and he will be judged. The post is sublime, if it is occupied with zeal and genius, if it is held by a man of compassion and talent. But if, on the contrary, it is badly conducted—what a contrast!

We're still marching for great stretches daily; we're hardly given enough time to rest or to water our horses, which are growing thinner and dying off as fast as you can look at them. Our underclothes and uniforms are worn out. All this would be agreeable if only we were pursuing the enemy, but as it is . . . ! ! ! And then, the awareness that the enemy is only 200 versts from Moscow is enough to give us the most depressing thoughts.

16 August, Vyazma

A pretty little city. Retreat is all the more painful the moment one passes through a city, since it's a tight squeeze getting through and everyone pushes ahead to be the first to pass. There is no lack of supplies; on the contrary, there's a glut of everything since we pillaged the city. Our camp is two versts on the other side of the city. The weather is fine!

17 August

At last, a day of rest. Jacques is with me. We've bought some wine. Everyone at the camp has abandoned himself to the pleasures of the good life; they seem to have forgotten that the enemy is only twenty versts away from us. After a long time I've finally seen some women. The armed peasants are doing the enemy a great deal of damage because they remove their supplies, and since they know the terrain they often attack in the shadows of the night. There are 15,000 of them in Moscow Province. There's a lot of talk about Kutuzov being named Generalissimo of all the armies. Maybe things will go better.

18 August

What a day! It rained for twenty-four hours steadily. I'm drenched to the bone. I can hardly hold my quill up. Kutuzov has just arrived.

19 August

Our retreat continues. This morning I was despatched to make some levies and get some supplies. Passing by the little city of Struzha I met some of the wounded; among them I saw a face I knew. I went over to greet him but a crowd of natives and marauders who were fleeing at the approach of the French and who were crying out "Here they are!" separated me from the poor officer. The enemy's arrival astonished me; I thought I was a long way from them. Heavy cannon fire finally told me that they had attacked and cut through the centre. The disorder was extreme; everyone was fleeing. Finally the cossacks appeared, and the French, who were already in the streets, were obliged to fall back. I had sent back my command under the non-commissioned officer. Curiosity held me back. The city looked like a nest of ants. Everything was in confusion. The houses were empty, the windows and doors broken. The streets were filled with barrels, beds, and furniture. The inhabitants, running, hiding, shouting, and begging, added to the horrors of the place and to the tumultuous scene of the soldiers fighting. Anyone who has not been present at such a scene could never imagine it. I should have dearly liked to help, console, save, and hide people, but it was impossible. Quite undone, filled with pain, I turned my grey and tried to get back to my camp, where everyone was serene.

20 August, Nikolayev

This morning I witnessed a really touching scene. A few versts from our camp we passed a detachment of prisoners, among whom I perceived a number of Polish officers. The face of one interested me, it was so noble and spiritual. He seemed to be suffering, but he had an expression of resignation. I was about to approach him when I heard him give a cry and saw him making his way through the crowd. He was trying to reach a Russian officer, mounted with his back to him, who was talking to the quartermasters. The moment the officer turned towards the source of the exclamations and caught sight of the prisoner, he leaped off his horse and flung himself into the man's arms. The upset and surprise produced by such an unusual scene soon turned into admiration and interest when the Russian officer told us that this was his only brother, who had entered the service of the Poles. This touching meeting led me to some reflections on the military condition and on wars in general. How cruel and vain are honour and ambition!

21 August, Rzhatskoy Pristan

A charming little city. The houses are so well built and so clean, the streets of such pretty symmetry. Everything was still in the most perfect order, except that the inhabitants had already left their dwellings. The city had been abandoned to us, and everything was taken away immediately. We were like famished lions that after a lengthy quest had found something to sate their hunger. We left camp to fling ourselves into the shops and on the supplies assigned to us.

News from Moscow tells us that the inhabitants there are leaving.

22 August

A march of thirty versts. We've set up camp at Borodino. The word is that a general battle will take place shortly. May God shield us! It is time to measure ourselves against the subverters.

23 August

Here I am in a palace of greenery, lying outstretched on my coat, which is coming apart, and drinking a kind of tea made from lukewarm water and leaves soaked in honey. I give myself up to my thoughts. I feel a pleasant satisfaction (quite unusual), a pure and tranquil repose. Though bereft of everything, sharing the mourning that has descended on all Russia, with no news of my loved ones in Reval, I have a premonition that uplifts me. I often had the habit, when we were retreating, of seizing my sabre and cursing our inactivity, and of conceiving all sorts of sinister plots and unforgivable extravagances, but this evening I am submitting myself to the higher powers; I clasp my hands and pray fervently! May the Almighty grant victory to the Russian army; may He give me strength and fortitude at the decisive moment; may He give me the courage to endure the blows of my fate, if I am put to the test; and finally, may He protect my absent family and friends!

24 August

Everything is being readied for a major battle which will determine the triumph or the shame of Napoleon. Rostoptshin has armed Moscow. At six o'clock an attack was launched against our left flank. It was a rather warm engagement; losses were 1,000 dead. Our batteries are well mounted.

25 August

Spent the evening at Headquarters. I was aide-de-camp for Barclay de Tolly. Everything is calm: the silence before the storm.

*On 16 August Kutuzov was appointed Commander-in-Chief.
He at once extended the retreat as far as Borodino, where he called
a halt and had an entrenched camp set up on the Moskva River on
both sides of the Borodino Monastery. The principal combat force
of the French army, with Napoléon, reached Borodino on 24 August.*

*The sixty-seven-year-old Kutuzov had only recently been honoured
and fêted as the conqueror of the Turks. He had stood against
Napoleon at Austerlitz and lost. In Napoleon's eyes, nevertheless,
he was the only opponent among the Russian marshals who was to be
taken seriously.*

26, 27 August. Midnight. Between Borodino and Mozhaisk

Oh, day of massacre! Oh, day of horrors! I'm still alive—
and I prostrate myself to thank God for it. Jacques—what
is he doing? Is he still breathing, or not? Perhaps he's
wounded, and I'm far away from him, unable to bring him
help! What cruel uncertainty!

I was still in Barclay's suite at four o'clock when the
enemy's offensive was announced to us. The General Staff
mounted up at once to follow the two generals, who were
already giving their orders. The weather was magnificent.
The sun was about to rise and its first rays heralded the
battle. An enemy battery mounted on a hill near the
Borodino Monastery opened fire, sending us its challenge.
At once *everything* began moving. The sharpshooters clashed,
the infantry advanced in square formation, and the cavalry
stationed itself in reserve. The flying artillery occupied the
gaps and, together with the stationary batteries, hurled
death into the ranks of the attackers. Our position was
superb; the centre was heavily manned and fortified. The
right wing, though well defended, was almost out of the
battle. But the left, alone, had a great deal to do, and it was
the position that suffered the most. Our regiment found itself
at the centre. I was very grieved at being separated from my
comrades. The minister, his aides-de-camp, and I made off

KEY

A. Napoleon's Guards and Reserves, who were turning our flank.

B. Infantry columns, deployed. *f.* Light troops

p.p. The monastery and town of Borodino. *ö ö* are movable batteries.

C. The main body of infantry. *Z.* The main body of cavalry, hidden behind a rise on the ground, which attacked our centre at 11.30.

L. is the river Moskva.

d. are the Russian batteries.⚞⚟movable batteries.

0. The Russian army, drawn up in square formation.

⚞⚟ Cossacks on the right flank. *x.* Light troops who tried to turn the French right flank but who were repulsed by the enormous batteries.

b. Artillery positions *a* are the Guards and Reserves. *X.* Troops marching directly to Mozhaisk. *y* the road ▨▨▨ Movable bridge.

Planche. de la position

A. Les Gardes et les Réserves de Napoléons, qui tournoient notre flanc.

B. Colones d'Infanterie, qui déployent les troupes légères.

P.P. Le Monastère et le bourg Borodino. ## Sont des batteries mouvantes.

C. Gros d'Infanterie. D. Gros de Cavalerie, qui attaque

notre centre à 11½ heures, et qui était caché, derrière une hauteur.

L. est le fleuve Moskva

⊃ Sont des batteries russes. ## batteries mouvantes

⊃ l'armée russe formée en bataillon carrés.

⋀ Cosaques sur le flanc droit. ⋏ troupes légères qui veulent tourner

le flanc droit des fr. mais qui sont repoussés par des batteries enormes.

P. Parc. Q. sont les gardes et les réserves. K. des troupes qui vont droit

à Majaïsk. Y. la chaussée. ≡ Pont mouvant.

Le Camp & la Position de Borodino

at a fast gallop as far as the river, where Bistram was fighting
in the water with the French.

The novelty of this whole scene, the whistling of the shells
and bullets, the clatter of the hand weapons, and the noise
of the fighting men—all this bewildered me and had a
singular effect on me. Our chasseurs were finally thrown
back, and the French, drunk with joy and liquor, scrambled
up the shore and overran everything before them. We were
very close to the fighting. My horse, usually a fiery beast,
was hit by a lump of mud thrown towards me by a bomb and
reared. At eight o'clock I was sent back to the regiment
because the officer relieving me had arrived. I found the
regiment inactive. But the cannon shells were reaching us.
At 8.30 we were put on a hill, where we were quite exposed
but could see everything. The spectacle was most majestic,
most impressive. Before us 300,000 men were squeezed into
a narrow space, fighting with fury and tenacity. The
cannon fire increased from one minute to the next. The
defensive firing could hardly be heard. The whole plain was
covered by smoke. For three hours we stood there motionless, looking, trembling, and losing patience. The shells hit
and killed a great many horses, fewer men. At eleven o'clock
the massacre grew general; the earth trembled, the air
darkened.

Suddenly the noise stopped! The enemy cavalry, 25,000
strong, charged our columns and batteries. The reserves
started moving. Our cavalry moved off, with Shevich at the
head of our brigade to lead us to victory. Hurrah! We
attacked! The earth trembled and groaned beneath the
weight of the cuirassiers. There was a collision, but the dust
prevented us from distinguishing our adversaries. It was the
carabiniers and the lancers. The carnage lasted five minutes.
The horses trampled the dying and the wounded. The enemy
had been repulsed, but we had scarcely formed our squadrons when the fire from a disguised battery nearby decimated
our ranks. The trumpet assembled us. There was a second
attack, with less success. The enemy meanwhile had forced

the left wing, and we were despatched across the battlefield. The sight of the dead and wounded was frightful. A description of it would be futile, since it would be too feeble. At four o'clock the fighting slackened. But at six it began with redoubled fury. The sun would not set today. My mouth was full of sand and blood. We had lost twelve officers. At nine o'clock the victor was still undecided, but at 9.30 our left flank was broken through and repulsed. Instead of flinging himself on their right wing Platov had left his post; this is how we have been forced to fall back again.

Today saw 68,000 men killed on both sides, and 1,200 officers on our side. We could have won the battle if the right flank had acted vigorously, but—alas!—it is lost, and we are going to abandon Moscow to the fury of these bandits!

Chapter IV

KUTUZOV SAVES RUSSIA

The night following the Battle of Borodino, Kutuzov, who had lost no more than the outworks of his positions, summoned his field commanders to discuss whether the following day a renewed attack by the 120,000 French troops against the 70,000 Russians still remaining was to be risked, with the safety of the country at stake, or whether the retreat should be continued in order to lure the enemy still farther into the interior.

He addressed the assembled War Council as follows:

I am well aware of the great value of the sacrifice being made. The ancient city of the tsars, which has been the pride of our realm for a thousand years, filled with the relics and the sacred objects of our faith, will fall. The loss of our holy city is great, but great, too, is the danger that threatens the whole Fatherland. This war is being waged not for Moscow, but for the Fatherland. Accordingly, the lesser must yield to the greater. So, since all means of saving Moscow are exhausted, let the city fall into the enemy's power, but in such a way that it will at the same time become a memorial worthy of the honour of a great and luckless people and an eternally luminous example for future generations and centuries.

I, however, shall lead the army sideways off into the fertile countryside of Kaluga, and after it has swiftly recuperated there, while hunger and the northern winter will have weakened and worn down the foreigners, I shall then seize them from the rear and the sides, and I hope, trusting in God and in the courage of the army, that they will pay for all the atrocities they have perpetrated and will leave our holy soil in disgrace.

The War Council agreed. Kutuzov withdrew beyond the Moskva and encamped on the road to Mozhaisk.

28 August, Mozhaisk

What joy, what happiness! Jacques is well, except for a little contusion. His regiment lost a great many men; he conducted himself well. Our meeting was most satisfying.

28 August to 1 September

We've been running back and forth like madmen, sometimes to the right, sometimes to the left. We are finally beneath the walls of Moscow! Here it is, that splendid capital, Mother of the Motherland; the ancient dwelling-place of the tsars and home of the grandeurs of Russia. What pain, what rage to know Moscow is in the hands of Napoleon! Bitter tears flow from my eyes. My emotion is too turbulent to endure. I'm going to see this mournful city, which soon will be the victim of flames. They are winning, those French dogs! What fires they're making in their camps! What sounds of joy and merriment we can hear! But patience! We shall see who's going to pay for the broken china!

2 September, Moscow

I've gone through the city on horseback. How beautiful it is! How big it is, how lively it must be in peacetime. But now only marauders can be seen, or the infirm, and sirens, who are swimming at present in their element. Everyone is laying in supplies. I've seen the Kremlin and have been to some well-known squares and buildings, but the churches were shut.

3 September

God! We have passed through Moscow and abandoned it! My Fyodor was taken captive. My hand baggage has been lost. Everything is converging to destroy my last hopes. We've marched all day and are encamped forty versts from Moscow, but we can make out the flames. The brightness they produce is unbelievable. The entire army is as though undone. There is much open talk of treachery and traitors.

Courage has been undermined, and the soldiers are beginning to revolt. What a prospect! I'm completely exhausted.

4 September

We're swinging around and changing direction. Kutuzov is still cheerful and confident. What will the end of all this be? We lead the life of animals. Our food is repulsive, our bed is the earth, our pleasure is sleeping. And with all this, no hope for the future. What a situation!

5 September

We're bearing south. Our march looks like a funeral procession. Today we were tormented by thirst. It was very hot. We made twenty-eight versts. Our camp is on the highway from Volodimir to Ryazan. There is an abundance of supplies and the peasants are giving us all sorts of help. I've seen one of those camps of fleeing peasants; there were about 250 carts set up in a circle and the families stayed in the centre. The nights are very cold.

6 September, Stupia

A day of rest. How we need it! Everyone is at the end of his tether. The artillery is barely dragging along. Approaching a village in order to get some supplies, I saw a French prisoner sold to the peasants for twenty rubles; they baptized him with boiling tar and impaled him alive on a piece of pointed iron. What horror! Oh, humanity! I groan over it. The Russian women kill with hatchets the prisoners and marauders who pass by their houses. But measures have already been taken to put a stop to this barbarity. The saddest thing of all is that our own soldiers spare nothing. They burn, pillage, loot, and devastate everything that comes to hand. All around, for a circle of 100 versts, you can see immense fires which indicate the road taken by the enemy troops and our own, since we have vowed to leave nothing for the enemy. Bread, fruit, supplies, animals—everything is wiped out. The wells and streams are ruined, and the foragers don't dare show themselves for fear of being clubbed down by the partisans.

7 to 12 September

In the evening. It's impossible for me to keep up my Diary as I should; my ink powder has got damp and the paper is wet. We came by the Serpukhov road, where the enemy pursued us. But we are still avoiding him by making a semicircle toward the Kaluga road. We tell each other anecdotes, some of them worth noting. A Russian peasant who had stayed on in Moscow and like his comrades had had the letter "B" branded on his left hand (that is, Napoleon had branded the letter "B" on the hands of all captured Russian peasants), escaped and went straight to the French Headquarters. After he questioned one of the officers as to what the letter that was burnt into his left hand meant, this was explained to him. Suddenly he took a hatchet and, holding it with his right hand, cut off his left; he presented it to the officer, saying, "Take your Bonaparte, I don't want it, I'm staying Russian!" Wonderful!

I was also told of a French detachment that had been looking for supplies in a manor house and, finding a cellar full of fine wines, had gone inside to drink. The peasants of the neighbourhood, having waited for a favourable moment, had shut them in and then, as a token of their meritorious action, had cut off their noses.

13 September, Podolsk

A pretty little city. The army is beginning to pluck up its courage again. The enemy is getting weaker day by day, and our reinforcements are reaching us in small detachments. It's believed there will soon be a big engagement. Cannon fire can be heard.

14 September

I've had the misfortune to lose my pretty mare. It's a great loss. I loved that horse so much; she was so beautiful and docile. I wept like a small child at seeing her stretched out lifeless on the ground. The animal was unique! She knew me perfectly! She ate everything from my hand— sugar, sandwiches, even an omelette. She liked punch, and in Borodino she had unseated a French colonel. There was no horse in the regiment that jumped with as much lightness as high as my beloved Mashka. So I had her buried; her memory will always be dear to me.

15, 16 September

We're on the road to Kaluga. If the enemy manage to overcome us, and to enter Little Russia,* then we are lost, for there is an abundance of everything there and the climate isn't so severe. But if they are compelled to go back by the same road, the cold and the hunger will ruin them. It's already being said that supplies and food have come to an end in Moscow.

17 September

An armistice is being discussed; that would be bitter. Our motto must be: either exterminate them or perish, for the enemy is a Hydra that sooner or later will be reborn if a single head is left. Bonaparte declared war on us because we had made peace with the English. He wanted to force us to continue the war with a people he thought he was going to smother by depriving it of all possibilities of trade. But it was impossible. We had to improve our finances; we were obliged to raise the rate of exchange of our money and to stimulate our languishing trade; and that was how peace was made with Great Britain after four years. Since she needed us she paid us subsidies for the expenses of the war that soon enveloped us without Bonaparte's having warned us either by a declaration or on the pretext of some broken treaty. Hence Napoleon crossed our borders without any formalities. He armed Poland against us, and he believed that by proclaiming freedom in Russia he would get the

* *I.e. Malaya Rossiya,* an old territorial division of Russia (Ed.).

people behind him; but he made a mistake, because he didn't know that the love of the peasants for their God is inseparable from that for their ruler and that they prefer honourable poverty to ill-gotten gains. Napoleon will never be able to forget the things we resort to in order to conquer him, which somewhat resemble the behaviour of savages. If he spends the winter in camp and his troops have time to rest, it will be the end of our glory and our prosperity; I hope these rumours of peace and armistice are false. The only danger is the proximity of Prince Bernadotte, who might well be able to take advantage of this critical moment.

A country like ours, which is still in a virginal and primitive state, is difficult to tame or subjugate. Napoleon made a tremendous mistake in venturing as far as the centre of Russia. Everyone is beginning to appreciate the wisdom of this retreat that has been so criticized. Barclay has fallen back; a great deal of wrong has been done this man. The number of prisoners is immense and these poor people can scarcely drag themselves along; they are escorted by cossacks, who kill them with lances the moment they no longer have the power to walk. The prisoners tell stories about their Emperor amusing himself in Moscow, and how they are soon going to take St. Petersburg. As proof they show military bulletins full of lies. This arrogance is the most absurd and miserable thing in the world. But such is the character of that nation; it is manifested everywhere. Among the prisoners can be seen Bavarians, Spaniards, Italians, Saxons, etc. What an enormous army, that of the Allies! It's said that twelve peoples are fighting against us. It's like a crusade. But our hour will come. It's true that the Gauls inundated the Roman Empire; but the Slavs will one day swallow up the French Empire.

18 September

Reserves are being formed everywhere. Hundreds of officers have been sent to Murm to organize troops. A corps of 25,000 cossacks has just arrived from the banks of the

Don. Everyone has been given a free hand: we are pillaging and looting all over in order not to leave anything for the French. I've seen a peasant with a torch in his hand burning his hut in order not to abandon it to the French. The estates of the gentry are a source of great pain to me. How many valuable things have been broken and stolen! Among other things, I've seen in the anteroom of a pillaged château the works of Linnaeus and of Buffon (the vellum edition, in large quarto) lying on the floor trampled by the feet of marauders. What a loss!

19 September, Tarutino

It's being said we're going to take up a strong position here. It's often very cold. I feel very remorseful for having maltreated a soldier this morning in a fit of ill temper about a trifle.

20 September

It's claimed that we're going to be lodged in the villages; I don't believe a word of it. I've just bought a blanket cover that takes the place of everything for me. Meyer and Jacques are with me.

21 September

We've been given seven houses for the regiment. Our army has taken up a very favourable position, and from what I hear, we're going to stay here four weeks in order to force the enemy to fall back by the same road. I'm quartered in a bathroom; it's better than nothing!

22 September

A negotiator has just arrived. Miloradovich is going to have a conference with Marshal Ney. Both sides are quiet. We're holding some hills and a vast plain divided by a river. Our pickets and outposts are on this side, the enemy's on the other. To pass the time we all get together at the place of one or another of us; we amuse ourselves playing cards, smoking, or drinking. I'm quartered together with one Durov and a Mr. Thomson; I make plans, draw, and we play all sorts of games together. What a sad occupation for warriors!

23 September

The word is going around that the French are already eating their horses and that 10,000 cavalrymen have been turned into infantrymen, because the lack of fodder is killing the horses. Jacques comes regularly to see us. He's a very nice boy. He's very attached to me and shares everything he has with me. I'll always love him with all my heart.

24 September

I've managed to get hold of some books out of an old building that seems to have once contained a fine library— the life of Nestor,* in Russian, and *Le Grandison*,† in French. A Russian camp follower has also got us a game of lotto, which we find very amusing.

25 September

We're still in our camp at Tarutino. I've been to see some people I know at Headquarters. There's a great deal of talk there about an armistice, peace, and about the great revolutions taking place in Europe. Figner and Zeslavin, two famous partisan leaders, are doing the enemy a great deal of damage, especially Figner.

26 September

The life we lead is beginning to bore everyone. The inactivity is unendurable. An occasion has presented itself to write to Reval. What a joy it will be to write to my family! In the evenings we play all sorts of pranks and laugh a lot. My couch, though hard and dirty, is a very good one—I'm sleeping in a broken oven and must climb inside to sleep.

---

* Russian monk and author who died in 1114 (Ed.).

† *Sir Charles Grandison,* novel by the English writer Samuel Richardson (1689–1761) (Ed.).

27 September

I woke up with a start tonight. A poor cuirassier, who had apparently got cold, came to take refuge in the half-rotten roof of our little hut. The beams that supported our shelter against the fury of the wind and frost collapsed and fell on top of my oven. The noise was terrible. I thought I was at the Last Judgement, or had been attacked by the enemy. Luckily nothing hit me, and I got away without anything but a fright. We had some fun fishing today. The weather is passable, and the officers were all together. In the evening we went to hear camp retreat.

28 September to 1 October

I've just come back from a little excursion. On the 28th I was despatched to look for supplies for the whole division. I had 160 cuirassiers under orders. I'd never had so many under my command before; my pride swelled up, and I thought I was at least as powerful as our colonel. At the head of my cohort, devising vast plans and proud as a king, I left camp. We started off in the direction of Kaluga, where the enemy had not yet appeared. We soon reached a village where we found a peasant who was immediately nominated leader of our column. He seemed to me a little unhappy about his new duties, but a few blows with the flat of a sabre turned him into the politest man in the world. He promised to lead us into a very rich area, and he kept his word. We passed through a big forest. After a march of twenty versts we came to a region of radiant, lush country. A splendid château came into view. I despatched a nego-tiator to announce my arrival to the master of the house. But we had already been seen. A number of peasants armed with guns and hatchets appeared, but their wrath soon gave way to more peaceful feelings. I harangued them, speaking of God, Fatherland, the Russian troops, Moscow, and our discipline. A second Cicero, I succeeded in touching their hearts. I was surrounded, taken down from my horse; my cuirassiers were quartered in the villages nearby, and I was led in triumph to the château, where an old steward received me, cap in hand. Good quarters, good food, good wine, charming bed—nothing was forgotten to make my stay agreeable and useful. The following day I was given oxen, 100 sacks of oats and several carts full of hay, fruit, vegetables, etc.; everything was given in abundance. I despatched twenty cuirassiers for each regiment to escort this caravan, which started moving off and soon disappeared. I found myself excessively at ease and I determined to stay another two days in this paradise; I finally returned from my trip this morning. Thanks to the supplies I had brought, the colonel held back a little reprimand I more than deserved.

Today is Papa's birthday. God preserve him for the happiness of his family and for the welfare of his province!

2 October

This evening I had a most curious adventure. At six o'clock I had gone on horseback to see Meyer at the camp. Coming back, it was already growing dark and two glasses of punch had made me dizzy. I got lost. Running first to the right, then to the left, in order to avoid the river that separated us from the enemy, I caught sight of some dying camp fires surrounded by sleeping men. I passed them noiselessly, thinking they were the camp followers. I came to the stream that separated us from the enemy outposts. Just facing me I saw by the light of a camp fire some cavalry chasseurs sitting around drinking. They had scarcely caught sight of me when they started shouting. Our cossacks, who took me for a Frenchman, leaped on their horses and set out after me, their lances up. I got frightened. The thought of being killed seized me with such force that, forgetting to yell out to them in Russian, I started off at a breakneck gallop. My grey, bounding over ditches and bushes, finally managed to get me away from the cossacks, when *splash! splash!*— there I was, up to my ears in a great swamp. After a great deal of toil and a great many detours I got to my village, filthy and drenched to the bone, and stiff with cold and dampness. Next time, less punch and more attentiveness. How well I shall sleep!

3 October

Still at Tarutino. Jacques's been made an officer—what joy! He deserves it. I've just been awarded the Order of St. Anne 3rd Class. So here I am, a knight! Splendid!

4, 5 October

There's word of an attack we're going to make tomorrow. The French are exhausted from hunger and fatigue. All peace proposals are being rejected and Wittgenstein has completely defeated Macdonald! What joy!

6 October

A very remarkable day! At four o'clock in the morning we attacked the French camp. Everyone there was still asleep. After a fight that lasted six hours we captured 3,000 prisoners and took some cannon, ammunition, and supplies. The enemy has fallen back, and we're going to attack them again!

7 October

We've done forty-eight versts. What a march! Everyone's asleep. The cold is excessive; I can't sleep. The bottle has become my favourite companion.

8, 9 October

Yesterday cannon fire was heard—between eleven and noon. Soon the engagement started. The enemy had entered the city of (new) Yaroslav the night before, having crossed the river. The 4th Army Corps, under the command of Doktorov, had been ordered to repulse the French. The attack was lively, and we were very lucky; the city was soon delivered from the enemy, the mobile bridge was burned, and they were forced to fall back. But they resumed their efforts, and oh, what a miracle! A new mobile bridge was built under the murderous fire of 150 guns that belaboured the French with shell. At six they managed to finish it. It was at once filled with troops; the French sharpshooters forced their way into the city. There was fighting in the streets; the carnage was horrible. Our regiment was on the right side of the highway on the left bank of the river. I was despatched to Ostermann, who kept me until nine o'clock in the evening. He sent me to the centre of the city twice. The sight there was indescribable. The cannon shells were shattering the walls of the houses, which were burning and collapsing. The streets were filled with corpses and the wounded. The hubbub was frightful. The French had taken the city eight times, but they were always driven off again by our gallant grenadiers and chasseurs. Finally, on the ninth try, they were totally beaten back and our people remained masters of the city. Throughout the night we were disturbed by bombs and rockets. I was exhausted with hunger and fatigue. My greatcoat was pierced through by two bullets, and my grey was scarcely breathing. And what a torture this morning at four o'clock when we were given a drubbing by a hail of shells that killed a great many men and animals. Our division covered the retreat. At five o'clock in the evening we were finally able to rest. The enemy was forced to retreat by the same road. What glory! What a triumph!

10 October

The enemy are running away as hard as they can. The artillery is diminishing every day. The cavalry is dragging along on foot and they're all very discouraged. Long live Russia! Long live the Russian arms! We're going to chase the Hydra outside our borders. We shall kill it, perhaps. May its principal head not elude us!

Twenty-sixth Bulletin of the Grand Army at Borovsk:

The Russian Army is leaving the highway of Kolomna and taking a cross-country road toward Kaluga. The smoke of Moscow had struck them in the face; the mood of the Russians was sombre and religious. The King of Naples* and Poniatowski are guiding their corps to pursue the enemy. Lauriston has been sent once again to the Russian Headquarters.† Meanwhile a sort of cease-fire had taken place at the outposts. But the cossacks interrupted this. . . . The siege of Moscow, which is now a veritable sewer, has been raised. All stores that could still be saved have been brought to safety. On the 23rd,‡ at two o'clock in the morning, the Duke of Treviso exploded the Kremlin and set off for Verezha. . . . The Emperor is going to lead his army to the province of Smolensk, to its well-deserved winter quarters; the Russians will not dare to disturb this march, which will be executed in the greatest order. The Army is in the best mood in the world; it has an excess of everything and is being wonderfully well favoured by the weather.

11 October

Moscow has been retaken. The occupiers have turned their backs; we're in hot pursuit! The weather seems to be backing our efforts; it's severely cold and snow is already covering the fields.

12, 13 October

We're chasing them, but apparently the cold is making them leap so well that we can't catch them. You see unfortunates everywhere, congealed with cold and half dead of hunger, begging for help.

14 October, Vyazma

Sometimes, because of the lack of cavalry, we take outpost duty, and that's how I took thirteen prisoners today—and two horses, one of which is very pretty, a mare. But it's impossible to write, everything is so frozen.

15 October

There's been an important engagement. The cossacks are

---

* Murat (Ed.).   † For peace negotiations (Ed.).
‡ 11 October in the Russian calendar (Ed.).

pillaging everything left by the French. We're finding a great many things of value and sometimes money, too. I've just bought a sheepskin coat; it's doing me a lot of good.

16, 17, 18 October

Our position is rather critical; we have nothing to eat. I just made myself a soup of lukewarm water with some tallow; if we ran out of schnapps we'd die of misery and hunger. Yesterday I encountered a poor wretch. He was a French officer and a Mason; he was in a terrible situation. I would have so much liked to help him but I myself had nothing, so I was forced to abandon him. We're catching up with a great many women who had been following the French army. Some of them are very pretty. I also saw some children, but they're all going to die, because everything for 100 versts around has been ravaged. Our horses are eating nothing but straw; they look like cows.

19 October

The horrors we're surrounded by make mankind tremble and move the coldest and most cruel of men. Imagine a whole army in rout, in the most frightful disorder, feeding on horseflesh and God knows what, fleeing and attacked during the nights, deprived of rest and clothing, and you will have a feeble idea of what has become of Bonaparte's redoubtable army.

20, 21, 23 October

The enemy's latest efforts have failed. The Battle of Krasna has annihilated the fear-inspiring courage of the French army. The poor Germans filled me with the most compassion. The battle was fierce. Some 18,000 prisoners and eighty cannon are our takings for this memorable day.

24 October

What misery! What horror! This retreat looks like a rabbit hunt. The wrath of Providence is manifesting itself and is punishing the bandits. Oh Kutuzov! Oh Barclay! What wrongs have been done you! Oh, the catastrophe that Moscow was burnt! But let Moscow, Petersburg, and every other city in Russia be burnt as long as the Fatherland is saved!

The parts of the country we are going through look like deserts. Men and horses are dying of hunger and exhaustion. Only the cossacks, always lively and cheerful, manage to keep their spirits up. The rest of us have a very hard time dragging on after the fleeing enemy, and our horses, which have no shoes, slip on the frozen ground and fall down, never to get up again. The artillery, especially, is suffering a lot.

25, 26 October

We're going back along the same road we marched on this summer. What a contrast, and all in the space of a few months! We're doing thirty to forty versts a day, moving towards Polotsk at this great pace. The life I'm leading and my clothing are too unusual not to say something about them. My underwear consists of three shirts and a few pairs of long socks; I'm afraid to change them because of the freezing cold. I'm eaten up by fleas and encased by filth, since my sheepskin never leaves me. During the day it's underneath my greatcoat, and during the night it serves as blanket. The food I eat is disgusting; since we lack everything, we grill the meat in the fire and swallow it, half raw and blackened by smoke, without salt or bread. Only hard liquor keeps us going.

27 October

How cold the nights are! We can't sleep, so we sit around a fire to warm ourselves, but our backs are ice-cold; then we turn around to warm up the back side. The most disagreeable thing is the smoke; the wind drives it into our eyes, which give us a lot of pain. But this gypsy life doesn't prevent anyone from being very happy. We all get together around the camp fire, chatting, singing, playing pranks, and all in the best of tempers.

28 October

Polotsk has been taken again. We're supposed to be assigned quarters. May God grant it! Today a cossack offered me a small redwood box, without a key and double-locked. He wanted forty rubles for it; I offered him ten. That made him angry; he took out his sabre and slashed the box open. I was very disappointed, because it contained diamonds that were worth at least 10,000 rubles. How I regretted my hesitation! I immediately offered him 100 rubles, which I intended to borrow from the general, but the cossack saluted me affectedly, said he would soon find someone else to buy it, and went away.

29, 30, 31 October

I've got a high fever. Really, what a sad life we lead. We've turned into cattle. These blasted camps are soon going to do me in. Our situation gets worse from one day to the next, and there's no hope of its soon ending. It's been a long time since I saw Jacques. Could he be ill? We've moved through Polotsk; there's talk of a great battle that was fought between Chichagov and Wittgenstein, and Napoleon.

10 November, Sklov

We've moved off the highway, crossed the Dnieper, and have been assigned lodgings. What a pleasure! The van-guard is going to pursue Napoleon; we're moving as far as Vilna in short stages.

The Battle of Borisov has taken place. The three army corps attacked the remnants of the Allied army, which lost its entire artillery and all ammunition crossing the Berezina. But he, the Corsican, the terror and scourge of Europe, was able to escape and avoid final defeat. He's fleeing towards the border and has left the remnants of this once so large and glittering army to their own devices. About 120,000 captives have been counted, including 2,000 officers and twenty-eight generals; 700 cannon have been taken. Everything dragged out of Moscow has been won back, and the treasures found in individual war chests are immense. The cossacks have a great deal of money and jewellery. To compensate us for not getting any spoils, we are being assigned quarters. So everyone gets something. What a difference between Poland and Russia! Here there's no lack of anything, and all around, you can see that the Polish traitors love the French. But we'll set them right soon enough: everything left them by the French is being taken by us.

11 November

We're marching in short stretches daily. The quarters are very bad, but they're still quarters. You at least can change your underwear and get warm by the oven. At Sklov we took in supplies. Everyone looks radiant. Only the Grand Duke's arrival depresses people. The enemy army is completely dispersed. The fighting is over. The French are running away like madmen, with us running after them. Bonaparte, that marvel of politics and tactics, has found himself without resources. His fame resembles a rocket that dazzles everyone for a moment through its brilliance, and then disappears immediately. The stubbornness of the English, the wisdom of the two commanding generals, and the gallantry of our troops have punished the monster's crimes. Providence has completed the task by wiping out his slaves. But how many innocent victims there have been!

12 November, Parets

A small town. The Jews everywhere look upon us as their liberators. They hate the French and help us in whatever way they can. There's nothing as comical as seeing these detachments of prisoners we meet every day. It would be difficult to tell they were soldiers. You see the most peculiar clothes—cuirassiers with feet wrapped up in sheets and rags, cannoneers in woman's clothes and muffs. All this disorder is accompanied by cossacks constantly slogging prisoners with a knout and calling out: "Allo, marcher, Camerade!" I have a high fever that's consuming me.

13, 14 November, Smalevits

The nearer we approach our destination, that is, the capital of Lithuania, the more we feel the need of rest. The cold is intense. Though the village is thirty versts from the highway, everything here has been pillaged already—our predecessors did a fine job of cleaning out the villages. The inhabitants are to be pitied; absolutely nothing has been left them. The houses have been deprived of their roofs, which serve as fuel for the soldiers who still must camp here, since the number of houses assigned us is so small that even the officers can scarcely find room.

15 November

A day of rest. These always become holidays, because everyone rests *and* gives in to indolence. I've just been handed some old letters from Reval. What pleasure mail gives one! Thanks to Providence everyone at home is well.

16, 17 November

We're now in Radiskevich, a little town in Vilna Province. It's teeming with Jews, buying and selling. Shouting, noise, fighting, arguing—all without any rhyme or reason. But it amuses me. I've just been present at a duel between two Jewesses that ended with their beating each other up. My poor Peter has frozen feet; he has to follow the regiment in a sleigh. So I have no servant. What a situation! Jacques has been ill, but he's feeling better, thanks to Govorg, his regimental physician.

18 November

We are in camp again. What a cruel fate! I'm frozen through and half dead with hunger.

19, 20 November

I've a great desire to tear up my Diary and stop writing; it bores and inconveniences me endlessly. Jacques is with me.

At ten o'clock in the evening of 23 November Napoleon left the army to return to Paris. He gave the supreme command to Murat. He shook hands emotionally with all the generals, embraced each one, and drove off in his usual carriage with a sledge following immediately.

On 29 November Napoleon arrived in Warsaw. There he declared, in the presence of his ambassador, de Pradt, M. Stanislaus Potocki, and Finance Minister Mathusiewicz:

I thrive on unrest; the more unrest I have the better I feel. Only indolent kings get fat in their palaces; I get fat on horseback and in the camps. From the sublime to the ridiculous is only a step. The army is magnificent, I have 120,000 men, and I have consistently beaten the Russians. They no longer dare to stand against us, they are no longer the soldiers of Friedland and Eylau. A stand will be made in Vilna. I'm now gathering 300,000 men. The Russians' good luck will make them rash. I'll give them two or three battles on the Oder, and in another half year I'll be back at the Nyemen once again. On my throne I mean even more than I do at the head of my army. . . . I can't stop the freezing weather; every morning I'm told that I've lost 10,000 horses. Very well, then, *bon voyage*! Our Norman horses are not as tough as the Russians'; they can't stand less than 9 degrees, just like the men themselves. Just look at the Bavarians—there's not a single one of them left. It may be said that I've stayed in Moscow too long. That may be, but it was fine weather after all. The bad season started sooner than usual, and I was waiting there for peace. I was thinking of going to St. Petersburg. . . . A stand will be made in Vilna. I left the King of Naples there. Ha, ha, this is a great political spectacle; nothing ventured, nothing gained. On 6 November I was still master of Europe; on the 14th I no longer was, I could no longer recognize my army. So does the sublime border on the ridiculous. . . .

21 November to 1 December

On the 21st we went back to the main road, and the last week we've marched on it as far as Vilna. We had scarcely come onto the highway when the most frightful sight presented itself to my horrified gaze. Overturned wagons, cannon, kegs of powder, carriages, etc., were scattered about all along the road. On both sides of the road you could see poor wretches either dead already or in the throes of death, wearing the most grotesque clothing and in the saddest situation. We passed by all these phantoms, all these corpses, without a feeling or a shudder, we were so accustomed to the horrors of this destructive war. *From Osmian to Vilna 6,000 corpses were counted.* Passing by a tavern I saw inside a heap of dead bodies, all naked, piled up one on top of the other, and living people were sitting on their comrades, gnawing away at the flesh of their companions and roaring with pain like savage beasts. Oh humanity! Where hast thou hidden! But what an advantage that the cold is so intense that the air cannot become infested so quickly; otherwise the plague would surely be upon us. For eight days we watched all this, and for eight days I was surrounded by these terrors; for eight days I couldn't shut my eyes; these scenes will never be erased from my memory. How cruel man becomes the moment he loses his compassion and pity! The cossacks continue playing tricks on these wretches.

1 December, Vilna

We've finally arrived. What happiness! What joy! Our quarters are good, and we have been given a month of rest. You must never despair in this life, for the more critical or unhappy the situation, the closer the moment approaches that will end our miseries. Our entry, which was supposed to represent a triumph, looked more like a masquerade. The costumes of the various regiments were really burlesque, and the Emperor, who had arrived a day earlier and before whom we paraded, couldn't stop himself from laughing. I had to search for at least an hour before finding the number of my lodging. Finally, after many false starts, I was so happy to take possession of it! The house was pretty and well furnished, though very small; my horses and servants also found a niche for themselves. As an extra piece of luck, chance—or rather my lucky star—got me a charming hostess who instantly gave me the best room, touching on her own, and promised to feed me and my servants for 100 rubles. The offer was accepted, and I am installed. A good bed, good food, good company, and a rather good piano to boot! What more do I need, to believe that I'm the luckiest man in the world. Everything is forgotten—danger, hunger, thirst, misery, cold, and fever. I think only of the present and bless the Heavens that seem so benevolent to my tiny being.

2, 3 December

My hostess is called Mme de Zidlerova. She's a widow twenty-three years old, a piquant brunette, ravishingly pretty, sprightly, and gay; to a charming bearing and appearance she joins a rather cultivated, rich mind. She has a number of talents, which she shows off with grace and modesty; her conversation is interesting and very animated. She lived only six months with her husband, who, being old already, died soon after an indisposition. Widowed for a year, she had not abandoned the pleasures of this world; a second Ninon,* she gathered together in her little house all the best people in Vilna. These visits and gatherings naturally had to stop, and, taking advantage of all these dispositions for my own benefit, I finished by promising her, for my part, to be constant. Languell, who lives with me but whom I've managed to keep at a distance, eats with us and spends the day in our company. Jacques has arrived; what joy!

4 December

I've spent the morning going about the city seeing all the sights. The streets are laid out well; there are some handsome buildings. Vilna is surrounded by high hills that dominate it. The river passing by its outskirts is small and dirty, but the houses are well built and clean. There is an enormous

* Anne Lenclos, seventeenth-century French lady of fashion known as Ninon de Lenclos (Ed.).

number of Jews, and, in general, business doesn't seem to have suffered from the headlong retreat of the enemy, for the shops are well supplied, and for money you can get anything you like. The city itself has suffered only a little; just the outlying parts were plundered and damaged. The huge number of dead bodies and dead horses make the air very unhealthy; it produces a sort of pestilential illness that is killing a lot of people.

This evening I visited the theatre; though I couldn't understand everything being said, I could easily see that the theatre wasn't worth much; as for the orchestra, it was terrible. There was a big audience, though most of the nobility have retired to their estates. The number of those women who carry their morals in their pockets and their virtues in their bonnets is quite large, but they repel me since I am paying court to my widow.

On 5 December Tsar Alexander arrived in Vilna. He addressed an appeal and a manifesto to the soldiers of the Russian Army:

Your courage and your endurance have been crowned by a glory that posterity will never forget. Your name and your deeds will be handed down from mouth to mouth by your sons to their children and to their children's children to the last generation. There is no longer an enemy to be found on the soil of our land. You have made your way over their bodies and their bones to the borders of the realm. Now you will step over those borders, not in order to make conquests or to bring war into the land of your neighbours, but in order to secure a desired and enduring peace. You are Russians, you are Christians! As such, need you be reminded that it is the soldier's duty to be courageous in battle and gentle on the march and in the land of the enemy? That is demanded and expected by your orthodox religion, by your Fatherland, and by your Tsar.

5 December
Military movements have stopped for a while, but politics and diplomacy are beginning their game again. Austria

seems more or less neutral, but Prussia is going to join us, and the Poles are obliged to put on a good face. Mlle Dorothea, my widow's companion, has just arrived. Her friendship is useful to me. Jacques dined with me; how thin he's become, the poor boy. This evening we played some music.

6 December

The proximity of my lovely neighbour inflames my senses and my imagination. Her bedroom touches on mine. She shares hers with Mlle Dorothea, who acts as her duenna. How seductive she looked this morning on getting up! The mourning she still wears heightens her colour, and the most beautiful hair you can imagine shadows her lovely forehead, on which two ebony eyebrows cry out to be painted. Her mouth, lips, cheeks, and eyes are charming, but her figure, her bearing, and her throat are quite ravishing. What a treasure! What an encounter!

7 December

We spend the day laughing and joking; my lovely hostess, after the fashion of her compatriots, sometimes sits on my knees and caresses me unscrupulously. I must confess to her my passion, in order to accelerate my victory and her defeat. She seems to have a good heart, but her liveliness sometimes frightens me. There are moments when she seems to be dreaming. But I soon draw her out of her meditation to play with her. Her voluptuous nonchalance, her vivacity and dash, her seductive mind all put me beside myself.

8 December

Tender avowals, by both parties, have been made without any ado. My heart is doing *entrechats* and my passion consumes and burns up anything that comes near me. Eyes moist with pleasure, she's just called me her love and her lover. True or not, I'm satisfied, and my happiness is complete.

9, 10 December

Just imagine my situation: loved by a charming woman, adoring her in return, passing whole hours speaking to her of my passion and listening to the expression of her own; and then judge my ecstasy accordingly when I say that I've passed in the arms of Celestine one night, but a night belonging to God! I was just about to sink into sleep last night when I heard a soft knock at my door. With one bound I was at the door leading to her bedroom. Fearful of Mlle Dorothea's proximity, I held back my indiscreet breathing and opened the door with utmost caution. You could see nothing, for the night was dark and I was quivering with voluptuousness; I listened and heard a sigh, which echoed in the depths of my heart. An invisible light led me forward, and finally I touched the bed that contained so many charms, so many treasures! Two plump, rounded arms received me and pressed me against a breast softer than Persian silk, palpitating with pleasure and anticipation. A mouth burning with love sought my lips, which were already devouring the most secret of her charms. To slip beneath the cover, to press myself against her divine body, and to swoon with lustfulness took but a moment. But what is the use of portraying a headiness that can never be described, but can only be felt. The night passed in the most splendid frolicking, but our indiscreet bed betrayed us to Mlle Dorothea, who began coughing. Poor old girl! Apparently she envied the fate of her cousin. This morning, Celestine having gone out for a moment, I found myself alone with this virgin of forty years and had a talk with her. I begged her pardon for the noise I had made and proposed a little consolation to her which I carried out so well that I found favour with her.

Things will go on as before; but I'm afraid they will go on too quickly and too often for me, for I've been weakened, and my constitution may be ruined by all this "too often" and "too quickly".

This evening I visited, together with a number of comrades,

the hospital for the wounded and the sick. I've never seen anything more pathetic. There were 3,000 Frenchmen squeezed into one house, with no food, no help, and no means! I helped wherever I could, but it was no more than a drop of water on a hot stone. How they've been punished for their arrogance!

11 December

I've been handed 1,000 rubles sent my by my parents. I needed the money badly; I had nothing of anything.

12 December

The Tsar's birthday. A great ball; masquerade. General amnesty for the Poles.

15 December

The Prince of Oldenburg has just died. His brother is awfully sad. My Celestine is the most amiable of creatures, and we spend our days in the sweetest *dolce far niente*. I've just sprained my foot; I shall have to report ill for a while.

16 December

A small scene. I struck her servant, which annoyed her; she sulked all day. Languell has been made an officer; his joy is indescribable. I'm going to try to persuade him to pay court to my belle; I want to see what comes of it.

17 December

She's taking the bait. Oh, these women! Nicholas is redoubling his efforts; I play up my indifference.

18 December

Wittgenstein is in Königsberg, Platov in Danzig, and Shaplit in Warsaw. We've been informed that the campaign is to continue and that we're to start off for Germany, which is all I can wish for.

19, 20 December

I'm returning to my dalliance. She seems to be ignoring her inconstancy. Jacques eats with me almost every day. My life is extremely agreeable.

21, 22 December

The infantry is on the march already. We'll be leaving Vilna on 1 January, but I feel some inner sickness burning within me.

23 December to 1 January

Languell has triumphed. Is it possible! I never believed this woman was so loose . . . but I'm consoling myself. For that matter it's better to believe only half of what women say. Adieu, dear Vilna, charming city! When shall I ever see you again?

Chapter V

FROM TAUROGGEN TO LEIPZIG

On 18 December 1812 the Prussian General York and the Russian General von Diebitsch concluded a cease-fire agreement in the mill at Pocherau near Tauroggen. General York informed his commanding officer, Marshal Macdonald, Duke of Taranto:

The Prussian troops will constitute a neutral corps and not permit themselves any hostilities against either one of both parties. Forthcoming events that may be brought about through transactions between the warring powers will determine its future fate.

General York wrote to the King of Prussia from Tauroggen:

. . . that I have been obliged to conclude with Major-General von Diebitsch in the service of His Majesty Tsar Alexander the accompanying convention, which I have the honour to submit to your Majesty. In the full conviction that had I continued marching I should have risked the existence of the Army Corps and the loss of its artillery and its baggage train, as has been shown by the experience of the Grand Army, I believed that as a faithful subject of Your Majesty I was entitled to consider your advantage alone without regard to that of your ally. . . . I should gladly offer your Majesty my head if you were to find my conduct blameworthy. Nevertheless I shall have the sweet certainty in my final moment of thinking that I shall be dying as a faithful subject, as a true Prussian, and finally, as a man who desired only the best for the Fatherland.

On 26 December Russian Field Marshal Prince Wittgenstein, General York, Freiherr von Stein, and Councillor von Kotzebue arrived in Königsberg. Prince Wittgenstein issued the following appeal:

The Russian people, worthy of honour because of its love for the Fatherland, its piety, and its steadfastness, offers you a firm hand for your emancipation from the bonds of alien tyranny; seize with gratitude this opportunity to re-establish German independence, trifled away by your disunity and irresolution, and to placate the spirits of your free forefathers. German priests of all sects, arouse courage and enthusiasm, and pray at the common altar of the Fatherland for the success of the sacred enterprise. Princes of German origin, it is to you that the nation has long been looking with expectation; break the chains that the alien conqueror forged upon you and yours with his sugary flattery when he loosed the sacred German alliance of princes. You free German burghers, above all, you Hansa merchants, rouse yourselves to the struggle for German freedom. The ancient German Rhine shall be drunk by free Germans alone, and the happy vines shall wreath its banks undisturbed. Whosoever speaks a German language, let your heart now be filled with new courage and faith! Let every German find in every countryman a brother and a companion-in-arms for German freedom and independence! I, too, a German, in anticipation of this heartfelt joy, already see the brittle chain breaking, the sacred expanses of the Fatherland purified of the tyrant's mercenaries, its tormentors.

On 28 January 1813 Tsar Alexander arrived in Warsaw with 8,000 men and set up his headquarters there. The Austrian Auxiliary Corps of the Grand Army under Prince Schwarzenberg fell back toward Galicia.

31 January 1813, Ortelsburg
From 1 January of this year I was so ill I couldn't write.

Before I go on with my Diary the past month must be entered, described as briefly and as well as possible, and preceded by a short but sad reminiscence.

Jacques and I—we took the march out of Vilna together —had hardly done more than three days' march when a growing fever, unnoticed on the first day, laid us both low. He had already caught up with his regiment, so he stayed there; but sick as I was, I still had to find my own. On the

5th day I found it. The regimental doctor, M. Habersank, at once said my illness was an acute nerve fever, but advised me to continue the march until I found a comfortable camp where I should have myself treated at once and stay until I was completely better. I was in the most helpless condition. With no money or underclothes and a sick servant as attendant, I lay there dragging myself from one night's lodging to another, foreseeing my certain death. We passed through Leipani and Orini to the Nyemen, which we crossed on the 7th at Merichi. With no help, no medicines, no care, rest, nor quiet, I already seemed on the brink of death. Just then my brother turned up; he had already recovered because he has a stronger constitution. He accompanied me as he used to do and gave me everything, though he had nothing much himself. Between Merichi and Seyny an incident took place that will remain firmly embedded in my memory. We were following the regiment slowly in a miserable sleigh. The weather was cold; my brother was sitting by my side and seemed to be exclusively busy with my unconscious, pathetic condition. His servant Maloshka was driving. Suddenly a regimental cart came hurtling down on us at an all-out gallop from above us—we were just on an overhanging of the mountain. Instead of making way, Maloshka turned the cart over, and it would have cost my life if Jacques had not quickly rolled me over into a ditch. After the danger was passed, Jacques's terror was transformed into fury at the stupidity of the servant; he drew his sabre and slashed the whole way through his arm. It went through my own heart like a knife, but I could scarcely cry out, and even less make a move. This sign of Jacques's fraternal devotion, though it was coarse, and the compassion that the fellow's scream of pain aroused in me buried themselves deep in my soul. And at night I would speak of it, in my feverish dreams.

Our route led us over Augustow, Raygrod, Wonsotz, Biala, Johannisburg as far as Ortelsburg, where my nerve fever got so bad that I had to be left behind in a miserable little hut, given up by the doctor, where I remained, for the most part, unconscious. Meanwhile my brother had fallen ill again and could no longer help me. So we stayed over here on the 18th, abandoned by everyone, in the most dismal plight you can imagine. In order to help his officers the Grand Duke had given the four of us seventy-five silver rubles, a generosity I shall never forget. Four days later the city Commission went to a little trouble for us, assigned us new and better quarters and sent us Dr. Quade, who did everything in his power to restore us. On the 23rd I became noticeably better; three other officers (I found that out only later) had also been left behind because of illness. These became our daily companions, and everything seemed to be going much better when suddenly Jacques became so ill that I lost all hope. Just then our saviour appeared, and without him we would surely have perished. On the 24th, in the morning, Jacques was lying there, a deep rattle in his throat, and both servants were lying stretched out on the straw, while I myself, wasted away because of lice and bad food, was scarcely conscious. I couldn't do anything; everything was flickering blue and black before my eyes. Just then a man came into our hut, in a Prussian uniform. I had scarcely enough presence of mind to greet him with a movement of the hand and ask him the reason for his visit; his lips opened, and a life-restoring balm flowed from his words over into my heart. "Comrade," he said, "do not despair, there is a power above watching over the days of your life. It would be sad indeed for one who has escaped death by bullets, like yourself, to die upon a sickbed. But be of good cheer, Quade is a skilful man and I want to be your friend and helper. Come over to the house of my father-in-law; we want to take care of you until you get better. There is no sacrifice too great to preserve the gallant saviours of Russia and Prussia." His eye rested on my wasted face with such firmness and warmth, his hand reached for mine, and though a huge moustache shadowed his face, his forehead expressed kindness, sweetness, and uprightness. My heart could find no words to express my gratitude, and half confused, in a half whisper, I stammered out to him my thanks. He left us proposing to visit us very soon again, and promised to take care of us.

Oh humanity—I would soon have lost all faith in Thee, but how quickly it has been restored!

Happinesses seldom come singly. On the 26th, in the afternoon, I was sitting at my brother's bedside chatting with him about home when in came—I could scarcely believe my eyes—my old Fyodor, who had been thought dead. Our joy was boundless.

He had to tell us at once where, how, when, and why he was there. His answers could hardly satisfy our questions. So in a few words he told us how he had been captured by the French in Moscow, how he had spent three weeks there in dreadful misery, how he had then gone on foot to St. Petersburg and Reval, and, finally, why he had been sent here again. My parents had learned from an earlier letter from Jacques that we were to march to Warsaw and so he had been ordered to look for us all over. On his way through he had been told that some sick Russian officers were here, and so he had come to ask them about us; by great good luck he had actually found us. Money, underwear, letters—in short, everything that can rejoice the human heart after long-drawn-out affliction was given us with a lavish hand. Thankfully we looked up to Heaven and thankfully we sent our thoughts back to our dear homeland.

On the 27th, in the morning, our excellent Prussian cavalry captain—his name is Rosken—visited us again, and stayed with us at least an hour. He and Dr. Quade were the only ones we saw, since we weren't allowed to go out. Jacques was getting better every day; I, too, improved visibly. On the 28th I went out for the first time; what bliss! The city of Ortelsburg is small and pretty, but all the food is very expensive. I made a number of acquaintances, among others two Prussian officers by the name of Strauss and Wedel and the Secretary, Foelkner. I also found books and music, which made a doubly agreeable impression on me since the piano was being played by a beautiful girl. The city is situated on a lake that is rather large. The inhabitants are peaceful, good-natured people, who seem to be fond of Russians. There is a lot of amber found here and the businesses dealing with it are considerable. Something that made a big impression on me is the so-called *accis*, or luxury tax. For every cart, servant, dog, etc., a special tax has to be paid. The state must have rather bad finances to have allowed things to go so far.

Rosken has visited me a great deal the past few days. On 1 February we mean to drive out to see his father-in-law, Baron Burckhard in Therewisch. The property lies only two miles from the city, just a stone's throw. Out of kindness I've been provided with a piano. I've also been received in a very friendly way by all the inhabitants of the city. I usually spend my evenings at Quade's; he has a most charming family. Molde and Hafke, two bourgeois from the city, have linked themselves to us and often give us luncheons. A serious illness from which he recovers can do a person a lot of good after all.

1 February, Therewisch

I'm being treasured here by these good people—it's as though I were in Abraham's bosom. The outgoing kindness, the sympathetic concern that is expressed by every single word they say binds me to them with ties of friendship and gratitude; how good it feels, after a long time, to meet domestic happiness and sympathy!

The family is rather large; they should all be described in some detail. The father, an old soldier with a well-fed body and straightforward, basic intelligence, combines the strictest uprightness with the most yielding good nature. A passionate amateur of botany and hunting and, especially, gastronomy, he is spending the autumn of his life in the bosom of tranquillity and comfort. His wife, married for the second time like himself, could sit for Teniers* as the model of an old-fashioned German housewife. A few airs and graces, an extreme precision in taking care of household affairs, strict disciplining of the children and servants accompanied by a benevolent kindliness all give her the look of a Beatrice. The two oldest daughters, Mme Stach and Mme v. Rosken, are dear sweet creatures, who live for themselves and their own sphere of activity, seem to love their husbands and children above everything, and otherwise let the world go its own way. The three young unmarried daughters, Lorchen, Minchen, and Julchen, are quite different. The eldest, a subtle, high-strung, highly sensitive girl, has a penchant for mooning about and has a good deal of education. The two younger ones are altogether children of nature; they're health and merriment itself, only with the difference that the first one, Minchen, is very quiet and modest, while the second, Julchen, seems very lively and a little flirtatious. The sons-in-law, two old swashbucklers, round out the picture and at the same time the family circle.

I spent today very agreeably; it passed in cheerful conversation, and evening was upon us before we were aware of it. A Jew came along with all sorts of things to sell. We bought some, laughing a lot. I asked him in passing whether he didn't want to buy honesty from me. "Oh," said the Jew, "that's sold to anyone bidding the most, but is not able to be sold. Just a short time ago, it was put into the pillory in Tilsit." Not a bad retort for a Jewish dealer!

2 February

Jacques and I have been strolling about this little town; Berg, the District Head, and our acquaintances were visited. In the evening there was a drinking spree at Molde's—so enough for today.

3, 4 February

We went to Volka and Therewisch again. The time we
_____

* The Dutch painter David Teniers (1610–1690) (Ed.).

spend there is too agreeable to be forgotten, the people too good not to be loved at once. But soon we'll have to leave them, since we're already feeling much better.

5 February

It really is great good luck to have a dear one in a strange place to whom you can cling and to whom you can reveal the most secret recesses of your heart; that's how it is with us two brothers. Far from our family, in a rather helpless situation, we try to find in our brotherly sympathy and friendship something to ward off all the attacks of grief, need, and bad circumstances. Our present serenity has been greatly added to by Fyodor's arrival and by the warmth of our reception in the Burckhard home; we've really almost forgotten all the unpleasantness, and from time to time we're deliciously happy. The day after tomorrow the baptism of the Stach baby takes place. I'm to be godfather, hold the child, and go to Therewisch. It's the first time in my life that I have to do anything like this; I shall assume a thoroughly stiff and solemn personality. Grangs, of the magistracy, gave me some things to read today, classical works at that. Reading helps a lot when you have nothing at all to do.

6 February

I must still have some sickness in me; I'm feeling very ill again. If only it's not a return of that nerve fever! If it is I'm lost.

7 February

The baptism went off all right; the little Christian has been baptized with the name of our Emperor and my own. During the ceremony I felt so weak I had to hand the child over to the Baroness to hold.

8 February to 1 March

I had a premonition it was going to happen, but Heavens, the difficult ordeal has been undergone for a second time.

For almost three weeks I lay unconscious in Therewisch. The relapse came so abruptly that there was fear for my life; also, the illness had become so malevolent that black patches showed up on my body. I knew little about my condition, since I usually lay in a delirium. But all the more did my dear Jacques and the sweet family to whose kindly care I once again owe my life feel the weight of my illness. In the old Baroness I found a second mother; in the daughters, my sisters; all of them, with heartfelt sympathy, nursed me at the risk of their own health. They sat up with me for whole nights and took care of my slightest need with loving haste. Words are quite incapable of expressing what was done for me by this unusually kindhearted family. Eternal gratitude, permeating my entire being, will bind me to these people, and their friendship will always occupy the place of honour in my heart—yes—until the end of my days.

The oldest daughter, Lorchen, seemed to be especially self-sacrificing on my behalf, for she endured my moods with the greatest patience and love, listened to my fantasies and sat through night after night at my bedside. I could marry her out of gratitude; she's so attached to me, she surely loves me.

2 March

Really, with all his fancied achievements, what a weak and miserable creature man is! Only two weeks ago I was on the brink of the grave, now I'm as merry again as though nothing had happened. My recovery is spreading general joy among my friends, too. Yesterday evening Lorchen came into my room with tears in her eyes, fell on my neck, and said to me so movingly: "My dear brother"—that's what everyone calls me here—"how I thank the Creator that you have been given back to yourself and to us; but do stay a long time here, for otherwise you might well have one last relapse, which would inevitably be your ruin." I pressed the good girl to my heart, called her my own, and a fateful confession was already on my lips when, as though frightened awake, I gently pushed her back and reminded her of her duties. Weeping softly she left me! Better to be honourable and hard than weak and ungrateful. I can't get the scene out of my head and my heart.

3 March

Jacques, who's been coming over from Ortelsburg often to visit me, was here today; he was as happy as a child when he saw me recovering. In the city the thought of the possibility and probability of losing me had driven him half crazy. In an attack of fever he had wanted to shoot the doctor, had tossed the gendarmes who had tried to arrest him because of this out of the door, and had done all sorts of other foolish things because he was convinced an attempt was being made to poison and kill me.

4 March

Though I'm still very weak, I'm so much better that from time to time I can come out of my sickroom into the living room and take part in the conversations of the assembled family. Then I usually sit down with my Lorchen and embrace her cosily; that way we often sit together until the evening lights are turned up or my warm bed receives me. But it must not go on this way for long, since I'm afraid both for myself and for her.

This morning, while I was getting dressed, my Fyodor asked me quite naïvely why there had to be masters and servants in the world, and whether in the next world there might not be a turnabout and I could be his attendant. Scarcely able to restrain my laughter, I answered him that yes, that might easily be, and meanwhile he should be a good servant so that one day I might also be one for him.

My illness has cost me a great deal after all, and the pocket money from home has shrunken considerably.

5 March

Rosken amuses us with his droll stories; though he often

exaggerates wildly, every story he tells turns out to be very funny, and so he is forgiven the dirty stories that occasionally slip into his anecdotes. Stach is more serious, a man of considerable intellect.

6 March

We're already taking walks; Julchen and Minchen go on ahead with Jacques and play their little pranks; I come limping behind with Lorchen on my arm. Meanwhile her mother prepares our favourite dishes and the father gossips with people from the office or drinks his old German tankard of beer and smokes his pipe.

7 March

The country and the people here are very like Livonia,* with the difference that everyone here is more broad-minded and educated. Today we are getting ready for a pleasure trip we're taking tomorrow, and they're all, especially little mother, running hither and thither in a busy rush. Lorchen, who divines our imminent departure for the army, seems sad and introverted; the best thing to do is to notice nothing and to go away very suddenly, for it's easy to deceive a poor girl, but finer and nobler to comfort her.

8, 9, 10 March

The little pleasure outing to Rhein, which lies seven miles out of Therewisch, was extremely agreeable. Mother, with Lorchen and Julchen, and I sat together in the carriage. We passed through Sensburg, a most charming little town, where we ate lunch. At night we stayed with a Major Bieberstein in Malschewen. The whole of the trip I sat opposite my Lorchen, our knees touching; our hands groped for each other and stolen looks spoke to our hearts more vividly than fine phrases. In the morning, after breakfast, we went on as far as Rhein, where we had been awaited by the old Burck-

* Region bordering on the Gulf of Riga and comprising a southern section of present Estonia and the northern part of Latvia (Ed.).

hard for a long time and were received with the greatest pleasure. The forenoon went quickly. In the afternoon my Lorchen had a tooth drawn, an operation that gave her the most frightful pains, but they passed away quickly and that evening we were all the merrier. This morning I said goodbye to old Burckhard, whom I'll probably never see again. In spite of myself, my tears moistened his honest face, and he squeezed my hands in his emotion. The trip back was quiet.

11 March

I've just read in the newspapers that Prussia and Sweden have come out for the good cause and mean to join with us in destroying the empire of tyranny and terror; also, that the armies are drawing together in Silesia in order to undertake new operations against France. I must be off, otherwise I'll miss this pleasure and may be harmed because of that in the eyes of my comrades.

It's decided! Next Thursday it's away! Off into the wide world, in the wake of the advancing army. This evening it was difficult for me to tear myself out of Lorchen's arms. God! How will it all end? I have no reason to reproach myself. That is why I must flee her as one flees danger.

12 March

Today we were invited to the Frankenbergs', where a lot about politics was babbled. This sort of jabbering is unendurable for me. People who sometimes have no vision at all, and often don't even understand what they're talking about, give forth arrogant opinions and apodictic criticisms. And when some little chit of a woman, who ought to be sticking close to her cakes or her larder, starts drivelling on about the *Mine* and *Thine* of whole nations, about the character traits and behaviour of great generals and statesmen, it so turns my stomach every time that I feel like rushing off.

Jacques is having a good time in Ortelsburg and hasn't been to see me for several days. But I've invited him over tomorrow; I hope he turns up.

13 March

My brother, who's just arrived, has brought the news that our regiment is encamped near Kalisch, on the Silesian border, that our army is handing out silver medals with a blue ribbon for the year 1812, and that negotiations are taking place with Austria.

14 March

No one in the house knows yet that we're to move off the day after tomorrow, but tonight the secret must come out though I die because of it! All my other comrades from Ortelsburg are gone; we're the only ones who have remained behind in this region. Doctor Quade has been richly rewarded for his efforts. The excellent Burckhards are more than happy because of their conviction that they have kept alive a defender of the fatherland, returned a loving son to good health, and won an eternally grateful friend for themselves. Fate will surely bring us together again.

15 March

The truth is out. It has pained everyone, especially a certain person who turned white as a sheet at the news. That same afternoon I had an intimate, exalting conversation with her; a final silent embrace united our souls, never again to be separated. Be happy, never forget me—these were the words that rose up in both our hearts at the same time. The evening passed in warm caresses; past, present, and future were touched on, and it was not until late that we parted, each one afflicted in his own way, to say farewell the next morning for a long time, perhaps forever. I couldn't sleep all night; I kept letting in fresh air, writing home, and finishing my Diary.

16 March

Parting from people you love, to whom you are bound by ties of gratitude and friendship, is too bitter a pain to be described; I shall content myself by saying only that there were many sincere tears, some sighs, and many wishes for a comforting future.

17 to 21 March, trip from Therewisch to Kalisch

Our trip as far as the Vistula took place without any events of consequence, except for an erotic spectacle in a cabaret. On the 22nd we arrived at Khizhno. Here we crossed the majestic river on a floating bridge. The Vistula reminded me of the shores of the Neva and of the follies of my childhood. When shall I see those shores again, I wondered, and shall I be less childish then than I still feel now? The water mills on the ships amused me very much. The different kinds of objects gave me food for thought; everything interested me. We didn't call a halt until late in the day; very tired, we lay down to sleep at once.

23 March, Gostynin

A small city, full of Jews. I noticed that spring was approaching with rapid strides; you can see grass and flowers coming up everywhere, and the leaves are already bursting through their sheaths; joyfully we breathed in the redeeming balm of the spring air. We had put behind us only three miles, but our stomachs were already complaining of hunger when suddenly, at the end of a lane in the woods, a pretty château appeared to our enchanted gaze. "Let's see what happens," I cried out, "and take pot-luck with the owner of this château!" "Splendid!" said Jacques, and there we were, galloping at breakneck pace towards the pretty place; already I felt transported to the dwelling of the King of the Djinns, already my imagination was enchanting me with days of glory and passion there, when *boom!* There we were, the heroes of the play, overturned by a huge stone in our way. My Fyodor, who was clutching his side, my brother, who thought he'd broken his head, and myself turned in rage against the coachman; and he, or rather his back, had to pay for the cruel attack on our limbs. Then we set ourselves right and we arrived fairly modestly at the entrance of the château. M. Shimansky, the owner, received us rather cavalierly, quite mistrustful of the nice things we told him; he was judging us by our carriage, which was quite mediocre. As I went in I was struck by the orderliness and the taste that prevailed inside the house. Everything was remarkably refined—the furniture, the dinner, the conversation. The clavichord especially amused me a great deal. After coffee we made our bows; now here we are, after a trip of four miles, in Kutno, a frightful village where we are very badly quartered.

24 March

Quarrelled with Jacques about a Jew I had had freed; he had been arrested by a war commissioner who was trying to swindle him out of a bribe.

At Gregorovich I had the pleasure of seeing the pyramidal poplars, and some wheeled ploughs; the country, in general, is well cultivated and the inhabitants seem happy and well-to-do. Towards evening we arrived in Kladova, where we were invited to go to a Mayor's Ball, which amused me endlessly. There were a few pretty women there and some caricatures good enough to paint. The ensemble gave me an idea of local society.

25 March

Saw the Catholic church before leaving; terrible weather; lunched in Kola, a small village; in the evening dined in Bradyevo. That's where we found the Lithuanian Regiment. I took leave of Jacques; we parted with tears in our eyes. My heart went with him; it was very heavy. But the separation was bound to come.

26, 27 March

Through Golno and Varta to Kalisch.

28 March, Kalisch

This morning I was presented to the Grand Duke. He was

very civil. I left him and immediately went to see some of my comrades, who welcomed me with joy and warmth. I like the city a lot; it is very pretty and full of trade. Took a turn around the outskirts. Saw a child with six fingers. On my return my thoughts went wandering back to my good and kind friends, the Burckhards; I thought of Jacques too. I found a package waiting for me; it was no slight pleasure. Good news and fifty ducats.

Tomorrow we cross the German border. I'm burning to know the country.

29 March, Militsch

What a difference between Poland and Silesia! It's as though I were in a different world. How clean it all is! What order! It's as though one were breathing completely different air. The countryside is radiant, with villages, suburbs, and castles scattered throughout. The roads are bordered by fruit trees, which are in bloom now. The fields are tilled so prettily, the inhabitants dressed so neatly, their houses built so well with such symmetry, the woods— and even the shrubbery—kept so tidy that everything seems enchanted.

The city itself was charming. Triumphal wreaths had been put up for the Emperor's arrival. Languell and I went to see an old Prussian major named Lepel, a fine chap with a charming family. We drank to the healths of both our monarchs. A former court chamberlain took us to his place and showed us his curiosities, including crystal and glass covered with inscriptions that would fit the events of our own day.

30 March, Trachenberg

How pretty the daughters of Silesia are! They enchant me with their looks and their graces. The village we're camped in is half a mile long. The mayor, who received us, lives like a great lord. His daughter, charming and pretty as an angel, accepted my homage, but repulsed me in a dignified way which pleased me very much and made me think with a sigh of our peasants at home.

1 April

Marched as far as Prausnitz. Prussian manœuvres. A party of four in the evening.

2 April, Wenzien

A triumphal arch had been set up for us at the entry to the city. In huge letters the following words could be read: "Welcome, defenders of the oppressed, victory and blessing to your weapons!" This gave us a certain amount of pleasure; the regiment entered in a parade. Our bearing and the beauty of our troops constantly evoked signs and expressions of admiration. My horse, too, pranced about in honour of the belles in the windows.

3 April, Lüben

This morning we crossed the Oder at Steinau; the banks are very pretty there. The King of Prussia passed us in review; he's a handsome fellow. His princes pleased me enormously; though still very young they were carrying swords and have already distinguished themselves. We had a chance to see the King's Guard, which impressed us with the simplicity of their uniform and their splendid bearing. This morning at eleven we had a review, attended by the King and the Emperor. The monarchs had a conversation. For the first time in my life I saw mountain peaks of snow. It was the Riesengebirge range. I was as happy about this as a child and decided to get a closer view the next day.

4 April

A day of rest. Took walks.

5 April, Gor

A pretty little city; lovely colours. This Silesia is a paradise. The houses are built all in stone; they're very durable. The

BORIS UXKULL'S PARENTS

(*above*) His mother, Elisabeth Uxkull, *née* Gräfin Sievers,
1776–1865, (*below*) His father, Berend-Johann Uxkull, 1762–
1827. From portraits by Gerhard von Kügelgen

SCHLOSS FICKEL

(*above*) Front view (*below*) From the park

peasants are rich. Our own received us splendidly. The furniture, the beds, the food, coffee, dried fruit, beer, and wine—all, in fact, exquisite. What a difference between this country and our own! The peasant women's dress is very pretty; their skirts are short, their legs well turned; a good deal of pinching here.

6 April

Horrible weather, an exhausting march, but good quarters and nice people. A trip with Colonel Protassov to the Grenzberg, a very pretty ruin built in 1370 that once belonged to the Counts Schellendorf. Frederick II turned it into a powder storage. The fortress was besieged for six months, but in vain. It was too strong. It took us half an hour to climb up. The sun was just setting. The view of this immense plain, with villages scattered about, enchanted us. The Riesengebirge was to our right. We turned away from it with regret. The evening passed very agreeably at the pastor's, a decent old chap who kept staring at our moustaches. His daughter was a miracle of sweetness; I was completely bowled over.

7 April, Bunzlau

A small city, very crowded and clean.

8 April

Here we are at the borders of Saxony already. The Grand Duke* invited me over to play the piano for him. I was praised a great deal, though I felt timid and my hands were numb; but I managed to acquit myself all right. We're camping on the outskirts of Görlitz, a charming region. I went to see the grave of Jakob Boehme.† The city, the Neumarkt, the waterfalls—it's all very pretty. We've been received in Saxony too with open arms; we're looked on as liberators. The French yoke must have been very heavy for the poor

---

* Constantine (Ed.).

† German theosophist and mystic (1575–1624) (Ed.).

Germans. The King's absence is much regretted; it's being said that he intends to stay allied with the French. The defeat of York is spoken of, as well as a victory carried off by Wittgenstein over the French at Magdeburg. Thorn has been taken by storm.

What a lot of pretty faces there are!

9 April

A day of rest. The lovely Landeskrone mountain range is still before us. Today we did nothing but sleep, drink, and chat with the village girls, which amused us a great deal. A parade in Görlitz. A crowd of the local people admired us. What a triumph!

An outing to the Landeskrone, which dominates the whole countryside. A visit to Major Gersdorf. A gallant escapade in the inn. Marie swooning; I left at ten o'clock singing "Long live the life of the soldier!" I rejoined my regiment in Weissenberg at a fast gallop: a splendid road over the Gretscher plain by moonlight. Good quarters.

10, 11 April

Hochkirch, celebrated because of Frederick II's victory.*
Arrival in Bautzen, a pretty, flourishing city. Bischofswerda. Evening at Saratchinsky's.

12 April, Pillnitz

A splendid city on the banks of the Elbe. A boating party to Dresden. The weather was magnificent; picturesque hills, covered with vines! What a spectacle for someone who lives in the north. Fruit trees all abloom. Not a trace of war! Not a trace of fighting! All I dream about is rustic love and lust.

Arrived in Dresden; the bridge is magnificent. Visited my grandmother, Princess Putiatin,† whom I had not yet met. She received me with all the affection of a tender

* Uxkull is in error here (Ed.).

† Jakob-Johann Count Sievers, Boris's grandfather, was married to his cousin, Countess Sievers, who was married for a second time to Prince Putiatin (Ed.).

relative. The Prince seemed completely original to me. He's quite witty and a wonderful talker. Fireworks in honour of the Allies.

13 April, Dresden

A big parade. We made our entrance as conquerors; there was no end to the hurrahs. The princess overwhelmed me with her kindness. I met up with Jacques. Took a walk about the city, which pleased me a great deal. The officers are amusing themselves in town. Much struck by Brühl Palace. Everything worth seeing was looked at, including the inside of the sedan chairs, which amused us very much. In the theatre, *The Vestal Virgin;** the orchestra was marvellous. The monarchs honoured the public with their presence. The theatre was pretty; the costumes, voices, decorations— everything pleased me. Supper at the Bavarian Hotel. A gallant adventure with Mlle Caroline Müller, a very pretty girl full of zest. She got quite tipsy. My Fyodor got as drunk as a pig.

14, 15 April

The Plau plain is enchanting. The morning was heavenly, the evening still lovelier. Just imagine a valley filled with gardens and houses, surrounded by rocks cut through by a river whose presence is broadcast everywhere by the noise of its falls. Jägersdorf; I visited the coal mines. Splendid machinery; magnificent water pump. Back to Dresden.

16, 17 April

The library, the gallery. Correggio's *Nightfall* and Urbino's *Madonna†* were ravishing; the Catholic church, the music you hear there—all made the day pass quickly. Much talk of a forthcoming battle. The French armies are gathering and uniting near Frankfort. Lunched at Grandmama's. At the theatre we saw *A Soldier's Fortune*, a play I thought very

---

* Opera by Gasparo Spontini (1774–1851) (Ed.).
† The Sixtine Madonna (Ed.).

amusing. Visited Caroline. Back to Tharandt. A lovely evening; I'm in a delicious mood!

Kutuzov died in Bunzlau (Silesia) on 17 April. He had undertaken the renewed campaign against Napoleon only halfheartedly. When the enemy had been driven off Russian soil Kutuzov regarded his task as finished. In addition, the hardships of the winter campaign had undermined his already enfeebled health. In the service of the Russian Army since earliest youth, he had distinguished himself most gloriously in the earlier wars against the Turks. He had lost his right eye in a storm attack at Otsakov. He also served his country as ambassador, first in Constantinople, then in Berlin. His victory at Smolensk had the most decisive effect on the outcome of the Franco-Russian campaign. Until his death his mind was active and lively, but his body, in spite of its iron constitution, had been completely exhausted by the exertions of his constant soldiering.

The supreme command of the Russian armed forces was taken over by Prince Wittgenstein.

18 April
Adieu! We are three miles out of Dresden, in Nossen. How things change. We're here in battle dress. It's said that Napoleon is advancing with a heavy army unit. He's risking defeat after twenty-six years of carnage; but before abandoning his cause he's going to put a finish to quite a number of thousands. He's going to try to wipe out with our blood the shameful defeat he suffered at our bayonets. But in vain; he will perish; God is for us and with us; He will destroy that monster, that scourge of the earth! Blücher's army is magnificent; there is a spirit of revenge among these Prussians that allows one to hope for many good things; they fought like madmen.

19 April, Rundorf
Everything is being readied for an imminent battle.

From time to time the dull noise of cannon fire can already
be heard. The poor peasants are very much to be pitied
because of the pillage that is going on everywhere. The
weather is magnificent. What a contrast! While nature is
lavishly adorned like a young bride, human beings go on
tearing each other to pieces and devouring each other.

22 April

We were peacefully asleep in our barracks last night when
a sudden trumpet call rang out and awoke us with a start.
Soon everything was moving. It was a dark night, no moon
or stars. A fresh breeze shook the trees; rain was coming
down in great drops. The steps of the horses, the clanking
of arms, the soft gleaming of our helmets spread a sombre
hue over this nocturnal spectacle. We marched six miles
without a stop. The horses were exhausted. At Borna we
called a halt. It's taken for granted that something is going
to happen tomorrow.

23 April, *The Battle of Lützen*

We are retreating. The French fought like Mamelukes;
the Prussians were less strong, and Miloradovich arrived too
late. The heart of the action was at Weissenfels. Our squadrons charged around the same stone that covers the immortal
remains of Gustavus Adolphus. Our right flank was beaten;
the Prussian losses were considerable. At night we camped
opposite the enemy, who were trying to reconnoitre our
positions with bombs and rockets. The weather was damp.
The groaning of the wounded froze me with horror. I went
close to some of these unfortunates. It's impossible to describe
everything I heard and suffered that night.

24 April

This morning I went to the outposts. There they thought
the enemy army was turning toward Leipzig. As for us,
we're marching toward Altenburg. I saved the life of a number of wounded I picked up out of the ruins of a village and

lifted on to my horse. We're camped near Altenburg. A forced march to Chemnitz. We've been brought some French prisoners; they're all young and lively. They're estimated at 48,000 men and 600 cannon.

25 April, Freiberg

I went down to visit the mines. We're running like madmen; I don't understand it. Quartered in Oberwahlen. A fine night, good quarters; we've come quite a distance from the enemy. The countryside is like a garden; it's all going to be devastated. We're not far from Dresden.

27 April

We've crossed the Elbe; everyone is retreating. The Dresdeners are in consternation; I went through the city at a gallop. The Prince's house was empty. Jacques and I went through the chestnut lanes that shade the Elbe; our camps are on the other side of the river. The din, the music, the camp fires—everything spreads a warlike atmosphere over this countryside that used to be so peaceful. There's a lot of talk about an alliance with Austria. Metternich, Mme von Colloredo, and Schwarzenberg*—the whole of this mighty triumvirate has already been won over, it's said. That would give us 80,000 Austrian troops.

30 April

We're still camped on the outskirts of Dresden. Took a horseback ride to the Augustinian area. Meyer, Jacques, and I got a little tipsy. We fired off some corks at the enemy. A sad piece of news has gone around the camp, upsetting everyone. Our liberator, Kutuzov, has died. He was worth a full army corps; I tremble at the thought of his successor. Perhaps Barclay. We've just made six miles. We're quite close to Herrnhut. I should have very much liked to visit

---

* Prince Metternich, Austrian statesman and diplomat; Mme von Colloredo, wife of Count von Colloredo-Mansfeld, field marshal and diplomat; Prince von Schwarzenberg, field marshal (Ed.).

the children of Count von Zinzendorf,* but I was despatched for supplies. The beautiful countryside is being ravaged; the inhabitants are in despair at our abandoning Saxony. M. Zimmermann, an old gentleman, amuses me a great deal with his apprehensions and his greed.

1 May, Bautzen

Here we are, back in Bautzen. Our position is magnificent. It's being whispered that we're doing badly and that we're going to risk a second battle here. In the evening I went over to the Prussian camp. General Roeder and his officers received me affably. The music was good, and the supper delicious. Their bivouac looks like a pleasure camp. The gleam of the firelight had a fairylike effect.

3 May

We've changed our position. My chest hurts. This morning I was adjutant to General Uvarov. The cannon fire can be heard; the night looks like a sea of flames. The army corps have assembled. Tomorrow there'll be more to say about that!

The spectacle of a camp like this gives rise to different thoughts. How many warriors have gathered together here on one small spot! The youth of all the countries of Europe are concentrated here, thirsting for glory. How many of these men are looking at the moon for the last time in their lives, how many tears will be shed! Oh Moon, looking through a veil of smoke at tomorrow's victims, at least spread tonight a sweet joyfulness in their hearts and draw their gaze up to Heaven, where the life of the dead is weighed and the death of the living is determined!

8 May

How memorable are these days in which the fate of our armies may be decided! We're completely defeated, and our corps is in a state of headlong flight. We have 32,000

* Famous religious leader (Ed.).

men left on the field of battle. The day before yesterday, at six o'clock in the morning, the enemy attacked our centre —but without success. The next day they renewed their attack with much better results, after the high points of our position had been taken by storm. The cannon fire was frightful; our regiment lost many men. After a few hours of rest Napoleon redoubled his attack; our batteries were taken, the right flank bypassed, and the centre beaten into flight. We ran back ten versts, and after a short pause for rest we continued our retreat.

16 May

We've passed again through Görlitz, Löbau, Löwenberg, and Goldberg; for several hours we've been camped near Schweidnitz—a strong position. It's hot. An armistice is being mentioned. Walked along on the Zobten. A splendid view; ruins.

20 May

We're moving on toward Nimptsch; I've just passed Reichenbach, a village that's a mile long. A truce has been made. The Tsar has gone to Braunau. We're going to take up quarters. Our reserves have just arrived. Koskull is here too.

24 May, Grottkau

We're camped here; a pretty little city. My quarters are in Märzdorf. I'm not well at all. Bernadotte has gone to Headquarters. The diplomats are in full swing. All the great names have withdrawn to Bohemia; I've just made the acquaintance of a pastor who has a piano, books, and a charming young hostess. Tomorrow we're going to Brieg.

28 May, Brieg

A charming city on the banks of the Oder. The surroundings are pretty, the women still prettier. They're so white and plump. One of them, the foster child of a Jew named

Alexander, has attracted my entire attention. Her name is
Christel. To a remarkable degree she possesses all the charms
that innocence and naïveté can give a young person. I'm
living with a M. von Beyer, who has a fine piano and a very
interesting family. I've just received orders to go back, since
there's to be a review. How cruel and stupid it is to torment
weary people so.

14 June

My Diary has had to hold its peace for over a fortnight.
During this period I was in Brieg several times. Christel is
all fire and flame. Mme von Beyer enchants me with her
wit. I ran into Massenbach, from Therewisch; he's a good
comrade, with a sweet and cheerful nature.

I've conceived the mad plan of abducting Christel; she's
agreed. What will come of it? I don't believe in it for a
moment.

An evening at M. Hoffmann's. Strandmann is paying
court to Mlle Steinacker, very pretty but a flirt; we play
music. Yesterday I made the acquaintance of the niece of
M. von Beyer; her name is Amalie Müller, and she plays
well. We were united by a kind of sympathy.

17 June, Brieg

I am again in this charming place. Christel woke me up
this morning. What a temptation! I took a ride on horseback
this afternoon. The peasants here seem rather civilized, and
this, added to a great deal of wisdom, makes it pleasant to
deal with them. They're generally rich; their houses are
clean, and everything has an air of ease and harmony. The
countryside is Catholic, but since Silesia lost its monasteries
and became an integral part of the Prussian monarchy the
prejudices have largely faded away, so people say. The
population is large; it's hospitable and musical. The nobility
is still rather rich, though it has lost many of its former
privileges. It is not ostentatious, but it is proud. The men like
horses, hunting, and wine; the women hold themselves

splendidly, have a great many natural graces and beautiful complexion. There is quite a lot of looseness in the cities, less in the countryside. The peasant women here are more faithful to their husbands, and the girls more inclined to purity in their conduct because they are more religious. The women have a lively temperament, strong imagination, and subtle and sly minds. They're generally pretty. The women's costume is tasteful, the men's heavy. In the cities there are a great many talented people, especially in music. Dancing is very popular. I find the signs on the taverns and on the workshops endlessly entertaining; there are some terribly funny ones; for instance: "Here is a broombinder's house, where brooms are bound to redden behinds and whiten houses. Praised be the broombinders, who correct behaviour and clean the floors."

24 June

I've moved in completely with M. Beyer. I'm living in perfect harmony with Christel and the whole family. Mlle Malchen is becoming attached to me; she's a sweet child, but I prefer Christel because of her innocence. Walks in the park. Our truce will soon run out.

25 June

There's a tremendous bustling about at Headquarters. Apparently we're going to be marching soon. A promenade along the Neisse. What delicious countryside. A troop of strolling players has set itself up in Grottkau. A tightrope walker performed his marvels. A terrific storm—a lovely sight. Back to Märzdorf.

On 25 June the King of Prussia addressed this announcement to his subjects:

The enemy has offered a truce that I together with my allies have accepted until the 20th of the coming month, so that the full national strength that my people has now so gloriously displayed will be able to unfold itself fully. Until now the enemy has been far superior to us in numbers: we could win back only our national honour; we must make use of the brief respite in order to become so strong that we shall be able to win our independence. Continue in your firm resolve, trust your king, ceaselessly work on, and we shall achieve this sacred goal too.

From his headquarters in Bautzen Napoleon announced the following:

Since the beginning of the campaign the French Army has freed Saxony, conquered half of Silesia, taken back the Thirty-second Army Division, and destroyed the hopes of our enemies.

27 June, Brieg
A rendezvous at the Neisse Gate. My imprudence . . . a tender attachment . . . declaration—long live love!

1 July
Brieg has enthralled me. I feel so wonderful here that I've forgotten the whole outside world. Mme Beyer is the only one here who keeps me guessing. She has a very deep character. I get on her nerves, and she avoids me like a rabbit. M. Beyer is captivated the moment one speaks of Jean Paul,* whom he's crazy about; he lets himself go, drinks one glass of Tokay after another, and ends up telling stories. Christel lets herself go along; she's made of pure love. Mme Müller is very reserved, with unusual intelligence, but she judges people by their services, also by their appearance. Mlle Amalie is very flirtatious and lively, but she very cleverly hides her temperamental shortcomings. Her conversation is rather precious; she's always showing off what she's read. Mlle Sophie, who's engaged, is a good child, but she's wanton, sentimental, and sometimes mischievous. Pauline, the youngest, seems to me the best of them all.

* Pseudonym of Johann Paul Friedrich Richter (1763–1825), German humorist and prose writer (Ed.).

On 1 July Napoleon arrived in Halle an der Saale and demanded as satisfaction from the town's dwellers, who had fired at French soldiers, the execution of at least six of its citizens within four weeks. Otherwise, the city was to be punished by having a garrison of 15,000 men quartered in it and a fine of four million francs. If this were not paid, the city was to be reduced to ashes. In connection with this, Napoleon arranged a military parade near Leipzig. On 2 July Napoleon and the Allies agreed to extend the truce until 28 July. From then on a six-day notice of its annulment could be given.

3 July

Mlle Amalie's birthday. I presented her with my bouquet. This attention pleased her mother very much; the ladies regarded it as a hidden declaration. In the afternoon we went to Abraham's Garden. In accordance with my time-honoured system I paid court to all the ladies, one after the other. Mme Beyer is very reserved; Amalie is aiming at marriage. She was charming, a little pale, to tell the truth, but languishing away like Clarissa. I pretended not to notice her little game; I couldn't have been gayer. She tried too pick a quarrel and sulked; I kept increasing my good humour. Our reconciliation by the light of the moon was thoroughly romantic.

4 July

I won't forget today for the rest of my life. Mme Beyer, Mlle Amalie, and Christel all showered me with their good graces. What an intrigue! In the evening I played the organ.

8 July

The troop of strolling players entertained us a great deal at Grottkau. Two plays by Kotzebue* were put on yesterday. No matter what one says about Kotzebue, he is the only playwright who has been able to master German comedy.

* August Friedrich Ferdinand von Kotzebue (1761–1819) (Ed.).

Mlle Kolter, the actress, paid us a visit. It can easily be imagined that she was well received by our officers.

Our truce has been extended!

I'm amusing myself reading the books M. Beyer has lent me, among others, *Siebenkäs* by Jean Paul.* It's very good, but hard to understand.

9 July

This morning we had a big review. The Emperor and the King had us parade. The troops were splendid; it seems impossible not to be able to crush the enemy with such forces.

Had an argument with Zalov about a debt; I'm selling my horse to pay him.

12 July

I took a short leave for an outing to the mountains with M. Beyer. Jacques has arrived; he's off to Bialystok. It was a great pleasure to see him again. I'm going to try to have him transferred to the cavalry.

14 July

Two magnificent days in Brieg. Amalie was ravishing, so was Christel. Strandmann has seduced poor S.

17 July

Three days on duty. The Grand Duke was extremely gracious. We're going to stay here for a long time, doing nothing; I'm impatient to measure myself against the enemy and to give free rein to my ambitions.

19 July

Spent a few days in Brieg. Last night I risked a declaration. Amalie couldn't have been more flattered. How will it all end? Mme Beyer is an angel; Beyer seems disturbed. I have

* Humorous novel by Johann Paul Friedrich Richter, known as Jean Paul (1763–1825) (Ed.).

no intention of disturbing his conjugal happiness; but Christel will be my lightning rod. Long live youth, long live love and boldness!

22 July

Here we are, M. Beyer and myself, going along in a carriage; we're on our way to Landeck. The conversation has been lively, the weather magnificent, the surroundings charming. We made a stop in Neisse. Up to then the terrain had been flat, but we had hardly reached the heights dominating the fortress when the mountains near Glatz appeared in all their glory. We crossed the drawbridge. I am incognito and pass as M. Beyer's secretary. This gives us a good laugh. The moment we arrived we went to see M. Beyer's brother, a man of matchless humour. M. Steckel entertained us with a lovely symphony of Beethoven. The piano was excellent. The evening passed by marvellously. Supper, beds—all wonderful. This morning we visited the fortifications. The buildings are a hydraulic masterpiece. They can put the right side of the city under water by forcing the river to take another course. Splendid view of the surroundings from the casemates. Promenade in the town. Visited Mme Schubert and Mme Dörring, charming women. An outing to Johannisberg is underway. We're all laughing about the agreeable adventure. We go to Ottmachau first, then spend the night in Johannisberg, a pretty little city with an old castle. Magnificent view of the mountains of Bohemia. Supper and some good wine at the chaplain's. Military fantasy on the piano in the drawing room. Some tall stories!

25 July

The two gentlemen are leaving us. I took leave of them with great regret; I haven't met such nice people for a long time. We entered a valley first that led directly to Landeck. I'm struck by the beauty of this place; I'd very much like to stay on here. Promenade to the baths and to the English gardens. The communal bath; I was astonished to see men and women pell-mell in it. But their costumes are decent. The water is clear. From above, the people look like monsters. I felt marvellously refreshed by a bath I took. Dined at the table d'hôte. Music in the living room; a Princess Biron sang like a nightingale. We're going to see the inspector, a highly respectable man, and Mme Berger, who has a charming daughter. Had supper at the "Potash Works", in a lovely garden. I thought the people quite select. The place is charming. Ran into Rönne, who told me the march was beginning.

30 July

After hurrying through Wartha and Frankenstein, remarkable for the pilgrimages there and the ruins; meeting a Silesian army corps that was on the move to Bohemia; sleeping in Reichenbach, a big village almost a mile long; we returned by way of Nimptsch, Strehlen, and Grottkau to our own place in Brieg, where I made preparations for my departure. Our regiments had already left. The farewells were very tender; I promised to come back soon; this was some consolation, though I didn't believe it myself. Christel wept like a mad thing; Amalie, whose face was pale, said to me: "That's how the young gentlemen are; destruction is their business, but a broken heart is just a joke to them. May Heaven keep you and never let you feel what I'm feeling now!" These words pierced my heart but—what can one do? The trumpet sounds, glory beckons. *Adieu, les amours!*

Napoleon is falling back. Moreau* has been called back from America. He's at the head of the army; the Emperor seems to want to keep him near to his own person. Wellington has beaten the French at Vittoria in Spain; the Austrians have proclaimed themselves our allies. Reverses for our

---

* Jean Victor (1763–1813), known as Moreau, French soldier exiled and living in Trenton, N.J. Mortally wounded upon his return to Europe at the Battle of Dresden (Ed.).

enemies everywhere. The good cause will, I hope, be triumphant.

1 August

By way of Münsterberg, Frankenstein, Silberberg, Neurode, to Braunau, where I met my regiment.

At the end of July Austria joined the alliance against Napoleon. On 3 August Emperor Franz of Austria, Tsar Alexander of Russia, and King Friedrich Wilhelm of Prussia met in Prague to confer on a general plan of campaign. On 4 August the Austrian army joined a Russian and a Prussian corps in Bohemia under the command of Prince Schwarzenberg. A proclamation of the Prince in connection with this read as follows:

A great day has come: Austria is speaking up with a loud voice for the cause of right and order. It is not against France, it is only against French force outside the borders of France that this great alliance has arisen. Battle as befits Austrian warriors, and you shall win!

Together with the Austrians the Allies now had 500,000 men under arms. Napoleon disposed of a combat force of 350,000 men.

At one o'clock in the night of 5 August the truce came to an end; hostilities began simultaneously at all points.

The headquarters of the Allied monarchs was Prague; that of Prince Schwarzenberg was Melnik; that of General Blücher was Jauer; that of the Crown Prince of Sweden (Bernadotte) was Charlottenburg. Napoleon's Headquarters was in Bautzen.

3 August, Horsitz

A day of rest. We are in the heart of Bohemia, a curious country with a Slav population. Our regiment is exhausted. The horses are sick; the country is mountainous, the terrain cut up, and the roads very stony. There's something wild about nature here, and the rocks, which you see all over, have bizarre shapes. Waterfalls can be seen everywhere, plunging from the summits of the hills into abysses covered with bushy forests. The peasants are poor and not very civilized. Their language is something like Russian; they understand us a little. The peasants' costume is unusual: black jackets, something like armour plate. The country, in general, is very picturesque. The sunset and the echo of the thunder are marvellously effective. The valleys of Aders-bach and Reinerz are incomparable; huge rocky masses that seem to mean to crush the traveller look like pyramids turned upside down.

7 August, Königgrätz

A fine fortress. We've crossed the Elbe. Today I celebrated my twentieth birthday. My thoughts were with my people in Reval. I also spent the day contemplating my past life and my present. It's no use trying to correct one's faults; the result isn't very brilliant.

8 August

Marched forty versts. We're camped at Elb-Kosteletz. A renewal of hostilities is being mentioned; also, it is said that the Austrians have come to grips with the French. There are rumours that the Spaniards and the English under Welling-ton have wiped out Napoleon's army in Spain. We're very near Prague. Marched sixty-eight versts. We're completely exhausted.

9, 10 August

Laun, a small provincial town, the home of Kreutzer,* the violinist. The Erzgebirge range lies before us in all its grandeur. We paraded today before Emperor Franz, who looks like a cobbler. We saw Postelberg, a magnificent castle which belongs to Schwarzenberg.

---

* Rudolf Kreutzer (1766–1831), violinist and composer to whom Beethoven's famous sonata was dedicated (Ed.).

12 August, Saaz

A charming city. I made the acquaintance of Dr. Leber, who received me affably. The Eger River has lovely surroundings. Mlle Lottchen kept me busy all day long.

On 11 August the Allies won a victory at Gross Beeren, near Berlin. The Crown Prince of Sweden, Bülow, Tauentzien, Borstel, Thümen, Kraft, Prince von Hessen-Homburg, and Cardell fought against Oudinot, Victor, Régnier, Bertrand, and Arrighi. The French fell back to Baruth on the Elbe.

On 14 August the Allies, under General Blücher, won a battle near Katzbach, not far from Wahlstatt. Sacken, York, Langeron, Horn, Huenerbein, Prince von Mecklenburg, Steinmetz, Korff, Charbatof, and Densisiev, with 80,000 men, confronted a French army of equal strength under Ney, Macdonald, Lauriston, Souham, and Sébastiani. The French lost 18,000 prisoners, including one divisional and two brigade generals, 103 cannon, 250 powder wagons, and 4 eagles. They fell back to the Bober River.

Early in the morning of the same day Napoleon arrived in Dresden. In the afternoon the Allies, under Prince Schwarzenberg, attacked the French entrenchments and positions on the left bank of the Elbe from three points.

15 August, Brix, Dux, Töplitz

Three ravishing places. We are nearing the enemy, who have entrenched themselves near Dresden. The area is pretty, but the weather is awful; it's pouring.

16 August, The Battle of Dresden

A French sortie; a column of Austrians has been captured. Moreau has fallen. Retreat . . . a frightful road by way of Giesshübel. We're beaten and pursued.

17 August, The Battle of Kulm

At four o'clock in the morning we left Altenburg. The

weather was stormy and presaged a day that would be no less so. The road and the passes near Kraupen, between enormous mountains, were hardly passable. We'd scarcely come down onto the plain near Kulm, yet we could already hear cannon and musket fire on every side, quite close to us. An aide-de-camp of Count Ostermann came galloping up at a breakneck pace with the order for us to move on instantly to the field of battle. The infantry Guards regiments were already at grips with the enemy, who were harassing their flanks. It was Vandamme's corps, 40,000 strong, pushing us toward Töplitz. The Russian, Prussian, and Austrian headquarters were still behind us, in the passes near Kraupen. Thus, it was a question of saving the monarchs from being taken prisoner, since the French lines had already reached the exits from the passes. I was appointed adjutant to the divisional general. The firing had begun; on every side cannon shell whistled above our heads, and grenades were exploding right and left. The general exposed himself to death; he lost an arm. General Golitsyn succeeded him in command. Towards evening the Semyonovsky and Preobrazhensky regiments were attacked by rapid fire. The carnage was frightful. Nightfall separated the combatants and put an end to a very peppery day. The 8,000 soldiers of the Guard had fought 40,000; by clinging to their terrain, they had saved three army corps and three crowned heads, all of which would have been lost if we hadn't stood our ground! Glory to the Russian arms!

18 August

The engagement resumed this morning with renewed ferocity. The battle was outside Kulm; we charged the enemy a number of times—they had been intending to outflank us. The hussars and the cuirassiers distinguished themselves, as did the infantry of the Guards. Towards noon Vandamme, in command of the French army corps, deployed all his forces; we definitely would have had to fall back if Kleist* had not attacked him from the rear. The Austrians and another Russian corps arrived in time to rescue us. The enemy were attacked from three sides and were routed so badly that they abandoned 81 cannon and 9,000 prisoners. Marshal Vandamme himself fell into our hands; he gnashed his teeth when an aide-de-camp had him surrender his sword. When he was asked to hand over his papers he retorted, "The only papers I have are for wiping my behind. Tell that to his Majesty." By four o'clock everything was over. The spectacle was magnificent. A countless crowd of prisoners marched in front of us. The Allied princes embraced before their soldiers' eyes. Joy transfigured their faces; the news of the defeat of the French by Blücher and Bernadotte added to our jubilation. Bonaparte's eagles will no longer invade Germany; they're going to go all the way back to France, never again to disturb the peace of Europe.

Yet this battle has cost the lives of many officers and of many fine friends of mine. The God of Battles will make a place for them!

19 August, Töplitz

A day of rest. A charming place. Took a promenade to the Schlossberg. The weather is superb; the army encamped 1,000 paces from the city; we're leading a marvellous life and fraternizing with the Prussian and Austrian girls, who, however, look at us somewhat askance.

On 19 August Headquarters of the Allies announced:

A French corps 40,000 strong, under Vandamme, has been beaten at Kulm and Nollendorf (between Peterswald and Töplitz) by the Russians under Ostermann, Grand Duke Constantine, Barclay de Tolly; the Prussians under King Wilhelm, Prince

---

* Count Kleist von Nollendorf, Prussian general and Corps commander (Ed.).

August,* Kleist, and Ziethen; and the Austrians under Prince
Schwarzenberg, Colloredo, Bianchi, and Prince Frederick von
Hessen-Homburg. There were 8,000 prisoners taken, including
Generals Prince Reuss, Montesquieu, and Dumonceau. Eighty-
seven cannon, 2 flags, 2 eagles, and 200 ammunition carts were
taken. On the side of the Allies, Prince von Pless has fallen.
Generals Ostermann, Karpovitsky, and Levashov were wounded.
The Preobrazhensky Regiment lost 700, the Izmailov Regiment
400, the Semakhov Regiment 900, and the Chasseur Guards 600
men. The Russian losses under Ostermann totalled 6,000 men.

From 5 August until today the French have lost: 38,000
prisoners, 750 officers, 246 cannon, and 415 army wagons. On
the battlefields between the Rhine and Dresden they have left
behind this month 35,000 sick and wounded.

*On 25 August, at Jüterbock and Dennewitz, a French army fight-
ing under Marshal Ney was annihilated by the Prussians under
Bülow, Tauentzien, and Borstel. According to their own reports,
the losses of the French came to 8,000 men and 12 cannon, those of
the Allies to 7,000 men. The Saxons, Württembergers, and Bavarians
were driven by the French into the firing. By the end of the battle
they had been destroyed to such an extent that scarcely even a brigade
could be formed from what was left of the Bavarians. Before this
battle the chief of the French General Staff had said to the commanding officer of the Württembergers, "You'll have to go on ahead, for
it is of some consequence to us that all of you be killed, else you'll
soon be fighting against us yourselves."*

25 August

I've been to see the Bilin cliff, which has a most remarkable
shape. The Blankenstein Castle near Spitzberg pleased me
greatly because of its splendid situation.

Yesterday, looking for supplies for the regiment among
the peasants, I was almost killed by the peasants; my
presence of mind saved me.

A French retreat is being spoken of. Our vanguard has
pushed the enemy back as far as Dresden.

* Friedrich Wilhelm Heinrich August, Prince of Prussia (Ed.).

26 August, Nollendorf

The Bohemians here are quite wild; we're marching along the Erzgebirge. Bonaparte is fleeing toward Leipzig. The plain of Töplitz was covered this morning by a whitish fog that looked like a sea of clouds. It was a magnificent spectacle.

30 August

I've just received some letters from Mama. Thank God, everyone is all right; what a satisfaction to know that one's family are well.

The weather is terrible; the camps are unbearable. Our vanguard has just been thrust back. But we fight every day with the Austrians, who don't want to declare themselves openly for our cause. May Metternich and Schwarzenberg finally come over to us! Will Austrian policy always be as perfidious as it has been in the past?

3 September

Every day we take a great many prisoners; from time to time cannon fire is heard. Napoleon's position must be very critical, for he's being pressed on all sides. From what we hear, the misery and distress in Dresden have reached a peak; desertion is adding to it, for whole companies are constantly coming over to our side. But in spite of this, Bonaparte's forces are estimated at 140,000 men. The Tyroleans have revolted against the Franco-Bavarian government and are going to make common cause with us. Freiberg has been taken by storm. The mobile bridges across the Elbe near Dresden have been burned by Blücher's vanguard. We're still camped on the outskirts of Töplitz. The surroundings are charming. I've found a pretty piano at a Jew's; it amuses me a lot. But there are no women; they've all fled from the approaching horrors of war.

6 September

Went to a military party arranged by the officers of our

division in honour of the monarchs. We were all very gay; the Emperor and the King attended. We were there as brothers and friends of the Prussians. Everyone got tipsy and we were all impossibly merry, but the party ended in a very tragic way, since a Prussian, Colonel Werder, in moving off in the darkness toward home, stumbled with his horse and broke his neck.

8 September, *The Ossegg Monastery*

I've just come back from a day of foraging. The monument to Chevalier de Saxe . . . the peasant who told me all the details of that famous duel. The monastery. The sight of the most profound peace amidst the ravages of war touched me. Some of the monks took me to see some remarkable things in the monastery. A painting by Guercino, the first of its kind I had seen representing the Holy Virgin, gave me a feeble idea of the beauty of Italian painting.

10 September

Poor Boris just missed being burnt alive! This experience, though almost fatal, was still somewhat ridiculous. My bivouac, made of wood and straw, caught fire during the night and I lost a great many of my things. Pilar, who was sleeping with me, shouted out at the top of his lungs; luckily we had time enough to flee.

Benningsen has arrived here with 65,000 reserves. He's going to take his place in our line-up. This reinforcement will decide the outcome of the passage at arms.

11 September

We're marching into the middle part of Saxony. The Eger is serving as a position; we passed Kratzav and Lobositz to arrive at our quarters. What bliss to find oneself at last in a room, among some splendid peasants, after six weeks of exhaustion! Koskull and myself are quartered with the village pastor, who amuses us because of his singularity. The village is prettily situated. The inhabitants, though somewhat wild,

are becoming accustomed to Russians. The Bohemian patois
is like Russian, so we can make ourselves understood. Old
Slavonic especially has a great many similarities to
Bohemian; the people have the same origins. The cook,
Mariko, has just learned a few words of Russian and she
annoys me. Her master irritates her, and she couldn't care
less about him. We make him drink and when he's tipsy he
gets rather ridiculous.

The ruins give me great pleasure. An adventure at the
tavern.

14 September, Prague

Two of the most radiant days of my life. This ancient city
has so many remarkable things in it; I've gone through it
zigzagging. This evening Koskull and I went to the theatre.
They gave Spontini's *Ferdinand Cortez*, which gave me an
idea of Italian music. The production was superb.

The Moldau [Vltava], which is quite large, divides the
city in two; the Hradcany castle and hill dominate the city.
John of Nepomuk and his splendid bridge astounded me by
their beauty, though the Dresden Bridge is even more
beautiful. The Cathedral is most impressive. Turning
towards the Old Town, I had myself taken to the Färber
Island, where I breakfasted. . . . An adventure with lovely
Theresa. At ten o'clock I went into a music salon, where
some plays were being given. M. Weber,* the great composer, received me very civilly and let me attend the
rehearsal. A conversation with Mlle Kührer.

At one o'clock I went back to my hotel, where I was
surrounded by a lot of do-nothings who call themselves
artists but who actually only empty foreigners' pockets.
In five minutes one of them cut out my silhouette for forty
kreuzers; according to him it was a speaking likeness.
Another declaimed some verses for me; that cost me,
willy-nilly, a gulden. A third slipped me, for several kreuzers,

* Carl Maria von Weber was conductor at the Prague theatre from
1813 to 1817 (Ed.).

a ticket with an invitation to a fine supper that some dancing girls from the theatre were supposed to attend. A fourth was a Jew who had all sorts of trifles to sell at double the right price. A fifth and some others finally made me lose patience: I kicked the rascals out. But they were scarcely gone before I was surrounded by women and girls who deafened me with their clamour. One of them was selling jewels made in Prague, another was begging for alms, another spoke to me of her virtue, which she seemed to be selling for an *écu*; another, a procuress, was singing the praises of her girls and trying to sell me some miraculous water that she said had the power to rejuvenate greybeards, etc. Wearied by all this nonsense, I went off to shut myself in my room and dine at my ease. The wine, which is a local one, is excellent; it's called Melniker and grows outside Melnik, a little city a few miles from Prague. It's dark red and looks like a Burgundy.

The Gothic buildings of Prague are of historic value. The fortress is magnificent; I was shown the place Frederick the Great took by storm with his Grenadiers. Music can be heard everywhere. Everyone sings and plays an instrument. At six o'clock we went to the theatre to see *A Russian Abroad*, a play that fits my circumstances and that I liked a lot. Countess Nostitz and Princess Cagliari were the targets of everyone's gaze; they are dazzling beauties. At ten o'clock we're going back to Libuchowitz.

17–21 September

During this past week I've spent the time visiting the countryside in a radius of ten miles and seeing some acquaintances I've met in the neighbourhood. Peretz Castle stands in a splendid valley, surrounded by high mountains covered with the most beautiful and variegated foliage, and cut in two by a stream with a number of waterfalls. The garden is most beautiful, a mixture of little shrubs and flowering trees, lanes of fruit trees, and deep clefts. The little villages breathe forth prosperity and freshness. The most remarkable sight is a hut, built into the rock above a dark pond surrounded by magnificent trees, inhabited by a family that is as virtuous as it is beautiful. A stream gushes out above the roof, adding to the originality of the whole scene. The village is note-worthy for a legend that goes back to 1083: while on a hunt the King of Bohemia saw standing next to a well (which I was shown) a peasant girl as beautiful as the day, washing laundry. He fell madly in love with her and married her. Ever since, the village has been called Peretz, which in Bohemian means washing. I was received very civilly at the castle; the young ladies of the house were very amiable. We were brought together by the piano, and I passed a very agreeable evening. Yesterday I came back to my village, since the Grand Duke is arriving.

22 September

Today was one of the most brilliant days of my military career, for I've just received my lieutenancy and at the same time the Order of St. Vladimir 4th Class. My Fyodor brings me some game every day; the pheasants around here have a marvellous taste.

23 September

Visited the Prussian camp; our German comrades received me very well, and I was treated to the local grapes, red and white, which are delicious.

24 September

We are on the march again. My Diary will suffer for it. We're in Postelberg. Terrible weather.

25 September, Kommotau

Our reserves have just arrived.

26 September, Saaz

A pretty little town; I'm quartered together with Sass, Dr. Leber, and the Howatke family; the older girl has a pretty voice. A puppet theatre that put on Goethe's *Faust* did a fine job. An adventure with Mme M., whom I saw at the theatre; on our way out she stepped on my foot and signalled me to follow her. Her escort left her at the porte-cochère of her house; I stayed hidden behind a column, where I waited a good half hour without losing patience. Finally a boy came over to me, took my by the arm, and began yelling at the top of his lungs; two torchbearers, accompanied by a number of other people, came out of the house. I was taken into a room where the master of the house, a professor, received me with the following words: "Thanks to the vigilance of my wife, you have been observed; you have evil designs; you want either to steal or to spy, or to have a gay adventure; you'll do nothing of the sort; I'm going to denounce you to the police in the morning and you'll be severely punished. This evening it's too late; you'll be imprisoned in a room on the ground floor." Flabbergasted by everything that had happened to me, I had scarcely begun apologizing when I was seized again, pushed into a dark room, and locked in. I was in a most disagreeable position, since my arms were tied. I had to be patient. A certain curiosity and a premonition kept me intrigued. I was lying on a sofa and sleep was already descending on my eyelids when a velvet hand woke me with a start. It was my lovely; the whole adventure had been nothing but a stratagem on her part. You can imagine how I made use of my time. This night spent in the arms of the most beautiful of women will always remain fresh in my memory. At four o'clock she gave me the signal to leave. I left madly in love with her. My unknown beauty had me depart softly; doubtless I shall never see her again; how we find and lose people! Woman is surely the Serpent of the Old Testament. At eight o'clock I left my hotel without having succeeded in hiding from the servant something of my little nocturnal.

28 September, Schmiedeberg, Marienberg

We are in Saxony again; it seems that the armies will soon

come to grips again, for we've received orders not to lose sight of our horses and our arms.

30 September, Langfeld, Zschopau

Little towns in Saxony. The country has been terribly devastated. Everyone is pillaging and looting; nevertheless we're received everywhere with cries of joy; it seems that Napoleon has no great friends here. The fruit here is delicious; we're stuffing ourselves to the point of incapacity. It keeps on pouring; a cold autumn.

1 October, Chemnitz

A real business town; pretty and rich. Papa's birthday; my most ardent wishes for his welfare.

2 October, Penig

This belongs to Count Schönburg, husband of my beautiful aunt. We're moving towards Leipzig at a great pace; the enemy are fleeing as fast as they can.

3 October, Altenburg, Meiselwitz, Pegau

We're finally in camp, on the old battlefield of Lützen which has already cost us a lot of blood. During the night we crossed the Elster and the Pleisse in order to join up with Wittgenstein, who's been marching in pursuit of the enemy along the highway leading directly to Leipzig. Cannon fire is being heard again; this music is becoming very familiar to us; it's a sad funeral dirge.

Towards noon the cannon fire doubled in intensity; the order came to be ready to advance. Soon we could make out the small fire and the clanking of weapons; we were moving forward at a fast trot; murderous fire was already appearing and the cannon shell was coming down on us! We galloped hard through a small village filled with wounded and had scarcely come out on the height on the other side when the battle appeared before our eyes; it was most savage. Our light division had already been thrown back twice by the enemy. The Tsar was in danger: the enemy had attacked unexpectedly. But our cuirassiers scarcely showed themselves when the French cavalry fell back. The cannon fire lasted a little longer, then everything stopped.

On 4 October Bavaria declared war on Napoleon. A Bavarian, General Wrede, assumed command of a combined Austrian-Bavarian army of 30,000 men.

Napoleon concentrated the entire French army, 200,000 strong, at Leipzig. Together, the armies of the Allies were about equally strong.

Prince Schwarzenberg addressed the following proclamation to his army:

The most important period of the Holy War has come; prepare yourselves for battle. The bond that unites mighty nations for one great goal will be tied tighter and tighter on the field of battle. Russians, Prussians, and Austrians! You are fighting for one single cause, you are fighting for the freedom of Europe, for the independence of peoples, for the undying glory of your names!

During the night Prince Schwarzenberg had three great white rocket flares shot into the dark skies to give the Silesian army on the other side of Leipzig the agreed-upon signal; soon afterwards, in the north, they were answered by four red rocket flares.

5, 6, 7 October, The Battle of Leipzig

This will always be remembered in the annals of war; I shall limit myself to a few words about it. The fate of Germany and perhaps of Europe has been decided; the enemy has been beaten. Their rout is total; they have lost almost 36,000 men, as many prisoners as dead. The Saxons have abandoned the eagles of Napoleon; our booty is immense. Prince Poniatowski was drowned in the Pleisse.* The firing began at seven o'clock in the morning; the battle was waged on all sides; it went on until midnight. Bernadotte

* Uxkull is in error here: Prince Poniatowski was drowned in the River Elster (Ed.).

decided the outcome of the battle by joining us with his Swedes and Prussians.

8 October

It's a horrible sight—a vast field covered with corpses, wounded, overturned wagons, and cannon; the fortification cost us the most blood. We've counted 30,000 of our soldiers dead. The noise was hellish; several high-ranking French generals have fallen or been captured—among others Bertrand, Reynier, and Lauriston. Almost 200 cannon have fallen into our hands. Our victory is complete. The Allied monarchs embraced in the great market square of Leipzig. The enthusiasm is general. We're going to pursue the enemy as far as the Rhine; I spent an entire night asleep on top of a corpse without knowing it. We're totally exhausted.

Chapter VI

THE MARCH ON PARIS

*Napoleon fled with his beaten army over the Saale at Weissenfels;
on 11 October he reached Erfurt. The great Allied army moved
along the highway from Naumburg to Weimar. The Emperor
of Austria had set up Headquarters at Gera. On 12 October the
King of Prussia entered Berlin to the jubilation of the populace.
It was the same day that the French, seven years before, had marched
into Berlin as conquerors. The King took part in a solemn service.
He sent the following letter to General Blücher:*

Your repeated victories have multiplied your services to the
state more rapidly than I have been capable of following with
proofs of my gratitude. Accept as another proof of that your
designation as General Field Marshal. May this dignity clothe
you for many years, to the joy of the Fatherland and as a model
for the army you have so often led to glory and victory.

13 October, Weimar

Weimar! We've been chasing the enemy, who are making
their escape at a great pace. We've passed Liebertwolkwitz,
Rötha, Groitzsch, Mölsen, Teuchern, Stössen, and Naumburg, where we spent a day. Then Pforta, famous for its
Gymnasium, from which Schiller and some of his contemporaries graduated; Eckartsberga (which was sacked),
Auerstedt, famous for the great battle of 1809. This morning
we entered Weimar in parade formation! We camped on
the outskirts; I intend to return.

15 October

It snowed this morning. A *Te Deum* in honour of the

victory. We've just taken up quarters; I'm lodged in Tanndorf. Marched through Plaue, Ehrenstein, Ilmenau— beautiful countryside, gigantic natural sights, the most romantic in the Thuringian Forest. On the highest peaks you can see snow, which is a marvellous contrast to the valleys and the fields bordering the foot of the mountains. The ruins, which bear the stamp of the Middle Ages, carry me back to feudal times. The cliffs and the waterfall are ravishingly beautiful in this part of the country; the inhabitants are gentle, civil, and very industrious. We crossed Goldlauter Mountain, where it was as cold as Siberia. At nine o'clock we arrived in Suhl, a pretty town, distinguished by the original costumes of the inhabitants.

18, 19 October, Themar

Gleichen Castle, famous as the residence of the Count, who married two women, and whose bed for three is still shown; then Henneberg, where we're camped.

20 October, Melrichstadt, Neustadt

The sight of vines was a pleasant surprise for me today. The grapes are excellent, the wine passable. Saw a manuscript of Charlemagne and Pippin* at the bailiff's.

22 October, Münnerstadt, Kissingen

Two pretty places. In the latter the inhabitants looked at us in amazement; they had never seen Russian cuirassiers before. They fought for the honour of receiving us; their welcome was as agreeable as it was novel. Messrs Bailmann and Goldmeyer showered us with kindness.

23 October, Schweinfurt, Werneck

We are in a fertile plain; a splendid castle that belongs to Archduke Ferdinand, brother of the Emperor of Austria. The local wine is excellent. There are some vague rumours about another French defeat at Hanau.

* German spelling for Pepin III, father of Charlemagne (Ed.).

(*above*) THE BATTLE OF SMOLENSK, AUGUST 1812

(*below*) THE CAMP OUTSIDE SMOLENSK

(*above*) ON THE ROAD TO VYAZMA
Engraving after the drawings of Albrecht Adam, war reporter
of the Napoleonic Army on its Russian campaign

(*below*) A PROMENADE IN VIENNA'S PRATER
Indian ink sketch in sepia by Vinzenz Georg Kininger

24 October

We're marching without a break by way of Würzburg, from where we could hear cannon fire; the fortress still hasn't been taken by our men. We crossed the Main on the other side of the city, which seems very well situated. Then we crossed Rossbrunn, Esselbach, and came to a halt in Aschaffenburg, a city I like a lot. "The Prince-Bishop has fled, but we are good Germans and are staying on to welcome the Russians," my landlord said to me this morning.

26 October

Ceremonial entry into Frankfort; this ancient residence of the emperors of Germany is very impressive. The Main cuts the city in two parts which are united by one of the most beautiful bridges I've ever seen. The outskirts have been severely damaged by the enemy, who retreated this way after the Battle of Hanau. We made our entry with sixty squadrons, led by our dear monarch. We were greeted by thousands of joyous outcries. The crowd was endless. Everyone fell all over themselves to be nice to us; we were quartered in Isenburg and Dreieichenhain, two villages just outside the city. This morning I received permission to take quarters in Frankfort.

28 October

I'm lodging with a M. Renner, a merchant who has a charming family. My room is pretty and I have a piano; the theatre and amusements are helping me overcome my exhaustion. The women here are charming, my acquaintances are increasing little by little. I've become friendly with M. Sponsel, a nephew of Renner's, a splendid fellow full of merriment and good talk. I intend to pay court to Mlle Elise, the oldest daughter of the house.

1 November

I feel very much at home already; I like the life here a lot. I'm paying court to my lovely, who is responding well to my teasing. The theatre, especially the opera, is enchanting. Mme Milder has an endlessly agreeable voice. I go back occasionally to my village, but only to come right back to Frankfort, where everyone is having a marvellous time. There is talk of peace, of an armistice; the French have abandoned the right bank of the Rhine, so Germany is delivered of these tyrants who pillaged her so. What a clash of interests there will be now; everyone will want to get back what he used to have; the Emperor is being flattered, but he's putting everything off for the future.

3 November

We are spending some very pleasant days with the Renner family; two Prussians, Gol and Neumann, are also staying here with my landlord. Promenade to the Cathedral; paintings, relics of Charles V. The miraculous clock shows the heavens. A rendezvous with Lisette; we're getting on at a great rate. Political conversations with the two Renner brothers, who make me laugh.

At an extraordinary session of the State Council in Paris Napoleon said:

All my allies have abandoned me; the Bavarians have betrayed me. Didn't they move to my rear to cut off my retreat? But now they've been slaughtered too! No; no peace until I have burnt Munich. A triumvirate has been formed in the North, that same one that partitioned Poland. No peace until it is smashed! I demand 300,000 men. I want to set up a camp of 100,000 men at Bordeaux, as well as one at Lyon and another at Metz. With this last draft and with what I still have, I shall have a million soldiers; but I want men, not young conscripts who will merely fill the hospitals or die while on the march. I can depend only on the inhabitants of old France. And Holland must remain mine; I'd rather sink it in the sea. Everyone must march. You are the fathers of families, the chiefs of the people; you must show the path of zeal. People are speaking of peace, I hear nothing but the word peace, when everything should resound with shouts of war.

4, 5 November, Darmstadt

A pretty place. The King of Bavaria was at the theatre with the family of the Archduke; the opera was *Joseph*, by Méhul;* a magnificent production. Mme Schönberger was delicious as Joseph; it's rare to hear a woman sing tenor. M. Fray took me to an art collection; these curiosities interest me.

In the evening I was sitting in a café reading the news of the day when two people came in quarrelling; I inclined my ear and witnessed for the first time a metaphysical argument. It had to do with the liberty of man. One of the two belonged to the Voltaire school, the other to the Leibniz and Wolf school; the gentlemen got lost in abstractions. The one who was for pre-established harmony seemed to be losing ground when the other floored him with an argument that was as cogent as it was vigorous. "God knows," he said, "what we're going to be doing in ten years' time; so if we do wrong He's allowing all the evil to take place. So where is the freedom of the individual?" "But," the other replied, "both things, freedom and necessity, can exist perfectly well together. God foresees the wrong action I'm going to perform in ten years because he is omniscient. But by virtue of my freedom of will I could nevertheless have behaved differently."

I broke my head over this thesis and antithesis; I did my best to dissipate the thick fog that envelops our intelligence. I believe that philosophy is going to interest me a great deal one day. There is no branch of knowledge more sublime, for it concerns itself with things that are of the greatest importance to man.

9 November

An adventure in Aschaffenburg; two Austrian officers on the other side of my door were cursing the Russian nation. My first impulse was to get up and shut their mouths for them, but I soon changed my mind and thought of how to revenge myself in the same way. Cursing the Austrians

* Étienne Henri Méhul (1765–1817), French composer (Ed.).

in a loud voice, I waited for one of these gentlemen to come in and provoke me; but nothing happened: the noise stopped and I fell sound asleep.

I've finally been relieved of my duty as quartermaster; I'm returning to Frankfort this evening, where I shall go on with my old style of living. Lisette and I chat, embrace, and are very attached to each other; the little one comes to my room often and covers me with her caresses; she's of a ravishing innocence; I cover her with kisses in return and we get on so well together that the hour for dinner or suppertime comes without our even noticing it. She has a body of velvet, lovely great eyes, and a very lively mind. If I came from Frankfort and were a salesman I'd marry her at once, but I like her too much to abuse her; I respect her virtue and her innocence. Each time I leave her I am seized by sadness; each time I come from Dreiersheim back to the city my horse is covered with foam. I love every amusement the moment I can share it with her. Nevertheless it is all illusion; we're going to be off soon; I shall leave her, we shall weep a little, then forget each other.

It is only because of Thee, oh sweet illusion of the imagination, that man can be happy. Let us therefore rejoice in the present, and may each pleasure be adorned by the blossoms of a brilliant imagination!

It is true that the happiness of the moment is often spoiled for us by the thought of its falseness, but let us smother the painful suspicion that happiness is unreal; for life is short and the time of blossoming still shorter. And if honesty is not opposed to it, let us enjoy the present, not think much of the past and still less of the future. Nevertheless my dream castles are most agreeable; I already see myself free, liberated from the ties of the service and established in this beautiful country I like so much. Having been all over the world and learned something of things and people, I'll be better able to guide my tastes; my reason will be shaped by study and I shall become a thinking man, whereas for the present I'm no more than a puppet.

20 November

Since I was busy with the regiment's papers and my own I found it impossible to carry on my Diary; but I'm resuming it to touch on a few political topics. One hears so many things being talked about that it is hard to find out what the truth is; the French have crossed the Rhine, and our own army is going to cross it at three points, to plunge into the heart of France. All the French corps that had stayed in Germany to man the fortresses have more or less surrendered. The only thing left for Napoleon to do is to collect another army. The northern army has delivered the Netherlands from French rule. The king has fled, with all his wealth. Switzerland has proclaimed its neutrality!

Marching is being spoken of; I don't believe a word of it, because I don't wish to. Yesterday we had such a good time together again; Lisette couldn't have been sweeter. In the alcove we swore to love each other eternally; we caressed each other so much that I was afraid of the consequences. Her younger sister Betty saved us in time, as did little Gustave, who is going to be very intelligent one day.

24 November

Tomorrow we march. Everyone is in despair. Lisette is weeping. But Glory gives the commands—adieu Love! Adieu Lisette forever. . . .

26 November, Ober-Roda, Obenburg, Miltenberg

A rather painful march; but here we are in the duchy of Baden. It's very cold, but the countryside is magnificent. Very mountainous. I visited the ruin by way of distraction. There I met a man whom it will be just as hard for me to forget as it was for me to make out his character. He was living in the castle with his family. He received me very civilly and showed me the remains of his ancestors' dwelling place and some gigantic pieces of ancient armour. This man had a most charming family and everything that could make him happy, but his nature was sinister and contrasted in such a baroque manner with the gaiety of his family, above all with the mad gaiety of his pretty wife, that he gave me the shivers.

I came back home to write to Lisette (and here's manly constancy!) when I saw my landlady, Clara Müller, whom I liked so much that I began burning with impatience to have her; she was pretty, piquant, and provocative. At first she played the prude, but later, after I had offered her a gift and treated her to some punch and a few bold caresses, she took off her mask and promised to go to bed with me. "We poor girls with a certain temperament," she told me, "are the most unfortunate creatures in the world if we're not yet married at my age. Obliged to keep up appearances, we're in eternal torment, consumed by our passions. I'm considered very well behaved, but that's completely false. You'll be my fourth lover. I'll be waiting for you at midnight; adieu and au revoir." I was completely astonished by such frankness. The play was a good one; I had to see it through to the final curtain. At the hour of the rendezvous the door opened and I saw my lovely coming in, in a pretty négligé. I shall be silent on the sequel. The temperament of the blonde German woman is easily the equal of that of the most piquant brunette. All the nuances of feeling—priceless!

We spent the next day laughing and chatting, and towards evening caressing. We ended up weeping at the news of my imminent departure. But the sources of the anguish will soon be dried up.

1 December

We're going through fine country. It doesn't feel like winter. The Neckar enchants me with its radiant banks. Rotenau, Hornberg (the castle of Götz von Berlichingen), Neckarsulm, Heilbronn (a lovely Gothic cathedral), Bietigheim, and Ludwigsburg. I like Württemberg a lot; the country is so radiant and so well populated. I'm quartered with a nice old woman; my knowledge of the country and the language made me the acquaintance of Pastor Christmann, who plays the piano well.

In Paris Napoleon opened the legislative assembly, saying:

I have drafted and executed great plans for the well-being and happiness of the world. Nations can allow themselves to enter safely into negotiations only when they unfold the full force of their power. My peoples will never have to fear that their Emperor's policy will betray their national glory.

8 December

We're leading a very peaceful and agreeable life in this pretty countryside. It gives me enormous pleasure to talk to these good Germans, who, though a little pedantic, are very well educated and profound. Visited Lachmann* in Marbach, Schiller's birthplace. Coming back from my promenade (I had been to see Schiller's house) I made the acquaintance of the daughter of the house, Wilhelmine Krauter, a very pretty girl.

10 December

Parade in Stuttgart. The King of Württemberg gave us a banquet; the champagne flowed. He's very fat, this prince. We're staying on here a few days. The court is magnificent, everything here breathes of opulence. The theatre is superb. They were giving *The Vestal Virgin*. The cold is beginning to sting; we shall have to run.

25 December

On the road to Tübingen I had the misfortune to sprain a leg when I fell off my horse. I was forced to stay on in Rottenburg, from where I was taken to Tübingen; there I was put in Klotz's house, where I put myself in the hands of Professor Frohrieb. I was recommended by the Grand Duke himself, which got me a marvellous reception. My sprain was very bad; I spent fifteen days in bed, during which time I had the occasion to meditate on the future and the past. Unable to write, I limited myself to reading. Now

* Karl Lachmann (1793–1851), German classical philologist (Ed.).

I'm better, thank God, and en route to Basel, where the regiment is going to cross the Rhine.

Reminiscences of Tübingen: Doctors Frohrieb, Stofacker, and Hirsch; Mlles Kaufmann and Klotz; Fyodor drunk as a pig. A visit to Mme Schubart, widow of the great poet.* Said farewell to Frohrieb; what a noble trait: he refused my money, the last I had!

26 December

Travelled from Tübingen to Basel, by way of Hechingen, Altingen, Tuttlingen, Engen, Deichingen, and Schaffhausen.

The countryside is lovely. The celebrated Black Forest gave me the shivers. The wine and fruit are delicious, the game excellent. The inhabitants of lower Swabia are good-natured and kindly, generally robust and industrious, but a little stupid. The local dialect is horrible. The King is hated; everyone is delighted with the departure of the French and the progress of the Allies. A witticism of the Grand Duke of Baden about the King made me laugh. "The King," he said, "has done everything in his power to ruin his people, but hasn't managed it. And I've taken all the pains in the world to make my own prosper, but in vain!"

In Schaffhausen I went off at once to take a look at the waterfall. It's very beautiful, but I had thought it would be bigger and more impressive.

Made the acquaintance of M. Schwarz; we're going to leave for Basel together. I was a witness of his farewells to his family; his sister made me feel close to him. We're going to make a detour by way of Constance and Zürich.

The Allies declared that they would not lay down their arms until Switzerland had recovered its ancient freedom and its ancient borders. A convention was concluded at Basel concerning the march into Switzerland: the Allies agreed that true neutrality could exist only when the state that proclaimed it was free of any alien influence.

* Christian Friedrich Daniel Schubart (1739–1791).

At this point any acknowledgment of Swiss neutrality would do no more than give a shield to injustice while presenting an obstacle to those whose only aim was to restore the independence of all states. The peremptory influence hitherto exercised by Napoleon on Swiss affairs had made Switzerland's declaration of neutrality completely null and inadmissible, and had justified the march into Switzerland of the Allied armies, who were determined to re-establish the ancient, complete independence of the Swiss confederation.

29 December

Schwarz and I left Schaffhausen early yesterday morning. The weather was fine; the Swiss postilion gave us a splendid ride. We drove along the bank of the Rhine; towards six o'clock we arrived in Constance, which was well situated. The city itself is very old. The evening and the sunset were delicious. What luck to be able to while away the time here in this beautiful Swiss countryside! The ground is covered with a light carpet of snow, which has a reddish look. The old castle, the water pumps and the saltworks were remarkable sights. The following day we continued on our way through Frauenfeld and Winterthur to Zürich, where the sight of my first glacier gave me boundless joy. I'm treated with the greatest regard everywhere since they think I'm wounded.

31 December

Today we passed quickly through Zurzach, Laufenburg, and Rheinfelden, and arrived at sunset in Basel, where I was lodged with a M. Turneisen, who gave me a splendid reception. The sight of the Rhine from the mobile bridge, the army corps that are being carried to France, made my heart quiver with joy. In Hüningen you could hear the thundering of cannon!

The niece of my host, Turneisen, has a fine collection of stamps. It's said that because of the intercession of La Harpe Switzerland is going to keep its ancient republican institutions. I feel beside myself with pleasure at the thought that my feet are treading the same soil made famous by the exploits of the Swiss heroes, in this cradle of the political and moral freedom of Europe. In earlier years I used to love to let my imagination hover over these heroic scenes of the Middle Ages.

1 January 1814

The New Year finds us in France! There are two things worth noting here: 1) The passage over the Rhine at Basel; 2) The success of the campaign pushing us towards Paris. The New Year promises a splendid future for all of Europe. The regiments of the Russian and Prussian Guards paraded today, before the eyes of the three monarchs, across a fine drawbridge thrown across the river. Shouts of joy rang up to the heavens. The inhabitants, who were standing along the route, told us they had never seen anything so splendid. The countryside doesn't look very fertile; the German spoken here is a bad dialect. Very few young people, lots of old ones. The inhabitants are quite oppressed.

4 January

We've just crossed part of the countryside around Mont-béliard and the Upper Rhine, which are quite different. The city of Montbéliard, which is prettily situated, has a handsome castle. There's a great deal of poverty; the towns are filthy, but the inhabitants seem to be kind. In Vallaret we halted for a while at the frontier of the Franche-Comté, where you can already hear good French. It's being said that the united corps of Blücher and Wittgenstein are moving closer to Paris. The weather is awful. I'm numb with cold; the roads are practically impassable. We're staying with Tatishchev, who is very intelligent and has a good memory, but like all Russians is frivolous and sensual.

6 January, Vesoul

A charming little city; a fine inn full of officers. Met Mlle Josephine, the neighbour's daughter. A few wild oats . . . . Some conversations with the mayor. Very friendly with two Prussian officers.

7 January

Day of rest. The two Prussians came to see me this morning and we talked a lot about campaigning and about war; then we went to see the mayor, who showed us a fine portrait by Van Dyck. I take great pleasure in objects of art, but I lack any knowledge or any occasion to educate myself and my taste will never be able to develop. The peasants of this part of the country look rather wild and are not very outgoing to strangers. They wear wooden sabots, which are heavy but economical; they're better than our leather sandals, but half a dozen of these people walking make a devilish noise. There was a scene between one of the officers and a soldier who had tried to escape. Napoleon is not particularly popular in this part of the country because he has exhausted the resources of France. It is high time for God to lay him low. We shall see!

8 January, Pont-sur-Saône

A nice little place, with a pretty bridge; the river is broad and handsome; the countryside looks fertile. Passing before our camping place our dear kind Emperor stopped a moment and chatted with us. How affable and gracious he is; may God protect him!

9, 10 January, Saintrin

Bad quarters. Spent the evening with the general. There's talk of peace negotiations. In my opinion nothing should be done until Paris has been taken! God grant that we may soon have peace, but only peace with glory and honour.

11, 12 January, Plateau of Langres

Forced march over Grifollettes, Longeau, and Baissez. Escapade at headquarters. Sass and I amused ourselves chatting with the high military of the three powers. Our adored monarch makes himself beloved by his affability; it's said that he's giving himself over a great deal to religious exercises.

13, 14 January

It seems our cavalry is going to be stationed here a few days. I've taken quarters at a baker's; he gives us all sorts of tidbits. The city is gay, well built, with textile factories. Passing by in front of a shop I saw a pretty woman; I accosted her. Mlle Adèle was from Paris and told me a great deal about the great capital. Then I offered her some champagne, which she gracefully accepted while entertaining us with her pleasant talk. Salza, Pilar, and Languell shared my amusements, and made me laugh a lot by talking about their prowess.

15, 16 January, Chaumont

We left Langres with regret and arrived quite exhausted in this place. Nogent-en-Bassigny, which we visited en route, is a pretty town where we were treated to a first-rate wine and supper.

17, 18 January, Colombey-les-deux-Églises

The Prussians are making a clean sweep of all the supplies; the town and its inhabitants resent our appetite. It's my view that we ought to treat these poor people better. The weather is frightful, and the winter is just as "Russian" here as it is at home. We are in the heart of the Champagne district, which is, however, good for nothing but its wines.

19 January, Bar-sur-Aube

Today we marched before the enemy, whose camp fires we could see; you could hear cannon fire. Napoleon is waiting for us in Brunne; the mud is frightful. Tomorrow we're surely going to have some heavy skirmishing!

21–25 January

It was a fierce engagement under generals Blücher and Sacken. The enemy lost 53 cannon and 2,000 prisoners. The French army is retreating to Troyes. Our regiment made counter-movements; we crossed Bar-sur-Seine. The place we're camped in is pretty and rich in vineyards; we're given any amount of food we need.

28 January, Saint-Bar

We are camped on the banks of the Seine, which flows beneath my windows; how everything changes! Two years ago it was the Neva, a year ago the Vistula; today it's the river that cuts across Paris, where ·we shall shortly make an entrance as conquerors, I hope. May God grant it!

29 January, Troyes

Troyes is taken; the great captain has been thrown back and there is talk of a truce and of a congress in Châtillon-sur-Seine.

A duel: I was Languell's second; the affair ended when his opponent received a slight wound.

30, 31 January, Frénois

A day of rest. A fierce war on the chickens, pigeons, and sucking pigs, of which we've made tabula rasa. These endless plains of the Champagne weary the eye. The agriculture here seems to me neglected, except for the grapes; the vineyards are very well taken care of and show a profit. The livestock is run-down; the peasants seem poor and drunk. The fields are poorly taken care of, and there's a shortage of wood. On the other hand, the iron and steel workshops look fine; you can buy fine blades of any size at a good price. The town dwellers seem to have a kindly disposition; they're frank and amiable, though also ignorant; they're short, but lively and courageous. They are attached to the old régime and to the Bourbon dynasty, or pretend to be, but I believe that in their hearts they're republicans. In general, the French are devoid of religion, but not of honour, which takes the place of the former. They have common sense, but no feeling. I prefer the character of the Germans. The middle class has a good education in France and makes up the kernel of the literate people. It is only this middle class that has its own opinions. It is quite different from the way it is with us, where the nobility has the enlightenment and the wealth; here in France, the nobility has lost its prestige and influence. The artisans, the merchants, the manufacturers, and the farmers in France all have an appearance of prosperity that is very attractive; they know how to talk about everything, with much wit. Greed for money and immorality help make them prosperous. It is quite painful to see beautiful France occupied by foreigners, but she has richly deserved this punishment, for since the revolution of 1789 she has done nothing but wallow in her own passions. Ambition, pride, and dexterity have brought her far, but also within a hair's breadth of destruction by smothering within this splendid people the seeds of happiness and humanity. The women, in general, are amiable but not very sure of themselves. The peasant women are docile and diligent, but gossipy and light-minded. The city women are flirtatious, calculating, and not very pretty, but they are witty. Their education seems to be very superficial and frivolous; conjugal happiness seems rare, and to me marriage seems borne rather like a grimace. The women of good society must be better; I haven't met them yet. As for industry and trade, I can hardly judge, since in wartime you never see anything of it. Provincial products are sometimes very expensive; bread and meat are expensive compared to Germany. Disorder and dirt are everywhere and spoil everything. The administration and the government seem everywhere to be well organized and centralized. France is divided into departments, as Russia is into provinces. Each department has its prefect and subprefect (governor and vice-governor), its Court of Appeal, magistracy, and chief of police. Every commune has its mayor and his deputy, who are elected by the majority of the votes cast. The laws of the country are made in the Parlement and are laid down in the five Codes of Napoleon. The Catholic religion is served by the curés, who are paid by the state. However, there are Calvinists everywhere. Consciences are very liberal, and there is general tolerance, especially in matters of faith and morals. I found a great deal of indifference everywhere with respect to religion, which is a great misfortune for the common people, since they need a firm moral base. French manners are agreeable, since the

Frenchman is supremely sociable. Great store is set by appearances. Comfort is very close to luxury. The literature seems to be rich.

1–3 February, Troyes

With drums rolling and fuses alight we passed through this city, capital of Champagne, which seems very old. The city is on the banks of the Seine; it has three beautiful bell towers that make it outstanding. Troyes has 25–30,000 inhabitants. It is dirty, with narrow streets. The weather was splendid. There was some astonishment at the fine bearing of our troops, especially since everyone expected Asiatic hordes to appear. Tatishchev and myself are quartered with a good-natured farmer who, even though he had been under some pressure from the officers before us, is treating us well. The house is completely white from the chalk that is found here in abundance. I've just received some letters from my family and friends; what joy it is to get good news from one's home. May God preserve them!

4 February, Nogent-sur-Seine

This place has been completely pillaged and burned. We got here by forced march. The Seine in these parts rolls its waters across a rich and beautiful plain, settled in villages. A fine countryman said to us today in answer to the question whether it was still far to Paris, "A good mile, gentlemen." He was right, for we were thrust back yesterday and today as far as Montereau-fault-Yonne, near which we're camped.

5, 6 February

The cold weather has started again, and there's not much to eat. The horses are exhausted. Paris is still *twenty* good miles away!

On 6 February Napoleon attacked the Allies at Montereau and forced them to retreat. The uninterrupted shrapnel fire of the French caused heavy losses. For a whole day the Crown Prince of Württemberg with 12,000 men defended the bridge at Montereau against

60,000 Frenchmen. This gave Prince Schwarzenberg time to gather his army and lead it back. According to French reports, the Allies lost 6,000 prisoners and 5,000 dead; according to their own, it was 3,000 dead and wounded. Field Marshal Blücher joined the principal force of the Allies at Arcis-sur-Aube.

The Allies despatched Count Paar to Napoleon's Headquarters at Montereau to offer a truce. Napoleon sent Paar back with the retort that he himself was "nearer Vienna than Paris".

7 February, Langres

Here we are back in this place again. There's something about this retreat that reminds me of Tarutino, where the country and the surroundings were devastated. The bivouacs and the countermarches and especially the nights are very disagreeable.

8–20 February

We're all rather crestfallen. The shouts of victory were premature and hasty; we had to fall back 140 versts. What must be cannot be avoided; the Devil take it! It was very cold, and we were short of everything. It's said that our retreat was a feint, but I don't believe it. The old eagle took to his wings once again and hurled himself at our phalanxes, which had to yield. After thirteen days of suffering we're having a relatively good time of it at Langres!

21 February

What bliss, to stretch out on a good sofa, warm yourself in front of a good fire, treat yourself to a good dinner, and sleep between two sheets—after two weeks of camp! Accordingly I've lavished the best of everything, in the joy of my heart, on everyone around me, down to the horses!

In town I made the acquaintance of a family, Meunier and Jacquemont, who gave me a splendid reception and with whom I had some relief from the vagabond life I'd been leading. We found a piano, which was a real treat for me; but taste for music is dead in France, which recognizes only concerts of drums and trumpets! What a difference between France and Germany, where everyone loves music. Nothing of the sort here, except for some gay ditties. The only thing that stands up here is the language. If the peasant is filthy, coarse, and lazy and his wife is stingy and false-hearted, the way they talk still is often very pleasing. There's a great shortage of young men because of the heavy draft.

23 February, Boulanger

We're moving ahead again. Thank you, Mars! Blücher—"Old Forwards!"—has resumed the initiative. Our rein-forcements have arrived, and here we are again, chasing after our enemies and new laurels. We've just outflanked them and attacked them from every side. Bernadotte is advancing with his Swedes. Troyes was taken again by bayonet; a lot of blood flowed. Visited the general. An adventure with lovely Jeannette. Masha, my poor mare, is far from well; I'm nursing her as best I can.

Blücher beat Napoleon at Laon. The French lost 25,000 men and 90 cannon.

After the battle Blücher addressed a proclamation to the French:

The sufferings that France has been groaning under for some months are the same that Napoleon has forced on Europe for the past twelve years. They arise from the horrible system of war he initiated and then imposed on us. Napoleon calls himself your sovereign. A sovereign is a father. What father would, for his own advantage, strangle his last child? What good sovereign would reject the honourable and advantageous peace offered him merely because that peace offended his personal pride and ambition? So, forward! If you will not follow the voice of righteousness, woe unto you!

26–29 February, Donne-Marie-en-Montois

Chetvertinsky and I are quartered very well in an old dungeon; the rest is doing us good. The last hours of Napoleon have come; his army is on its last legs.

21 March, Montmartre, Paris

For three weeks my Diary has been languishing; there was no time to touch book or pen. We've been harassed the whole time: battles, countermarches, outposts, bivouacs —and all this without a break. Now we're quite near Paris, where we can see from afar the smoke from the roofs and the outlying areas. The inhabitants are for us and the Bourbons, and the counter-revolution is going to deliver us the keys to the city.

But so many remarkable events call for attention. After reconquering Châlons-sur-Marne, Vignory, Cirey, Remilly-sur-Seine, Brienne-le-Château, and Bar-sur-Aube, we suddenly abandoned our line of operations in order to rejoin by forced marches Blücher's army corps. Bonaparte thought we were still on the main road; he exposed his flanks and was encircled and beaten at Vitry-le-François and then at Fère-Champenoise, where Macdonald's corps was attacked and scattered after a short but intense engagement. Our regiment took their cannon after a fine charge in which we had considerable losses. The victory was complete. We pursued the enemy by way of Sézanne and Meaux as far as the gates of Paris, where after one final effort the enemy army was forced to abandon the city to us.

Our entry yesterday was brilliant. The people received us with jubilation, foreseeing the return of the Bourbons, who are going to rule France again. The ex-Emperor has retreated to Fontainebleau, where he will have to surrender. Our regiment is going to be encamped in Grenelle. Barclay has been appointed marshal. There are many promotions and medals; I shall have my share. The sight of Paris, especially of Montmartre, where the cadets of Saint-Cyr and of the Polytechnique fought very well, made a strong impression on me; I circled the fortifications of this modern Babylon with an inexpressible feeling of joy and pride. The seizure of the city and our entry into it will be indelibly engraved in my memory! Thank God and our armies!

Chapter VII

BETWEEN DUTY AND LOVE

On 18 March the Allies, under Blücher, Barclay de Tolly, the Crown Prince of Württemberg, Prince Hohenlohe, Langeron, York, Kleist, Horn, Pirch, Kluex, Vorontsov, Müffling, Rayevsky, Kaptsevich, and Butsevich (the last two of whom stormed Montmartre) drove off 40,000 French troops with 150 cannon under Marmont and Mortier. The fighting went on from 6.30 A.M. to 3.30 P.M. The central section of the Allied army, with Russians, Prussians, and Badensien troops, took by storm the heights of Belleville, while the Blücher army took the entrenched area of La Villette and Montmartre. The Russians under Lambert, Wirth, and Gorchakov relentlessly pressed on through a murderous shrapnel fire in the vicinity of the King and the Prince of Prussia* against the entrenched positions of the French; they drove off the cavalry with bayonets, swept over the trenches and the cannon, and with a loss of 69 officers and 13,000 men flung the enemy back into the city of Paris.

Tsar Alexander accorded an audience to the maires *of all the city quarters of Paris, addressing them as follows:*

The fortunes of war have led me here. Your Emperor, who was my ally, deceived me three times. He pressed into the interior of my Empire and there he left devastation whose traces will be apparent for a long time. I followed him here in order to defend myself, but I am far from any intention of making France pay for the wrong he perpetrated in my borders.

Tsar Alexander gave freedom to 200,000 French war prisoners for whom Louis XVIII had already solicited mercy. The Prince Regent of Great Britain followed his example and freed 70,000

---

* King Wilhelm and Prince August (Ed.).

prisoners. The French army at Chaumont, Joinville, and Saint-Dizier and several French marshals came out against Napoleon, whose last bulletin from Bar-sur-Aube read:

His Majesty the Emperor had entrusted to Paris the pledges of his love and of the national honour, and Paris has scandalously betrayed them. The 800,000 people, if they had been inspired by courage and love for the fatherland, could have made the foe tremble. There were 40,000 men standing in their defence before the gates, and the Emperor himself was hastening there with an unconquered army. The city could have become an abyss that might have swallowed up the enemy, but it preferred to yield to him all its resources. The Emperor has ordered it to be struck off the list of his good cities; henceforth his camp will be his capital. He has no doubt of his good fortune and cannot bring himself to cover with shame a throne that is adorned by so many brilliant triumphs. France will have no peace if it is to be purchased with dishonour.

On 21 March the Senate in Paris, by a majority of 115 votes to 34, decided to deprive Napoleon Bonaparte of any claim to the throne of France and to annul the hereditary rights of his family, as well as to free the French army of its oath of loyalty to him. On 23 March hostilities were stopped and a line of demarcation set up between the armies.

Tsar Alexander repeated his suggestion to Napoleon to take the island of Elba as his residence, with a budget of six million francs a year.

1–25 March, Paris

I haven't the smallest intention of giving a description of Paris here; it would be as futile as it would be boring. But I should like to try to give my impressions, as they are so strong and the number of things to see is so great.

The panorama of the city from above is very impressive; the Seine cuts across the inhabited quarters and has a number of bridges for the traffic. The boulevards, the squares, the palaces catch one's eye at first, then attention is drawn to the Tuileries but fades as one approaches the city limits. Place Vendôme, the squares of the Obelisk,* of the Carrousel, of Victory, of the Concorde, and of Louis XV are really fine. Everywhere one encounters the history of this singular people. The quais alongside the Seine are quite comfortable, but are hardly anything at all compared with those of the Neva. Paris has few churches, and they are well decorated, especially Notre Dame and the Invalides. With pleasure and curiosity I visited the palaces of the Louvre, the Luxembourg, and the Tuileries. Taste, luxury, and elegance are found everywhere, but nothing is very majestic.

The noise and hubbub in the streets are terrific; 800,000 people are colliding and intermingling; added to these are 150,000 foreign soldiers. All this, in a space less than that of Moscow, is bound to block the streets and increase the confusion. I keep myself amused the whole day by wandering around the streets, going into the shops, the cafés, the reading rooms and art shows. But the Palais-Royal is what offers the most distraction, as well as the most temptation and danger to youth. I find these girls, who though lost are graceful and seductive, extremely dangerous. I was unable to resist their provocations and went to see a few of them, especially the Negroes and Creoles, whose nature is so different from our own and whose ways are so piquant and curious.

I visited the Napoleon Museum, the Panthéon, and the Louvre, which gave me a great deal to observe and to think about. It was only there that I understood what charm there is in the cultivation of the fine arts, as well as the strength and power of the genius that was able to create and to gather it all together. Though I could approach with respect all the monuments that contain the ashes of the great men of France, I nevertheless discovered a great deal of vanity and illusion too.

* Not the same as the obelisk erected in the Place de la Concorde in 1831 (Ed.).

In short, there is so much to see in Paris that one hardly knows where or how to begin one's day. Luckily, my squadron chief lets me do whatever I like and doesn't torment me with duties, so I have all the time I need to follow my inclinations and look for adventure. Paris is a great gathering point and a mingling of everything in France that is curious. Paris is, as it were, all France put together. For it is towards this centre, towards this head, that all the juices, the blood, and the money of the entire kingdom flow, while its members languish and decline in the same measure that the head grows bigger. It's like those precocious children with water-heads who sometimes are more intelligent than others but rarely live very long; they eat a lot without thriving. Might not this be the future of France?

It is far from rare to see people with an income of 100,000 francs ruining themselves, only to have another fortune leap up out of nowhere; then to see them fall back after a short time into nothingness, and so on. It's the same thing for ranks, jobs, and reputations—everything gets lost in the crucible. And you have only to wander about the vast subterranean catacombs of the city, where there are skeletons and skulls of the thousands who have disappeared, or to look at the great Père-Lachaise cemetery, where other thousands are sleeping peacefully, to get an idea of this immense "succession and disappearance of generations".

This capital is enhanced by being seen and contemplated at night, from afar or from a height, when thousands of streetlamps light up its shadows. That is when it gives the impression of being a real fairyland. Then again, I like to see it in the morning, early, when life begins to spread out and manifest its movements and noises. That's when it often looks like a thousand-headed monster, eating with a thousand mouths and crying out with a thousand throats, blaspheming, twisting, contorting, and making noise. It reminds me of the Apocalyptic Beast that St. John describes in hideous detail. Extremes meet here in a disgusting way. Extravagant opulence side by side with misery, and vice in rags. How can this immense number go on living for any length of time in this horrifying inequality? But there is a diamond in the dung heap that is bound to remain intact and luminous—it is the spirit, the genius of the French people, represented by its thinkers and virtuous men, who are acted upon and moved by the grandeur of God!

I love promenading along the boulevards studying the people passing by beneath the trees, or along the Champs-Élysées, where you can watch all the grand and beautiful people of Paris passing by in carriages, on horseback, or on foot, or else in the magnificent Jardin des Plantes, where so many objects of natural history have been brought together. Evenings are devoted to the various shows or theatres of Paris. The opera attracts me especially, mostly because of its orchestra. Its repertoire is unique. The vaudeville is highly diverting, just as the national theatre is interesting in its choice of classical plays. The other day I attended a performance of Racine's *Britannicus*. The monarchs were there in the grand loge opposite. In the midst of a scene that echoed present-day circumstances the audience shouted and divided into two sides, of which one —the one that was for the restoration and the Bourbons— was absolutely determined to knock down the eagle floating above the stage! The racket was horrible, but the whites prevailed over the reds and managed to climb up on an improvised ladder leaned against the balustrade and to knock down the emblem of the defeated dynasty to cries of "Down with the hen!" "Down with the griffin!" "Down with the scoundrel!" It was a veritable bedlam, an infernal bellowing that stunned the crowned heads, scarcely accustomed to such scenes in their own capitals. It took a long time for order to be restored; the play lasted until midnight. Zinsky, the quartermaster of our regiment, found me a good lodging with a legal expert by the name of Rousseau at No. 7 Rue du Jardin; he has a charming family and is smothering me with friendliness. I'm very well off here!

26 March, Paris

I'm living the life of a prince in Paris! Mornings go by quickly, too quickly. I run around back and forth, sometimes to the courts, sometimes to the museums and shows; then I dine with some friend at Véri's, or at the Provençal Brothers, and afterwards I ride on horseback or in some cabriolet outside the city, to Saint-Germain-en-Laye, Versailles, Marly-le-Roi, the Bois de Boulogne, etc. The evenings are devoted to the theatres, and I don't go home until very late; that's how it is every day. I would like it all to last a year or more, but alas! our departure is already being mentioned. This morning I took a Chinese bath and then breakfasted with one of those pretty little hussies that make the hours pass by like minutes. This doesn't at all prevent me from frequenting the salons of Mme Rousseau and Mme Lauris, a charming woman I met at the home of Chicherin's mistress, a Mme de Hanot, who keeps open house where people come together to gamble, dance, and play music. The interesting thing about these get-togethers is the conversation with the women who are always surrounded by their ardent, elegant lovers. Mlle Adèle, Mme de Hanot's niece, is extremely amiable, she has a very pretty voice and allows me to accompany her; her friend, Mme Dunquerque, is very seductive; I've accompanied the ladies to the opera and to the Odéon and have had a very good time in their company. The ballet dancers at the opera also caught my eye at once, but it is all a trap; you have to stay on the lookout, or you'll be a purse or two short! I've just rented an apartment for one of these enchantresses, whose mother has been very helpful. Marie has a slender figure, eyes *à la Madeleine*, and a sweet voice of admirable timbre. It's costing me a lot of money, but there's no risk of catching some fatal sickness here, as many of my comrades have done.

1 April

Spent the morning at the Jardin des Plantes, where the menagerie and the hot-houses interest me a great deal.

Yesterday's parade was made glamorous by the arrival of the Emperor of Austria. The Comte d'Artois* has just arrived. The Bourbons are being fêted and spoiled everywhere. Napoleon has surrendered unconditionally in Fontainebleau and is to be transported to the island of Elba; what an immense fall, but everything passes and withers in this world, especially in France, where one lives only for change! The whole country has just put out its white flags and the white cockades. It's one of the few counter-revolutions in the world.

Yesterday Mme Duménil gave us a fine ball. We danced the contredanse and some quadrilles. Mlle Aglaé treated me to a waltz; the Prince of Bavaria was there too.

5 April

I divide my time between the service, the École Militaire, and the pleasures of this life of leisure. On getting up I riffle through the various cards of invitation; then, after breakfast, I take a turn on horseback or in a cabriolet; I visit one of my lovelies, then I dine at five o'clock at the Palais-Royal. Then I meet the ladies at Fédeau's or at the Variétés; then to a rendezvous at Tortoni's, from where I go off to supper tête-à-tête with Marie or Lucile; I get home about two o'clock. Mme Lauris always receives me when her husband is not there; it's very convenient. I vow my eternal love, then I go from her to her neighbour, La Duny, whom I find even more agreeable. This morning I received a letter from Mama, which made me reflect a little on my way of passing the time; it gave me a great fit of remorse and repentance.

The King of France is supposed to arrive here any day. Uncertainty will be at an end and peace will be proclaimed. This morning I visited the museum of antiquities together with Mme Tremouville and Chabrillon. I saw the celebrated statues of Laokoön, the Belvedere Apollo, and the Venus of Medici.

* Younger brother of Louis XVI; later Charles X (Ed.).

8 April

I seem to prefer living women to those beautiful marble statues, for they speak, sing, dance, and are charming, while the statues are silent and remain impassive. Perhaps I shall find them more interesting when I am further advanced in my knowledge of the *beauté idéal*. But this morning I chose to pay court to Mlle Aglaé rather than go back to the Louvre. I found her in a reverie, pale and less beautiful than usual. Speaking generally, Frenchwomen are more pretty than beautiful, more seductive than tender, more superficial than solid. They prefer distractions to housekeeping. One can win the heart of a Frenchwoman more quickly by a compliment than by a sincere feeling. They don't like sentimentality much, but they do like wit and talent and whatever is piquant; they understand a man's merits only through his appearance. Character is of small account; reputation means a lot. In speaking ill of some women, in arousing their jealousies, you often manage to fascinate them.

The dinner dance at Mme de Hanot's last night was very lively. There were a great many pretty women. In the light they look fresh and lovely, all the more so since their toilettes are exquisite, but all you have to do is see them the morning after a ball like that in order to be disenchanted. We taught a number of these young ladies the mazurka, which they found delicious; they learned the twists and turns of this dance too very quickly and well. The Russians are treated very well, but that doesn't stop us from being made to pay through the nose for everything. The cabriolets cost fifteen francs a day. The coachmen are great rascals, but they're accommodating if you let them see a heavy purse.

I've been to Saint-Cloud and Versailles, where the terraces, the trees, and the interiors are magnificent. Everything there is historic, from the paintings to the furniture. The Sèvres porcelain interested me a great deal, because of its perfection and the great diversity of the objects. The rooms were filled with the loveliest vases. In Versailles the souvenirs of Henri IV and Louis XII fascinated me enormously. I liked the library of the kings less, because I couldn't understand a thing. But the orangery held my attention much longer. The palace, especially, and the park, with its 1,000 fountains, were very curious to see, but in a style that was too regular and monotonous; the eye is wearied by all the geometry. The little and the big Trianon are charming, much more modern and graceful. The landscape shows a ravishing variety.

15 April

King Louis XVIII made his ceremonial entry today. What a sensation, to see the Bourbons come back to Paris, that same Paris that twenty-five years ago put the King's brother to death on the scaffold! When I think of everything that's happened in front of this same equestrian statue of Henri IV during the past twenty-five years! Yet I've been here, I've seen with my own eyes the same people that at the time of the Convention clamoured at and condemned its kings, applaud the arrival of the illustrious exile! But God is great! And his vengeance certain! The people of Paris had to be seen this morning! There was no end to the shouts of "Long live the Bourbons!" "Long live Louis XVIII!" The enthusiasm was general, perhaps artificial or paid for by the legitimist party. The people are light-minded and characterless; they bend to the wind like a weathercock; they need constant change. I should have liked to see this same Paris the day the Bastille was stormed or the day Napoleon was crowned Emperor!

The city was like an immense fair. From the gates to Notre Dame, to which the King proceeded together with his whole train, it was teeming with people in different costumes, of all ages, making as much noise as they could. The women were wearing white hats and dresses embroidered with lilies. The carriages and riders and our army were all in gala costume. It was really *beautiful*, and curious to see. I changed my own costume and, dressed as a simple bourgeois, followed these motley groups. On every face you could see curiosity and expectation, a mixture of false pleasure with secret thoughts. Towards two o'clock, after making the tour of the city, I entered that lovely and ancient cathedral, which, though extremely spacious, was filled with people. I slipped through as far as the centre in order to see the king and his train pass by. The Senate, the legislative corps, the upper civil and military officials filed by before me. The chorus galleries and the balconies as far as the altar were adorned by beautiful women, which gave the scene the look of a magnificent tapestry of flowers! At three o'clock a confused noise—sounds of bells, fanfares, music, rolling carriages, etc.—announced the arrival of their majesties! I climbed up on a bench to see better. Soon I saw coming forward the old man with a crown, accompanied by the duchesses of Angoulême and Berry, by dukes and princes. The dome rang with outcries and shouts. A young person who had stationed herself near me stumbled; I held her up; she embraced me so as not to fall, and after seeing everything she came down from the top of the platform and thanked me naïvely for having protected her so well with my embrace. I paid her a few compliments, which she accepted in an amiable way; she allowed me to lead her out of the church. Very soon I had eyes and ears for her alone, and while chatting with her I took her to her home, where she lives with an old and disagreeable aunt, who received me with grumbles. But once the acquaintance was made I proposed to continue it; indeed, I had nothing to regret.

On the bridge, beneath the equestrian statue of good Henri IV and in front of a pretty arch of triumph adorned with flowers and pretty women, I found a very good place from which to watch our regiments and this whole procession of the day pass by. A gilded chariot, or carriage, all gala and drawn by eight white horses, advanced at a trot along the pavement smothered in flowers. The royal family were in it, dressed in finery and saluting right and left; the ladies seemed to me a little embarrassed. Rockets were being fired off on all sides; a Blanchard balloon* with banners rose up in the air; the public waved handkerchiefs in the air. Even the king in marble appeared to be smiling at this splendid occasion and spectacle and to be lending himself to the triumph of his great-grandson, whose misfortunes and trials had made him worthy of this restoration. At the Louvre, as well as at the Tuileries, there were receptions and festivities; the day ended with magnificent fireworks, a general illumination in which, however, the Napoleonists took no part at all.

19 April

My affairs, my way of living, so independent and at the same time so instructive, and my experiences in society are too various to be described. I shall limit myself accordingly to the plain facts. The houses and families of Mme de Hanot, Lauris, and Dunquerque have become home for me. I go and come as I please. My conscience, however, is not clear with respect to all these people, for I, together with all these play-actresses of society, am playing a comedy; I have pretended to love each one of them without feeling anything. Yet I have not taken advantage of them, and that should be enough. In any case, my senses are occupied elsewhere: Adèle, my little orphan, has been able to capture them and my heart as well. Mme Lépinois, whom I see a lot of too, is charming; she keeps close watch over me.

It gives me a lot of pleasure to study music at the conservatory; there are some teachers and artists of merit who let me attend their concerts. Barracks duty couldn't be easier; we do just as we please and are away whenever we feel like it. The French soldiers have a depressed look; they try to quarrel with us whenever an occasion arises. I amuse myself by attending the manœuvres of the National Guard in Paris, which is made up of good burghers whose uniforms are sometimes highly original. Some Napoleonists

* Named after François Blanchard, who crossed the Channel in such a balloon in 1785 (Ed.).

teased us the other day in a café, and a fight soon broke
out that was as formidable as it was comical, for we fought
with chairs and chandeliers, bottles and dishes. Everything
was devastated in the poor tavern, and a number of duels
resulted, one of which concerned me personally and ended
tragically; the Prussian who was my second started a fight
with the second of my opponent, after I had stretched the
latter out, and was killed! But all this took place secretly
without the knowledge of the authorities.

I often go promenading in the Luxembourg garden, which
is extremely pleasant, especially in moonlight alongside
some lovely.

Yesterday we were in the catacombs, where a religious
play was given. The other day I attended a performance
at the Odéon of a Rossini opera which was charming. The
balls succeed each other, one rendezvous follows another;
it's enough to bankrupt a man—both physically and
financially. It's time it all ended, since health must be
considered!

Mme Bayon had her jockey inform me that she would be
waiting for me around eleven o'clock in the garden of the
Tuileries; I was there on time, and then—etc., etc. Long
live youth! Long live the enchantresses of Paris! Later
we visited Saint-Germain, which is very pretty in the
spring.

1 May

Neuilly Bridge is magnificent; at Malmaison I had to
hand over a letter from the Emperor to the ex-Empress
Joséphine, who was ill but who nevertheless received me for
several minutes. She seemed to me still very beautiful. Her
lady-in-waiting, Mlle LeNormand, did the honours of the
château; the garden is worth seeing; among other things,
the black swans are singularly beautiful. The big pump in
Marly-le-Roi attracted my attention on my way back to
Paris. The water of the Seine goes through this gigantic
pump over an aqueduct 400 feet high in order to bring it as

far as Versailles. The forest of Saint-Germain-en-Laye is beautiful and fresh; the terrace offers a fine view of the countryside and of the surroundings of Paris.

Yesterday we went to the opera; they put on the *Bajadère*,* with a ballet. I was in the loge of Mme de Hanot, who had lent me 1,000 francs a few days before; I find that very disagreeable now. Won't I have some obligations now towards a lady who may have an interest in taking advantage of them?

The day before yesterday, outside Tortoni's, a countryman gave me a letter from Mama. What good fortune to have a mother like her, what guidance for a new life! Yesterday I visited M. Chateaubriand and also Mme de Genlis, two celebrated persons whose appearance in Paris is full of meaning. M. Clément presented me to them. The first received me very charmingly; he spoke very well and gave the impression of being a poet. His knowledge and his manners are remarkably distinguished. Madame la Comtesse made me wait half an hour in her salon. I had complete leisure to admire her furniture and the portraits of the Orléans family, whom she taught. Her conversation did not make at all the same impression on me as I had received when reading her works. She seemed rather distraught, and at bottom had little interest in a young Russian officer who may have bored her. I went from her to Mme Clément, who shows me many signs of friendship. Both daughters are beautiful and are excellent musicians; their mother is extremely erudite.

10 May

Mlle Aglaé reproached me tenderly one evening for having neglected her a little lately. She let fall a certain mysterious veil that had been between us for a fortnight. She confessed that she loved me and that I could ask for her hand in marriage, whereupon I told her that the thought had never crossed my mind; she got up and left me with tears in her

* Opera by Ch. Simon Catel (1773–1830) (Ed.).

eyes. I haven't seen her since. Yesterday her mother seemed to me to be in a very disagreeable mood; I shall return her 1,000 francs, and then, adieu for ever. My Paris evening costume suits me very well; I step into the salons here as a real beau, smart and scented. I can understand how the life of a Paris dandy must have great charms. You run from one conquest to another, from one amusement, one dinner, one show to another, and you do that every single day without stopping. Today I saw the showing of the Panoramas, of which the one of Naples amused me the most. Fédeau's and the vaudeville are my delight, because of the immense variety of subjects. *La Gioconda* is making the tour of the whole world! My poor Diary is also suffering from all this, since I scarcely have the time to devote any attention to it, I'm so steeped in this maelstrom of dissipations!

Departure is much spoken of; high time, too, for Paris is enough to ruin you! The de Hanot ladies and I are reconciled; the lost young hoped-for bridegroom is no longer regretted!!

20 May

It's all settled, we're leaving Paris tomorrow. Leaving Paris is hard, very hard, but if I stayed I might just as well declare myself bankrupt. I have to pack and make my farewells now. It really gives me pain to leave all my good and amiable acquaintances. The saddest farewell of all awaits me at my sweet Adèle's; she wants to follow me to Russia. What madness! M. Rousseau, the servants Louis and Nanette, have blessed me, standing around my baggage. An end to all this; we must strike up the old grenadier's *Tiriliri!*

Yet I hope to see you again, oh scene of my most splendid adventures and military triumphs! Yes, I shall see you once again some day! May God, who is compassionate to the good, happy, and courageous soldier, forgive me my foolishness and make me better behaved—on condition that He lets me see Paris again one day!

21 May, Claye-Souilly

By five o'clock in the morning—it was a grey rainy day, exactly the same colour as my mood—I had already mounted my old Serko and was riding silently and alone through the desolate streets of the city, which were soon to teem with people as usual and which I was not to see again. I passed the Faubourg Saint-Germain, Rue de Grenelle, Pont Royal, and Place Louis XV. To all these familiar places I said a heartfelt farewell. In front of my darling's windows I stood still, saw a young man slip out of the house, had all sorts of thoughts about it, then gave my grey the spurs and was soon at the city gate. There I met my men and Fyodor. Jokes and the beautiful springtime landscape soon put me in a gay mood. It was said that the peace treaty had been signed and that we had received our marching orders for St. Petersburg. That suits me very well. On the march today all the scenes of the past eight weeks in Paris passed in front of my mind's eye like shadows on a wall; I was sad and thought of how changeable man's fate is and of all the follies I had committed, and I promised God and myself to be more serious and virtuous. In this way the day passed. Weary, I caught up here with the regiment, which had moved on ahead. I had the pleasure of seeing a number of my comrades again.

23 May, Meaux

All these places have recovered again; the war seems to have vanished without a trace. The little village of Taye, where we are halting, has a most charming situation. I had hardly finished with my duties and correspondence when I went off with a gun into the nearby little woods, more in order to listen to the nightingales than to shoot at the poor game. The evening was delicious and I didn't come back until about eleven o'clock.

Today was a day of rest, and I woke up with the finest intention of doing something very sensible; but this feeling melted away like freshly fallen snow when I saw the beautiful eyes of my landlord's sweet daughter, to whom I began to pay full-dress court. Paris, Adèle, and everything is forgotten. Oh what frivolity!

24 May, La Ferté-sous-Jouarre

A small place, prettily situated. I'm quartered with an old woman who, as a maid, carried the Comte d'Artois and the Duchess of Angoulême in her arms. She told me her whole life story.

25 May, Château-Thierry

This pretty place has suffered a great deal from the war. The best champagne grapes grow here in the region, and every day we get a little tipsy, which makes you sleep wonderfully well. Languell, who sometimes listens to me walking back and forth as though I were alone—happy to be alive and in the hands of God, with my bottle in my pocket, declaiming and singing aloud—calls me then the mad dreamer. I let him laugh and I stay immersed in my own thoughts. I think with emotion of the bliss of seeing my family again at home—but this march back is very slow and long.

26 May, Dormans

A town on the Marne, whose course we've been following since the day before yesterday and which has villages along the cultivated banks. We're given a friendly reception everywhere; the people especially see that we're leaving and that we've really saved them from the shame and despotism of Bonaparte. Recently I heard a Frenchwoman warbling a Russian melody. Against that, we sing *Vive Henri IV*, and that's how nations exchange their ways of life. Tomorrow, a day of rest, I'm riding out to Rheims; I'm making a little detour.

27 May, Rheims

I reported at noon today, after a six-hour ride, to my commander. An accommodating fellow, he had a pretty lodging cleared for me so that I would have every comfort and all the leisure to look at this ancient city. My landlord, a merchant by the name of Jacob, is very intelligent and has a most charming daughter, Clémentine, the fiancée of an artillery captain who is to receive as dowry 40,000 bottles of champagne and a pretty vineyard, the lucky fellow!

28 May

The origins of this city are lost in the greyest antiquity; apparently it bloomed even before the birth of Christ. At the time of Caesar Rheims was called Duro Cortorum, Tourville, and in the time of Constantine was the capital of the Belgians. Seven military roads led to the city, of which only fragments are still in existence today. There was also Attila's camp near Bar-le-Duc, and you can see two triumphal arches of the Romans, whose architecture interested me a great deal. The arena, the mountain, Jorin's grave are all very remarkable too. The gravestone of the latter is 5 feet high and 8½ wide, with lovely sculpture. I was equally drawn to the church of St. Rémi and the cathedral by their Gothic shapes. One of the towers has what they call here *le petit tremblement*; it always starts moving the moment the bell is tolled. I spent an hour meditating in St. Peter's. I was very interested in the tombs of Clovis I and St. Remigius. The city itself is spread out and has 35,000 inhabitants and pretty streets and squares. The lyceum, the ancient fortifications, and the hospital were shown me by my very accommodating M. Jacob. In the evening we played some music.

29 May, La Cheppe

Today I saw a rich coin collection and a big champagne cellar with 200,000 bottles, one of which from time to time would explode like a pistol shot. We drank a delicious sparkling wine. At eleven o'clock I said good-bye to these good-hearted people. M. Jacob accompanied me as far as the

Maison Rouge, and now I've ridden along the chalk cliffs in a rather barren region as far as this place, which I reached late and where I joined my squadron.

30 May

Since we had a day of rest, I rode over to the Huns' encampment, whose outlines can still be seen distinctly and where at the beginning of the fifth century the celebrated battle took place that freed Europe from Attila, "the Scourge of God". All sorts of utensils and skulls; even a cave can still be found in the ground. The walls are still quite high, the ditch is half a mile in circumference and now forms a rivulet. The camp might have contained some 300,000 men. Two entrances can be distinctly made out, as well as the hill on which, according to legend, Attila's tent stood. The stone bridge leading over the little river is very old. In short, the whole thing certainly makes the impression of an historic fact.

30 May, Châlons-sur-Marne

Today has been a holiday for me. General Diebitsch, under whose eyes we took a battery and pulverized it at Fère-Champenoise when our regiment was pursuing Macdonald, has proposed me for a decoration. Scharitzki, who got some grapeshot through his body during the attack but made a complete recovery from the dangerous wound, was rewarded today with the Anna Medal around his neck, while I got the golden sword "For Bravery". For this imperial favour we emptied a number of bottles of champagne, which, however, heated me up so that I had to lie down. I didn't get sober till I got here. From here I'm going to ride on ahead as quartermaster, which will give me the opportunity to see a lot the others won't be able to, since they'll have to march along the highway so slowly.

31 May, Vitry-le-François

After a ten-hour march, which took a lot out of me and

my grey, I arrived here and at once saw to quarters for the regiment. So I've got a lot to do and no time for making any notes.

1 June, Bar-le-Duc
The march today was just like yesterday's. If we keep up this pace we'll soon be at the Rhine. A brilliant banquet at the mayor's; his plump better half and the advocate Le Glaive did the honours. Marshal Oudinot's castle. In the evening we went to the theatre and then to the hotel, where there was a lot of stout tippling and political talk.

2 June, Ligny-en-Barrois and Domrémy-la-Pucelle
The house and bed of Joan of Arc; this Virgin of Orléans, whose history and tragic end are so well described by Schiller, is one of the most brilliant stars of France. Without her heroic enthusiasm France at that time would have become the booty of the English.

3 June, Toul
An old bishop's seat; celebrated cathedrals, Agrippa's grave; an unfruitful countryside; the peasants are coarse, filthy, and stupid. Bad herds of cattle; textile factories; good vineyards, not many woods. Self-contemplation about my lost paradise.

4, 5 June, Nancy
A pretty place, refuge of the exiled kings of Poland; lots of Germans, passable theatre. Made the acquaintance of the poetess Conti. Melancholy and out of sorts with myself. A history book about Lorraine. Beaumarchais.

6 June, Dieuze
Bad quarters with a cobbler.

7 June, Fénétrange
A tough march. German villages. Climbed a high mountain;

a view of Pfalz and Alsace. From Lipheim we greeted once again the Strasbourg cathedral; decided to visit Strasbourg.

9, 10 June, Strasbourg

This is what I call roving. Yesterday morning I climbed aboard a one-horse carriage and set out *en bourgeois* for the little town of Saverne, which has a most charming situation. The countryside is hospitable, well cultivated, and full of manufacturers. In Esslingen we made our midday halt. Towards four o'clock we were overtaken by a violent storm. We had to turn in and spend the night in a little place where I was extremely well looked after and shared the bed with Lottchen, the servant girl. This morning we were off at a fast trot to the fortress. On the way I had to take on two tired French soldiers, who told me no military personnel were allowed inside. But I wouldn't let myself be deflected; I sent my carriage off with the servants into the nearest village and sauntered in on foot through the gate, with my cane in my hand. I was asked for my passport; I put up a show, assured them I was from Strasbourg, but all in vain. I had to go into the guardroom; my escort left me very mockingly and now I, immured between four walls, had all the time in the world to reflect on this fateful situation. Luckily I had my medal in my coat pocket; I put it into my buttonhole and arrogantly demanded an audience with the officer on duty. When the latter saw to whom he was talking he politely gave me back my freedom, but advised me to put the medal away again, not to show myself publicly or by name in the barracks or the arsenal, and wished me a very good time. No one was happier than I. Soon an inn turned up, as well as company and an escort who took me to Kolb, a banker recommended to me. The brother-in-law of M. Jacob of Rheims, he was very civil; he showed me the sights of the city, especially the magnificent cathedral, the mausoleum of Marshal de Saxe, the promenades, and the casino. In the evening after supper I visited a French officer whose acquaintance I had made in the meantime.

11 June, Hagenau

Early this morning together with M. Kolb I ascended the tower, a masterpiece of Gothic architecture, from where I could see a magnificent panorama of the city and the countryside. It is 435 feet high, from the lantern. You have a splendid view of the Rhine and the Black Forest from there, as well as the Vosges. But finally I got dizzy and had to go down. I looked over the fortifications, then lunched with the Kolb family and drove here in pleasant company—a Spanish woman, a Pole, and a Badener—who all carried on a lively conversation. I applied myself to my Andalusian and didn't slacken up until she shared a room and bed with me in Hagenau—which seemed to me pretty exotic. Then I found my regiment again, and since it was a day of rest I was able to have a gay time with my comrades telling them what had happened to me in the meantime. The inhabitants here are well-to-do and educated, and they seem to like us.

12–14 June, Durlach

After we had crossed the Rhine at Port Louis and had gone through Stollhofen, Rastatt, and Ellingen, we took up comfortable quarters here. So now I'm back again on the dear soil of Germany. *Vivat!*

I used up the day of rest in Durlach, as usual, dallying with the fair sex. The daughter of my landlady was soon tamed, and since she had lost her head to the slender cuirassier officer it was not difficult to lure her into my room in the evening. She was beautiful, fresh, and lush—and as agile as an eel. I was longing for Alcmenean strength and for time, but the brief dream of a summer night went by only too swiftly. At six o'clock I drove to the opera in Karlsruhe, where *Cinderella** was being put on, really very well. Now I'm sitting in my room again, waiting for sweet Sophie, who is on the staircase already and wants to come in! So till tomorrow, tiresome Diary!

* Opera by N. Isouard (1775–1818), Franco-Italian composer (Ed.).

15 June, Bruchsal

The Empress,* sister of the Grand Duke, passed us in review today. She was very condescending to us and gave gifts to the soldiers; I was somewhat pale and was almost thrown off my horse. But I recovered. I sat more firmly on my little mare tonight. My parting from the latter was comical; she assured me very naïvely that I had pleased her best of all the officers of the other nations who had stayed with her father; out of curiosity she had run through them all in turn in her mind; now she was going to fast for a few weeks. What shameless pertness in a seventeen-year-old girl!

16, 17 June, Sinsheim Mosbach

Since this is another day of rest I can resume my Diary and note that we have come here over the mountains and across the Neckar and have had very bad weather, but were amiably received by the inhabitants everywhere. Since I've entered into the spicy period of my life I've also got hold of only spicy books to pass the time. Thus I'm reading a great deal of Ovid's *Metamorphoses*, which has inflamed my imagination—in any case, excited by the lascivious pictures alone—to a boundless degree. But then I'm afflicted by a certain melancholy; I reflect on God, on the teachings of my good mother, on everything I read in the Scriptures as a child. My enfeebled body reminds me that things can't go on this way forever and that you don't stay twenty-one years old forever. But this return to a better state of mind is unfortunately no more than transitory, since my frivolity, which is incapable of resisting any opportunity, always wins the upper hand again. That's how it was this evening too. My Fyodor is living with the baggage and the horses at a smith's, who has a single pretty little daughter, with whom I instantly began an intrigue. But her father noticed something; he locked up the girl. She wanted to cool off

* Elizabeth of Baden, wife of Emperor Alexander I, and sister of Grand Duke Constantine (Ed.).

with me at once, since it was a hot summer night, but she was guarded under lock and key and all I could do was to scrape the skin off my hands and knees climbing up in the dark. But it was no use: I finally wound up in bed alone. That's when I had the above thoughts about my sinfulness, which otherwise wouldn't have occurred to me. What a worthless fellow I am; when shall I ever be any better?

19, 20 June, Walldürn

Just a few notes in this celebrated place of pilgrimage. Yesterday we moved through the avenues of the Odenwald forests: exhausting marches. The region was romantic, but uninhabited and barren. Our route led us over through Ober-Mudau to Settingen, where we unsaddled our weary horses. The little village was charmingly situated in the valley surrounded by high cliffs. The good-hearted mountain people received us most benevolently. Superstitious but upright, they support themselves by watchmaking. My host, who is also a maker of wall clocks, told me all sorts of things about nearby Walldürn. I decided to take a short ride over there and don't regret having visited it; once again I had a marvellous adventure. Since the evening was so lovely and the moon was shining down so sweetly I decided to climb up a cliff in order to enjoy the landscape in the night light. Fyodor and my host had warned me against going up, since an evil spirit haunts the old castle ruin; I however, even more excited at the prospect, put on my loaded pistols and set out merrily on the road. After at least an hour—the clock might have already struck eleven —I was there in the ruins. My pains were well rewarded, for I had a splendid spectacle before my eyes. Sinking to my knees, I felt myself for the first time in a long time raised up again to ardent prayer; I confessed to the Eternal Spirit my sins and vowed that I would improve; I may have been sunk in this meditation for three-quarters of an hour, when a strange noise reached my ear from the nearby stones! I swiftly leaped to my feet, and to my considerable astonishment I became aware of a tall white form enveloped in the light of the moon and pointing northward with upraised right arm. But instead of waiting for the end of this strange apparition and for an explanation of it I plunged into my belt, seized my pistols, and moved towards the spirit. But the weapons failed. The ghost stood there motionless and I distinctly heard the words in German: "Tomorrow I expect you in Walldürn, at the high altar." Only now did the face vanish. I stood there as though rooted to the spot and had to recuperate before I could even think of going home. There, they were anxiously waiting for me; I acted as though nothing had happened, but decided to go to the place of pilgrimage the following day.

So today I rode there by myself. I had myself shown the altar and heard an explanation of the miracle; after the sacristan had shown me a red cloth on which, through a sacred miracle, the form of the Saviour with nine heads was represented, due to poured out holy wine, I heard the following (I'm putting this legend down verbatim):

In the year 1333 of the gracious birth of our Saviour, when John XXII was reigning in the Seat of Peter, it came about that a priest by the name of Heinrich Otti, wielding the high office, conducted a negligent Mass in the church of Saint George; he overturned the chalice, whereupon the cloth was splashed but at once took on the above-described shape. When the priest observed this, he was affrighted and hid the evidence under the altar. Tormented by pangs of conscience as he lay dying, he revealed the miracle to a brother priest. The cloth with the sign was found, sent to the Pope, who after an investigation confirmed the miracle and designated the place as an object of pilgrimage; from then it was visited from far and wide; and for centuries touching the cloth has cured all sorts of illnesses.

This whole affair is, to be sure, very strange, but it's also possible that there is some priestly swindle behind it. When I touched the cloth myself I felt an electric shock and could distinctly read above the altar the words: "Purify thy heart, thou sinner, by prayer and repentance, and then go thy way in peace." On the way back I thought for a long time of everything I had experienced, but the only conclusion I reached was the simple belief that only God can work miracles, yet man must guard against lack of faith just as much as against superstition!

21, 22 June, Würzburg

Yesterday our column moved through Bischofsheim and came to a stop in Wallern, where I was quartered with a priest who took me in hand and wanted to drive the Devil out of me, since I was a heretic. I let him have his way and laughed up my sleeve at him, but went off anyhow to see the young people of the village, with whom I danced and gossiped away the whole evening. The people here are good-natured, but strict Catholics. The girls wear their hair in braids with long metal needles and red ribbons, which are very becoming. Today we marched through the beautiful city into the next village, where we rested. I looked over the sights of the town, which is very prettily situated and is encircled by the Main; it has many towers, a magnificent castle, about 40,000 inhabitants, and a university. In St. Julius' Hospital I drank a bottle of delicious Leisten wine and took away a few bottles of Steinwein and some leather wine pouches supposed to be thirty years old. In the evening I went to the theatre; it seemed mediocre. Made the acquaintance of a lady and her lodging-house; she gave me a friendly nod; in the evening I slipped in to see her and was hidden in the study, where I spent a delicious night in her arms. In bed she was quite a wild thing!

23–25 June, Werneck, Münnerstadt, Römhild

Now we're moving through Bavaria; a peculiar and powerfully marked race. The quarters are good and comfortable. We're already at the foot of the Thuringian Forest. Today I took leave of the general for a few days and am thinking of making a tour through the mountains and visiting Meiningen, Schmalkalden, Eisenach, Gotha, Erfurt, Weimar and Jena, where I hope to catch up with the regiment again. I hired a coach and took supplies along for eight days; I hope to put them to good use.

26 June, Meiningen and Schmalkalden

It took me eight hours to get here. I had Peter with me. I like the castle and the city very much. The widowed duchess* was just receiving the home-coming troops of the area; there was jubilation and festivities. Towards evening I drove through a pretty valley, where I could have found lodgings in a good tavern, but since I had lodging certificates I took up quarters in the house of a merchant who gave me a very hospitable reception; he was one of the Moravian Brethren and told me various things about his sect and tried to convert me. But I simply enjoyed the dinner and didn't go to bed until late.

27 June, Eisenach

This morning I drove to Bad Salzungen and Eisenach, two nice little towns in the Thuringian Forest, and decided to spend the night in the latter place. Since I was tired I didn't fuss about but flung myself on the bed and slept like a log until eight o'clock. Without anything special happening to me I arrived in the evening, in the finest of weather, in Gotha, a most charming little town that seems to be bustling with business. At the post I had a meal, visited the castle and the surroundings, and at night drove on to Erfurt.

28 June, Erfurt

I looked at the fort and the church, revelling in the prosperity and cleanliness of the village and the inhabitants. I was assigned quarters with a lady by the name of Walratz, who received me amiably, has a nice daughter, and in the evening invited the neighbours and treated us to a little dance.

* Duchess of Sachsen-Meiningen (Ed.).

29 June, Weimar

So here I am again in this charming place, whose smallest details have so many memories for me. This seat of the Muses will always have the most sacred recollections for me, since it was here that the greatest poets of Germany lived, and one of them, the greatest (Goethe), is still living. I took an apartment in The Elephant and made my plans at once. I reported to the commandant, Colonel Engelhard, who received me rather uncivilly, for which I played a trick on him. In the afternoon my host drove me to the lovely park. I stayed awhile in Schiller's little nature-house, meditated on him and on his works, and in the evening went to the Belvedere, where the princes were brought up; then to Goethe's house and to the castle, which is arranged with great taste and where you can see magnificent objects of art. At Bertuch's* I found only the daughter at home. Just before sunset I went to the garden again, where I had the good fortune to exchange a few words with the Grand Duchess Maria Pavlovna, who immediately recognized me as a Russian and called me over. Going out I saw a lady sitting in a bower; I sat down next to her in the dark, started a conversation, and encountered a good deal of education, then sentiment, and finally sympathy; I asked for her permission to accompany her, which she gave me. In front of a fine house that she was about to enter I wanted to take my leave, when she invited me to step inside. We were now received by an elderly lady; in candlelight I now saw a wonderfully sweet little face and the grace of innocence itself. Bewildered and embarrassed, yet at the same time lost in admiration of such chaste charms, I could no longer utter a single intelligible word. The Mama, for that was who the old lady was, seemed to be gloating, half ironically and half triumphantly, over my clumsiness. The daughter, on the other hand, had hastened in and out of the room in one bound and had brought me, in a delightful goblet with a

---

* Friedrich Justin Bertuch (1747–1822), German writer, publisher and book dealer; translator of *Don Quixote* (Ed.).

delightful hand, a fine Rhine wine, recommending it in these words: "My dear sir, after such exhaustion you must refresh yourself." But I took my hat and slipped off home.

Today I wrote to Goethe and asked him for an audience. He told the servant who had taken my note that he didn't know me and was no freak animal to be gaped at. My vanity was more than a little wounded by this extremely uncivil style, but my request might have looked that way.

To console myself I went to see the court chapel, where I saw a lovely old German picture by Van Dyck that moved me deeply. Then I went to visit the vault where Schiller's, Wieland's, Herder's, and Bode's ashes are resting; I also got the autographs of these celebrated men from a young man of Jena whose acquaintance I made at the table d'hôte; then I went to Bertuch, to whom I had been recommended and whom I loved and knew from my childhood because of his picture book; he received me in a very friendly way and sent me a few maps from his office. I left the city at noon and in a few hours I arrived in Jena, after driving along the Saale.

30 June, Jena

Here, to my joy, I met a young cousin from Wolmar, with whom I spent a few happy hours and who showed me the city, the university and its collections, and took me to a students' spree and then to see Professors Eberhard and Schott. The tone among the students seemed to me coarse and vulgar. Today I drove to the nearby headquarters in the village of Timmern, where the regiment is resting. Our good Emperor happened to drive by on his way to Weimar. The heat is frightful. Tomorrow we're off to Saxony.

1 July, Michelstadt

Our march brought us here by way of Naumburg, a nice little town, and Freiburg. The whole region is familiar to me from the campaign of the year before. The Grand Duchess

Maria Pavlovna passed us in review today and was very gracious; but the men and the horses were very tired from the long march. I lost a horse that was very dear to me; for that matter, I don't understand just why we're running back like madmen or people who've been beaten. I intend to see the fair in Leipzig.

3, 4 July, Leipzig

This city, which in a great many respects is interesting and noteworthy, is a real focal point for Germany and its commerce. The book trade, for instance, has reached gigantic dimensions here; not least of all because of the fair that is taking place now, in which merchants from all the regions of Europe and as far as the interior of Asia have gathered together to exchange their goods. Last year around this time I caught sight of its towers and walls to the music of cannon fire and between clouds of smoke, but couldn't get inside. But today I'm visiting its streets as a peaceful guest and go about unmolested.

I stopped at a good and clean tavern where I intend to make myself comfortable. Early in the morning of the 4th I got myself out of bed and went up the tower of the Divinity School in order to get a good look at the panorama of the battlefield. The three fateful days of October and of the battle of the nations came fresh to my mind, and I should have liked to meditate for a few hours on the destiny of peoples, on the soldier's life, and on the dead, but the tower guard came along and reminded me of going home. So I went down to the marketplace into the tumult of the streets and traffic, teeming with all sorts of different nations. When my stomach reminded me of mealtime I went to the most popular place, the Hotel de Saxe, where I found a very elegant crowd. In the afternoon I drove into the suburbs, to the Grimma Gate—it was very hot there—and to the battlefield itself, and didn't come back until late— after visiting Poniatowski's grave—to my inn, where I fell exhausted into Caroline's arms and enjoyed her sweet kisses. I saw the university, the Rosenau, the principal church, the town hall, the theatre, and the splendid shops only in passing.

5 July

I consider last night one of the most fateful in my life and this morning the turning point of my moral consciousness. For after going to supper with Baron Rosen and some officers, where there was a great deal of champagne-drinking, I fell into the hands of a siren who wheedled away from me the talisman of the sweet Blanche Lauris and rewarded me with a poison which I recognized running through my veins as the venereal fire. Only, to be sure, was this a premonition of the imminent evil. After I had slept off the dual intoxication I was attacked by pangs of conscience like ravenous wolves; I cannot recall living through a more forlorn morning. But I felt well content that God now finally intended to punish me for my senseless and frivolous life. I flung myself on my knees and in tears begged Him for forgiveness for my sinful life. In addition, the thought of having dissipated my health with a harlot I had made purchased love with was unendurable for me. . . . After the bacchanalia in the arms of this strumpet I had the most horrible dreams, and when I awoke I found myself in a little attic room whose furniture indicated to me that I had spent the time in a laundress's arms, and everything still betrayed the disorder of the squandered hours. A shriek of revulsion, terror, and remorse burst from my lips; I leaped up from the couch, flung the disgusting wench my purse, and as though lashed on by the Furies fled to my room, where until noon today I've been undergoing one of those struggles that are worse than any battles, for I had to endure the feeling of my own worthlessness and to await the horrible consequences of drunkenness and lechery. I shall never in my life forget this lesson. It will have its after-effects in my blood and bones for a very long time. My pride, my shame, my fear of the consequences of my adventure are tearing

at my mind today in such a way that I can't work up any
desire to do anything at all.

The Tsar has just arrived; the rejoicing is general. I took
a bath, then went to the regimental surgeon and from him
to a clever Italian I had met, who's taken great voyages and
told me wonderful stories about them. But this distraction
did not alleviate the sting inside me. In the evening a ball and
an illumination.

6 July, Halle an der Saale

A pleasant day. Made the acquaintance of Mlle Unzel-
mann, an artist, in the loge. I was given a reprimand by
General Arseniev and recalled to the regiment, where I
shall report tomorrow most obediently.

7 July, Dessau

The march today led us here by way of Radegast. The
countryside is beautiful and tilled, cultivated. In Wörlitz
I spoke to the Duke himself in his magnificent park. He is
very affable. My fears were not unfounded; my Leipzig
encounter has turned into a catastrophe. Now the thing is
to mend my folly. But where and how?!

10 July, Treuenbrietzen

Nous voilà en Prusse! On the 8th we moved to Bossdorf
by way of Coswig, two nice little spots on the Elbe. Got here
yesterday by way of Niemegk; now we're resting again.
The provinces have suffered a great deal from the war here.
I'm stopping with a very nice schoolmaster, who is very
erudite but extremely pedantic. How many people you meet,
countries you see, and notes you gather when you travel
around as a soldier! This changing life has great charms
of its own.

13 July, Potsdam

My illness is getting worse. I must think in earnest of an
honourable retreat for a little while. On the 11th we moved

to Beelitz, on the 12th I drove here, and now here I am *comfortablement casé*. The city is symmetrically built, like Nancy, and has a fine castle that reminds one of Frederick the Great, especially Sans Souci, which I visited in the morning, and its splendid gardens. The obelisk, the picture gallery, the orangery, the library, Voltaire's room and manuscripts are all worth seeing. I met the Court Marshal Voss in the gardens together with the princesses. In the evening I drove to Marienfeld, where I was quartered with an old captain who talked a lot about his campaigns and who has a sentimental daughter who made a show of all sorts of poetry and foolishness. Tomorrow it's off to Berlin.

14 July, Berlin

After taking a good look round Potsdam and making a few acquaintances, including the tutor of the princes, a very agreeable chap, and after entertaining my squadron singers in style in the evening, I set out early this morning and got here by noon. The view from above, from the mountain, on to the magnificent residency is really majestic. It takes easily an hour from the Halle Gate to the Brandenburg Gate. The old city goes as far as the Kurfürsten Bridge, from there the streets keep getting broader and prettier until, passing from one surprise to another, you come to the Lindenallee, which together with the Kreuzstrasse and the Brandenburg Gate really leave nothing more to be desired. Today, too, I was in constant motion until nightfall, since the time for seeing and learning is so limited.

The five sections of the city all have their own peculiar character and have different sorts of people. On this side of the Spree River live the rich, on the other side the poor people and the ones who have to earn a living. On the whole, the region around Berlin is ugly, the air is heavy, and the water bad. In spite of its 22 squares, its 220 streets, 16 gates, 34 bridges, 30 churches, 5 hours to get around, and 230,000 inhabitants, it doesn't make the impression of an historic city and a great seat, though the architecture is noble and

grand. The most impressive buildings are the university, the
old castle, the arsenal, the opera house. Of all the squares
I like the Wilhelmplatz the most. At the post office in the
Old City I received a package of letters—from Paris; then
I went to the palace, whose interior was shown me and
which contains a lot worth seeing. In Monbijou, a castle of
the king that lies along the Spree, there's very little to see;
I didn't stop here long, nor did I in the Charité, a big
hospital the sight of which repels me even now. . . . In the
Tiergarten, in Charlottenburg, under the tents and in
Belvedère, on the other hand, I looked around all the more
industriously. Towards six I went to the theatre; I liked the
play very much. It was called *The Portrait of the Mother.*
After supper a number of comrades drove off to the notorious
Miss Bernhard and to the Traiteur de Max, where we had a
delicious supper. But I behaved in a neutral way, though
this was no more than forced behaviour or virtue, for the
Devil is still inside me!

16 July

All day yesterday and until evening today I have had no
time to jot anything down, there was so much to look at
and do. Among others I met the son of my benefactress
Burckhard from Ortelsburg, Lieutenant Massenbach. The
acquaintance ripened swiftly and cordially. Such moments
of grateful emotion are real beacons in our life! It goes without saying that as we chatted and poured our hearts out
there was a proper amount of champagne drunk, though
the doctor had strictly forbidden it. While going home I
collided with a most charming girl who was walking down
the street; my spurs got mixed up in her dress, she fell down,
and I almost fell on top of her. Loud laughter among all
those on the scene. The girl was very piqued, though I
helped her up to her sweet little feet and stuttered out all
sorts of excuses. Then I hurried off to see Friedrich Kahlen,
but I didn't find him in the room. But in the room next door
I heard some giggling; I looked through the keyhole and

to my not inconsiderable merriment saw a *pas de quatre* I'll never forget.

In the evening I visited a club where you could hear some good music. Berlin is quite amusing, but has no soul; the people are clever and witty, the women are lively and flirtatious, but there's no heart in any of it, just wretched money and vanity. They're all avaricious! Tomorrow it's off again to the northeast. Now even I will soon have had enough distractions; I need physical and spiritual repose— but where can these be found, in this soldier's life on the march? Farewell, Berlin!

17 July, Müncheberg

Yesterday we moved up as far as Neutempel, where I was quartered with the stalwart pastor Gilsecker. A cheerful evening. Müncheberg is a tiny little nest, but it's become interesting to me because of a very odd person who together with his clan was burnt out three times, became a beggar three times, prospered again three times; and then became an enemy of mankind because of various swindles of others, and finally became the happiest husband and father in the world—consciously an atheist and dreamer and finally at the end of this life story, a complete Christian.

20 July, Zorndorf

On the 18th we marched by way of Seelow to Altboden over bad roads, then yesterday by way of Küstrin, a substantial fort, to here, where we're resting tomorrow. The Oder flows by in front of our windows; it has very nice banks. But the countryside is sandy and desolate; the peasants and burghers are poor. This place is famous for the battle won by Frederick the Great. A crippled old veteran of the period showed me the old trenches that are still there and told how he had once taken a pinch of snuff from the great king's own snuffbox. In Dennewitz, where the divisional headquarters is and where the castle belongs to my good friend Dönhoff, I spent the afternoon with Tishkevich, who put me up for the night, since I kept feeling worse and worse; but I had to share the place with a young married couple who didn't have the slightest shame and completely stopped me from sleeping, so I finally went off to the horses, where at last I found some rest on top of the hay.

22 July, Landsberg

Yesterday and today we moved through Vietz and Boltz to Genin. The weather was damp, and I had a bad pain in the chest. Now we're resting here again, and I've been able to nurse myself a little. In the evening there was a ball and supper at the casino in honour of the good King's birthday; as many as 200 people were merrily twirling. A few old carriages brought all the ladies, whose toilettes and manners looked quite comical and middle class. There was no lack of beer or tobacco smoke in the adjoining rooms; the Prussian can't live for a moment without them. Ill as I felt I danced every dance, especially with the mayor's pretty daughter, Annie Glatteris, who found herself in a tiresome situation since her father was in his cups and the floor was very rough. At four o'clock the crowd broke up; I accompanied this odd family as far as the old man's house and didn't wake up today until ten o'clock.

23 July, Friedberg

The march was exhausting; the woods to the left of the military highway were on fire. It's already teeming here with Jews. Since we had a day of rest today I nursed myself as well as I could, but things can't go on this way for long, otherwise I'll soon remain stretched out somewhere; what a miserable illness!

26 July, Filehne

Yesterday we moved by way of Driesen on to Neu-Erbach, which is on the Polish border. It already looks Lithuanian everywhere; I'm very homesick!

27 July, Schönlanke

The road took us over Ascherbude and Stieglitz to a wretched nest of Jews, where I spent the most depressing day of my marching soldier's life.

28, 29 July, Schneidemühl

The quarters today are—if that is possible—even more miserable than yesterday's. Even the food is piggish. What a difference from Germany! Since we had a day of rest, out of sheer boredom I went to see a Franciscan monk, who babbled a lot of silly nonsense to me about his church. I pretended I was thinking of letting him convert me; he became quite insistent, especially after a few glasses of punch which I set in front of him. He told me how he had once caught hold of the Devil and driven him off, and had done it with a piece of the cord once worn by St. Francis, and lots more such tomfoolery. Then in my presence he also wanted to practise some exorcism on the two small sick daughters of the landlady, which was then actually attempted, to the accompaniment of the strangest antics. The oldest daughter, a seventeen-year-old, seemed to get on well with the good Devil's doctor. He had probably slipped another section of the cord into her sick vagina and so cured her nymphomania. What a monstrosity, to play in this way with the most holy things! I gave the little one a pretty present, pressed her to tell me everything exactly about how the monk had healed her; very naïvely, she told me the whole story, though in a veiled way, and advised me if I were ill to turn to him in the same way. I was horrified, and I decided to punish the pastor that evening for his atrocities. I told him I too was possessed of the Devil and that he must drive him out of me. When he then went about this exorcism of his, I held a pistol against his forehead, ordered him to confess, and after he, trembling, had admitted his whole fraud, I gave him a thorough beating with the flat of my sword, had my horse saddled, and rode off.

30 July, Grabowo

Yesterday's story made us all laugh, but I felt some pangs of conscience at having thrashed the fellow so, for he won't recover from his lesson so easily. Indeed, what is man on earth that he may punish his fellow for such a sin? Hasn't he enough of his own to correct? Mend your own ways first, Boris, and leave the punishment of others to God!

The quarters today are frightful. You see nothing around but sand, heath, bushes, and miserable huts. These are the results of neglecting the people's education, just as at home. So let the government and the landowners do something decent for the education of the lower strata of the people! And there's no point to all these compulsory chores and corvées, which exhaust the land and the people on it and brutalize them.

31 July, Wirsitz

We squadron officers are all staying with a Polish nobleman, who received us very well. We sang war songs at the piano. In the evening I read a travel description that I found gripping. I would surely be a first-class tourist, since travelling is my passion. This evening, out of a full heart, I prayed to God once again. That makes me feel better than reading novels.

1 August, Nakel

I've just received a leave of three weeks to ride home to my family, since we're already not far from the Russian border. But with what a conscience I shall have to appear before my dear parents! I'm very grateful to General Arseniev for this kindness. But I'll follow the regiment along the marching route as far as Tilsit, then I'll ride on from there alone.

3 August, Bromberg

Yesterday we got as far as the Vistula to this completely German and heavily populated place. Today we had a day of rest, and I could nurse myself. God, how art Thou kind and gracious!

4, 5 August, Kulm

We managed our passage over the majestic Vistula yesterday and touched the localities of Fordon, Strelitz, and Gigin; Sacken and I stayed yesterday with a hunt master, who received us in a friendly way; today we found several gentlemen in the neighbourhood who entertained us and drank the health of the Emperor and of our army.

7 August, Graudenz

Today is my twenty-first birthday; so I'm legally of age! But am I morally, too? Unfortunately not! For I'm still as light-minded as a child, as immoral as a Franciscan, and as godless and unbelieving as a Tungus—no, no, today I have not much cause for happiness! Would God that I become a different human being after another twenty-one years! But what is the use of moping if it doesn't produce any decision? After a day spent in solitude I drove off with Ed. Manteuffel to the city, which gave us and the Prussian officers' corps a ball that was very animated. Right now, and before I go to bed, I want to vow to God to suppress my passion—and to dedicate myself to virtue. But would you creep to the cross in this way if you were well? I must answer—certainly not! Riper considerations and the feeling of your duty to act in accordance with principles are not enough to make you happy. For what is needed above all is piety, and while you may have had that as a child it's now been lost in the maelstrom of life.

When I pass my life before my eyes it falls first into two, then into three main periods. My childhood until the age of twelve was pure, happy, and untroubled. My life became worse and worse and more and more impure from the twelfth to the seventeenth year, the end of my school years and the beginning of my army life and first period in the garrison until we marched off—a time in which I reached the highest degree of immorality. I wish I had never lived through that, I'm so ashamed of that time of lies and frivolity and light-mindedness. The third period, from my nineteenth year until today—that is, the period of the campaigns—has, to be sure, been a more interesting and useful one for me, but what byways I found myself on in Paris and Leipzig! So forward for the good, and for that matter, from today on!

Graudenz lies very prettily on the Vistula; it has a strong fortress, lots of traffic and life, respectable people; in the house where I'm living I met a lady who looks very like Mme Dellingshausen-Buxhöveden. At the ball yesterday I danced with her, and it put me in mind of Reval; her name is Julie Neiden and she is the daughter of the local school-master.

10 August, Ortelsburg

So here I am again with my old friends, who were more than a little astonished and delighted at seeing me again so well preserved. On the 8th the regiment had marched to Garnsee, and on the 9th to Summern by way of Riesenburg, from where I then came here in a light gig. In Therewisch I found fat old Burckhard sitting in his easy chair as he was just a year ago, drinking some beer out of a tremendous mug, and the excellent Mama ironing laundry and flitting about the house, the daughters singing and knitting, Rosken playing with his wife and children—in short, everything just as it used to be, and as though I had ridden off instead of to Paris only to nearby Ortelsburg, where I spent an hour or so today. On the way I had to battle against rain and a storm. The night descended, the horses refused to go any farther, Fyodor cursed and whipped them, and finally the wagon turned over and we fell into the ditch. Very laboriously we got to Preussisch Mark, where I took a post carriage as far as Liebemühle, where we arrived early this morning. The mayor, a completely charming man, fortified steed and men and expedited me as far as Osterode, a nice little spot where we feasted on eels and gooseberries. Towards evening we were in Hohenstein, which is half burned down; but since I was in a hurry we galloped on by way of Jedwabne here, from where I visited my old acquaintances the

Quades, the Bergs, and the Fabecks. Happiest of all were the Wedels, the Grangows, and the Wolknows and Molde; but old Stach had meanwhile passed on to his fathers. I found Stael, who had been badly wounded in Gross Beeren, cosily together with his wife, Burckhard's daughter. But little Bernhard, my godson, was missing. I quickly withdrew from these friends and in another hour and a half was in Therewisch, whose church tower greeted me from afar like a faithful comrade.

When we had had our fill of embracing and hugging we began questions, answers, and stories till there was no end to them. Our hearts' outpourings lasted until late into the night, the cloverleaf—Julchen, Minchen, and Lorchen—stuffed my cheeks and stomach full of cake, wine, and fruit, so that I have to get myself ready for an attack of indigestion.

15 August, Therewisch

For a couple of days I haven't been able to get at my Diary, there's been so much to tell about the war, until late into every night. My indisposition seems to have vanished. It really is a wonderful thing, friendship and love, and surely gratitude is the third one in the alliance. Everything has been forgotten—hardships, discomfort, and grief. Every day we drive out to Volka to meet Rotkirch, and there we find all sorts of political talk, music, and fun for his children. . . . Such a lovely married life, like this, is just what I'd wish for myself too. . . . My room and bed in Therewisch are the same as before, and everything is still standing in its old place. Yesterday morning when I got up I thought I was still a convalescent from the year '13: coffee, almond cake— just like then—the garden, the bower, the benches were as they had been; even when I walk about with the sisters hand-in-hand I feel as though I had never left. At the pastor's and at the post many an hour is chattered away, and that's how it goes, one day after the other; and now I've been here five days already and am thinking of riding off tomorrow.

The old folks are in a bad way; they lost their fortune in the war; if only they could be helped!

Burckhard's been away; our reunion was very cordial. Now there was something else to gossip about, and so the day went by on wings. We go to Ortelsburg together often and visit the invalid there, who is getting along much better. Then friends usually get together at Stach's, and there's a real spree of laughing and jabbering. But the chief topic has been Lorchen's engagement to young Völkner. Impulses of jealousy; a noble victory after the battle. I give my approval to the new enterprise too; and hurrah! The two others make eyes at me, but I don't raise a finger.

16 August, Bischofsburg

My parting today from this beloved family was a hard blow for me. My affection for them will stay the same to my dying day. They accompanied me as far as Kobulten, to the sister of Bernhard, and from there I drove on, after a tender, painful farewell, as far as here, where sitting in some Jewish tavern I speculated on the transitoriness of all human happiness; soon afterwards I caught up with my squadron, with which I intend to go on as far as Tilsit.

19 August, Friedland

Our march route took us past the places that had seen such important battles in 1807—Heilsberg, Bartenstein, etc. We're going to rest here tomorrow. Good for taking care of myself physically, since I must now prepare myself for the long and strenuous trip to Reval. May God give me help!

22 August, Skaisgirren

Our column has been moving in a very leisurely way along the Lithuanian border as far as here; we were badly quartered, and my illness got worse, more and more worrying. I must put an end to this business and tackle the doctor seriously; he's been treating me only with palliatives, merely teasing the lion, merely salving the cancer.

25 August, Tilsit

So here I am, with God's help, arrived at the place that like a crossroads with double signposts points out Russia's border and gives me a friendly fateful reception. It is most charming. Crossing over the Neman was fun, at the same time very impressive. I'm still supposed to ride to Tauroggen, I hear; well, just that one more stop, and then!

27 August, Tauroggen

Today we stepped onto the soil of Russia, whose boundary posts with their double eagles we greeted with jubilation. But now I won't let myself be held up any longer, for my heart and duty and health are calling me to Reval. And today too I close my Diary, which has become as dear and precious to me as a faithful comrade. Unfortunately the general also seems to have changed his mind, for he is requesting me to march as far as Riga together with the regiment, which I'll hardly be capable of doing, my limbs are all giving me such pain. Never mind—one way or another I'll soon be home. Only courage! In any case I am ending this book with today's date. May God give me help!

The venereal disease contracted in Leipzig was probably ulcus molle; *this also seems to be indicated from the successful cure later. This type of illness, which was curable even in the eighteenth and nineteenth centuries, was very often, until it was identified in 1850, confused with other well-known venereal diseases. This led to the fact that the others were also wrongly thought to be partially curable. In any case—as emerges from other notes—the author had completely recovered his health in about two years (1816–17).*

PART TWO

AND THE WOMAN

1818–1819

Chapter I

FROM HEGEL TO HELENE

At the age of nineteen Boris had gone to war a cavalry ensign; in September 1814 he came back to his home in Fickel in Estonia at the age of twenty-one, a first lieutenant. He was there when the news reached him that he had been promoted to captain. Soon after his return he was retired from active service.

He moved from Fickel to another family holding that his father had transferred to him to administer. But the life of a country squire did not suit him; he often visited nearby Fickel, whose library fed his thirst for knowledge and which he enriched with the works of contemporary authors. He also travelled a great deal to the provincial capital of the country, St. Petersburg, which after Tsar Alexander's victory over Napoleon was very nearly the equal of the other European capitals, Vienna, Paris, and London, in external brilliance and political importance.

Boris was in Estonia when he learned of the fiasco of the first Peace Congress of Vienna, brought about by Napoleon's sudden return from Elba to France and the dramatic "Hundred Days" that followed it, ending with Napoleon's defeat at Waterloo. This last test of strength against Napoleon was endured by the Prussians and British alone, without their Russian and Austrian allies, but in St. Petersburg preparations were already being made for a new march on Paris, in case Napoleon threatened Europe again. The news of Wellington's and Blücher's victory at Waterloo was a message of good tidings for all those who had fought against Napoleon, especially for the Russian people, which had not yet forgotten the horrors of the war in its own country.

In Russia Napoleon had never been fêted as the "great mover and innovator" he had been thought to be by many educated Europeans. The war against him, which, with the burning of Moscow had reached a climax of horror, had nipped in the bud any tendency to idolize him. Napoleon, indeed, just before surrendering to go to St. Helena, had said, "God save me from the Russians!"

After Waterloo, along the Rhine, too, and in Elba, Napoleon began to be looked on with other eyes. His pictures vanished from German middle-class homes and even the sixty-six-year-old Goethe turned his back on the man he had once sung the praises of as the "defender of civilization against the barbarism of the Slavs".

All admirers of Goethe in Russia—including Boris, in spite of Goethe's disdainful rejection of his request for an audience— sympathized with his abandonment of Napoleon. The myth of Napoleon fell out of fashion at all the princely courts in Europe, as well as in the European salons, as did the sneer at the Slavs as "barbarians" against whom the peoples of Europe had to defend themselves.

These first years of peace were spent by Boris—surrounded and cosseted by parents and family—in an atmosphere of mutual affection. In 1817 two notable events took place: his second youngest sister, Elizabeth, celebrated her engagement to her second cousin, Karl-Eduard von Sievers, and on the same day his parents celebrated their silver wedding anniversary. The whole country, especially the city of Reval, took a lively part in this double holiday. But this year of fêtes fell under a shadow: two of Boris's brothers, Alexander and Wilhelm-Eduard, had got themselves involved in an affair of honour and, after a duel with a Lieutenant von Rothkirch, Alexander lost his rights as a nobleman and was demoted to the rank of a common soldier, as was his brother Wilhelm-Eduard, who had been his second. A year later Wilhelm-Eduard was drowned while swimming in the Dnieper.

Very soon after his return Boris had begun making plans for his future. He wanted to study philosophy. In those days the land of the thinkers was Germany, where the fame of Kant and Fichte had not yet dimmed and the star of men like Schelling and Baader was brightly beaming forth. Hegel too had already become known in philosophically-minded circles for his Phenomenology of Mind *and his* Science of Logic. *In the autumn of 1816 Hegel had been called to the philosophy chair of the University of Heidelberg; in 1817 his* Encyclopaedia of the Philosophical Sciences *appeared. The effect exercised by Hegel on the educated people of his age rested to a large extent on the general hope that he would succeed in creating a synthesis between religion and philosophy. Taking theology as his starting point, he had undertaken in his first writings to free Christianity from all forms of dogmatism and to reconcile it with Kant's* Critique of Pure Reason. *For Hegel this attempt at throwing a bridge between the pure spirit of reason and the Holy Spirit of theology was neither impossible nor blasphemous. Consequently, "Hegelianism" was, at the time, not merely a philosophy, but the religion of all educated people.*

Boris wrote to Hegel and told him that he wanted to come to Heidelberg to become his pupil. This initiated a correspondence between the young Baltic baron and the great philosopher that was to last over many years. One of Hegel's letters to Boris, dated 28 November 1821, has been preserved; part of it reads: "Russia . . . carries in its bosom a vast potentiality for the development of its intensive nature."

Hegel, too, as a young professor in Jena, had paid tribute to Napoleon's demonic genius. He greeted the defeat of the Prussian armies at Jena and Auerstedt in 1806, which he lived through in the greatest proximity, as an emancipation from the "corrupt and arrogant rule of Prussia" and as a rightful punishment of history. He called Napoleon, the executor of that punishment, "the World Spirit on horseback".

This youthful sin was forgotten and forgiven twelve years later, when Hegel was called to the chair of philosophy in Berlin, empty since the death of Fichte. In Heidelberg Hegel had received 1,500 ducats as salary; in Berlin he was offered more than double: 3,000 thalers, a very high professorial salary for the time.

In 1817 Boris came to Heidelberg and attended Hegel's difficult course, "An Outline of the Philosophic Sciences". Two years later, when his master was preparing to leave for Berlin, Boris, for quite different reasons, also decided to say farewell to Heidelberg.

20 December 1818, Heidelberg

Some days in one's life are so rich in events that there is hardly enough room to contain them. I had one such day today, the 20th of December 1818. I had scarcely got up when I received three letters—two from home and one from Clary—which were very important. At midday another one announced the death of my grandmother, and in the afternoon I avoided a duel only with difficulty. In the evening, at six, I was led into temptation by T.D., as Joseph was by his master's wife, and at eight I made the unforgettable acquaintance of my Helene!

12 January 1819, Heidelberg

For three weeks no Diary, because of—Helene!

On the 22nd of December I pressed a little note into her tiny satin hand. A deep flush spread over her cheeks; she lisped, "Thank you." On the 24th I got a note from her, in which she wrote: "I love you." That evening, at V.'s, she said it to me. In the evening of the 25th Amor brought us together again; how her hand trembled as it rested in mine, how blissful was the sound of the words of love! Thousands of burning kisses sealed our union. How her bosom heaved! I unloosed her hair and played with her locks. The parting was interminable. On the 26th we wandered about the ruins in the moonlight. There was much loving talk, many caresses and kisses. Tears of melancholy flowed—my lips dried them. When I recounted to her merry adventures from the Garden of the Hesperides and tales of black-eyed maidens, she said solemnly: "A German maid loves differently." On the 28th we walked hand in hand into the fields. The Paris Gate was our rendezvous. At eight the bell summoned her to her mother. On January 1st, New Year's Day brought me a new joy: the slyboots met me, slipping away from the Argus eyes of her mother, and was at the door with burning ardour, without a word. On the 3rd our hearts beat together for a long time, over by the wall cupboard in a silent embrace, before any words could twist themselves out of our overcharged hearts. She gave me a lock of her chestnut brown hair. On the 5th she wanted to go to Vienna with me. What a torment, yet what bliss! A heavenly pleasure awaits me. On the 9th there tolled the happy lover's hour, so long fought for and so longed for, in the little inn on the mountain. The straw! She gave me her bosom, which inflamed me to masculine audacity. But just at the height of our most blissful oblivion the waitress came into the anteroom. We leaped apart and went home, silent and shamefaced.

30 March 1819, Stuttgart

I'm through with Heidelberg; I've left. It was high time too, otherwise I would have worked up an outright fit of melancholy. Sitting still had turned me into a hypochondriac. I had already become one; for the last two months I could no longer go to see anyone; all society seemed to me hateful. The only exceptions I made were the disputatorium at six o'clock, and every now and then a little dance with my dear Helene Hahn, who led me for many an hour out of the sphere of speculation into the lush and cosy arms of love, away from Plato's and Hegel's sombre dialectics into the sacred secret chambers of Venus. The word of God was completely forgotten; earthy lust was now streaming through my heart. Runaway Boris, now being awaited by new and blissful occasions for grace and glory in the proud city on the Danube. But during this winter I've been quite industrious. I must make this confession to myself, after all!

On the 26th in the evening, after I had an earlier chat with Helene and she had gone off, I left Heidelberg, but with a much lighter heart than I did last winter. Why?— I have no idea myself; was it that I couldn't see through people then as I can now, or had I really become a hypochondriac from having sat around so much? The last day was a genuinely vexatious one for me. The farewell visits, the packing, the debts. Yes, if it hadn't been for these three things everything would have gone better. The debts this time really vexed me; and my purse is in a pretty hectic condition—how will it hold out till July? Well, I suppose, just be healthy and of good cheer—the *nervus rerum gerendarum* will find itself of its own accord.

But that I should be making the whole trip to Vienna this time in the company of a young girl really does seem to me a little odd after all. Nothing like it has ever happened to me. But, Boris, don't you like her? Isn't she good and sweet? Aren't you making her happy?—all this I hear in my heart. In general, the last winter was a strange one for me. Ever since then my mind has been striving upwards, but my soul has receded somewhat. Was it concentrating its forces, or was it surrendering to my mind? No, that is impossible, otherwise I would have no ideals in my heart nor any thirst for knowledge and learning. After coming back from Italy last autumn I had become weary of roving about; but, inwardly more troubled than ever, my spirit made up for it by reaching out in broader circles, and threatened to burst certain restrictions laid on it by the accepted views and by art. I was drawn mightily to science, to philosophy, for which I had always had a decided bent. But Hegel had left, called to Berlin. I wanted to go after him. I bemoaned my ill luck; for no one was there to take the place of this titanic mind. Consoling myself once again, I decided to make up for it by pursuing ancient languages, history, and aesthetics; accordingly I set up three lectures and shut myself in; chance led me to Hinrichs. Only he could be a real Hegelian, as far as I was concerned. Very soon a disputatorium had been arranged; I was completely delighted. For five months, day after day, we studied Hegel's system. The session would often last until nine o'clock.

In the beginning the dialectic was very obscure to me, but later bright and beaming rays came shooting out of the deep and sombre abyss of speculation! When we came to natural philosophy I saw that the universe fitted into the edifice of logic, and with the philosophy of mind the circle of the sciences was closed. The final four weeks were priceless for me, though Hinrichs, sometimes approaching the subject wrongly, would often misinterpret Hegel, misunderstanding his ideas in a sharp and discordant way. What was boundless, titanic, in the philosophy of subject-object, the profundity in the speculation and in the dialectic of thought, unfolded gradually into an immeasurable tapestry of ideas, and it was then that I genuinely began to think. Everything around me, in me, above me acquired a new shape; earthly magnitudes vanished, and the mind lost its fantastic direction; it became more transcendent. The measure by which I assessed everything became greater, the point of view, the standpoint I had started from was much loftier. But there were many battles, and difficult ones, for the decrepit old building of my mind had to come down.

In languages, especially in Latin, I accomplished a good deal that winter. The grammatical sheath of this language finally burst, after many a sigh; the classical kernel was revealed, and I soon cast a soulful glance into the literary and political life of the ancients. Klindworth, a philologist of intellect, not a mere interpreter of words, not a syntactical hair-splitter—which unfortunately is what most of the linguistic scholars are—laid out for me the characteristic and intimate life of the Roman world; I was soon familiar with the beauties of Sallust, and through him, with the patriotic strivings and activities of the Romans. The poets, especially the erotic ones like Catullus, Tibullus, and Ovid, followed the prose writers. The charm, the refinement, the tender nuances in their diction and fiction were limitlessly attractive to me, and I conceived a great affection for the true Muse. With Tacitus we came to a stop. It was a pity that I had to stop in the middle of exposition and translation. The four months were priceless to me also in that my style improved and my views of history and language were purified. In a word, I saw more clearly. But I lacked the rudiments of everything, the prior knowledge, the classical pre-training, particularly the knowledge of the ancient languages. Indeed, what could a soldier know in general, who, in any case, had enjoyed only a very defective schooling, who at first couldn't see the woods for the trees, who was too vain, too light-minded, too mendacious, too superficial—in short, too *Russian*.

I did less in the way of aesthetics; why, I'm not entirely

clear even now; doubtless because every theory of the beautiful, however good, is of negligible utility in a practical sense. I got an eye and a heart from nature; the first sees accurately, well and truly, the latter has straightforward feelings, is warm and tender, and all that is quite enough for the enjoyment of beauty. Hillebrand, whose private lecture on aesthetics I was taking, is a highly intelligent and kind-hearted man; I listened to him too, attentively and with pleasure; but in his views and judgements of the plastic arts he was backward, which was only natural, since he had never seen any products of art or anything beautiful, and I could learn only a little from him. Meanwhile I have gained a completely systematic classification and idea of the sciences, *et cela me suffit*. What I needed particularly was the theory of the rhetorical arts, of which I had no knowledge at all. That of the plastic arts I had acquired in my manifold wanderings hither and thither in life.

I regard my own aesthetic notes as the best I've put in here. I showed the most zeal in excerpting historical and statistical works. I finally attained a certain facility that will be of use to me one day, I hope. The twenty-four volumes of human history by Johannes Müller, Heeren's ideas and modern political history, Say,* and others I wrote down partly in toto, partly in fragments. This gave me a rapid and acute eye for the finding, compiling, and putting down of data and facts. Critical self-illumination was my favourite absorption in studying. A few compositions gave me a certain facility in style and in the setting forth of my thoughts. Among the latter, I mention here the draft on the emancipation of the Russian peasants which I worked on at first with zeal and a great deal of enthusiasm, but soon gave up, since I lacked the necessary skeleton, the groundwork (historical as well as fiscal) of the essay, the time for its due thinking through and working out, as well as the requisite

---

* Johannes von Müller (1752–1809), Swiss historian; Arnold Heeren (1760–1842), German historian at Göttingen; Jean Baptiste Say (1767–1832), French economist (Ed.).

knowledge. But I'm not letting it alone. It will be elaborated, corrected, and published in Göttingen next winter.

And now a résumé of the last few weeks in Heidelberg.

In November 1818 I had arranged a disputational course with Dr. Hinrichs. Full of philosophical zeal I went there again one day and rang (it was on a Monday, and the third time); it was five o'clock; the door opened. I saw before me a girl, full of grace and sweetness, who while responding in a friendly way to my greeting looked into my eyes with such a strange expression that my innermost soul leaped up within me. The next day the same thing happened. I enquired casually who the girl might be; I was told she was Hinrich's sister-in-law, Mlle Helene Hahn, a merry, cheerful little thing eighteen years old, but rather an intriguer. Pah! I thought, why should you be afraid of her, how does she concern you? Talk to her nicely, exchange a few words with her if it comes to that, but as for falling in love—well, I thought, that's a good long way off for you. Firmly intending not to concern myself with her much, I went there the next evening, and found her on the staircase in front of the wall cupboard. I said hello. She looked at me half questioning, half melancholy. I stormed past the siren on my way to the professor's room. Then I didn't see her for two days, but one Thursday—the moment is unforgettable for me—she appeared again, and was more beautiful than before. By the cupboard she seized hold of my hand and said to me: "The doctor is not at home; you're looking for him, oh, and I for you!" And then, swoosh, she vanished through a side door. I stood there petrified. That, I thought to myself, is something no innocent and inexperienced girl would do. Watch out, Boris, this Circe is going to make a fool out of you, don't let yourself be blinded by your vanity, or one day you might regret having had anything to do with her; then I slipped off back home.

A few days later I was sitting alone in the half-light of the dusk, upstairs at Hinrichs's at the window, waiting for him; the door of the room swung open softly, and a female

figure appeared, flitted past me to the sofa and lisped, "My
dear Sophie, didn't you see Uxkull coming?" and then went
out through the door again. I was about to cry out, "He's
here, what d'you want?", but the words died out on my
paralysed tongue. The singularity, the strangeness of the
situation had struck me so that I had forgotten to speak.
Boris, you must put a stop to this, I cried, leaping to my feet
and, determined to write to her next day, I went to bed late
and troubled. With a reserved note asking for an explanation
of the vision of the day before I rang at the door the following
day at the same hour. It opened. My mysterious lovely
appeared, quickly and happily took the little note being
held out to her and vanished. No answer the following day.
I was dying of impatience. I encountered my sweet enchan-
tress on the street corner. "Tonight at seven in the Kloster-
gässchen," she whispered flutingly into my ear. Like a
madman I rushed over to Hinrichs's; if there was anyone
who didn't understand Hegel that evening it was I. I felt a
fire under my feet.

At a quarter to seven I was already at the place of my
longing; I could hear my heart beating. Towards eight
I finally caught sight of her. I flew towards her. Quite self-
possessed, she told me that she had already seen me a year
before, that since then my image had grown within her
heart and that I had been her guardian angel in dangers,
that she loved me truly, saw the happiness of her life in me
alone, etc. I regarded it as my duty to remind her of hers;
and I told her in so many words that she could never become
my wife and that I knew her far too little to answer her feeling with my own love, but at the same time I asked her to
grant me her friendship and to allow me to see her further.
Since then we've seen each other often. Her married sister
knew about her secret and favoured it. The girl displayed a
rich soul and a great deal of graciousness and intelligence.

I came to like her more and more, until one day up at the
Müller Tavern, during an intimate moment in which to my
grief she behaved almost like a coquette, we set fire to our

senses, which from then on were to go on blazing. I rented a room for us on the Schlossberg, at an old witch's who for filthy lucre would clear out of her little room and her bed for the hours of our rendezvous. Here in the arms of this lushly built, love-besotted girl I spent heavenly hours of sweet bliss. No longer as a virgin, which she had pretended to be at first, did I embrace this ardent girl, but as an initiate who had been robbed of her innocence through seduction, as she later confessed to me. Thus many enjoyable months full of pleasure went by in undisturbed happiness until the hour of parting, which we had always believed to be still remote, came upon the loving couple only too swiftly. She had often expressed to me the wish of becoming the mother of my child, and she had nourished that hope; during the course of our intimacy no cogent indications of this had developed.

One evening, after we had met as usual at the Paris Gate and then gone off to the old lady's on the mountain and had chatted of my imminent departure, of her future, and of other things cosily but sadly, she told me with embarrassment that she was sure she was now going to become a mother; consequently she begged me to protect her from her mother's wrath and to take her to her uncle in Vienna. Her claim seemed to me untrue, since I had proof to the contrary. The following morning there was a painful scene, which, however, turned out for the best. Our joint trip was decided on and a time fixed. The girl was beside herself with joy, and as though newborn. From that moment she swore truth and fidelity and assured me that she had deceived me twice and only out of fear of losing me. How we later met in Sinsheim, what a blissful life we led together on the journey, and how it is going to go with her and with me in future is all written down in this Diary.

But involuntarily, before I close, the painful thought pops up: what is really happening to this acquaintance, which is bound to have a decisive influence on her and on my future life? How, in my present oppressed condition, can this relationship evolve that seems to be penetrating so deeply into the orbit of my present and future? I have no idea; may Fate let us know!

In Sinsheim I found my girl waiting for me. The oddity of this isolated situation at first made us both embarrassed; but some sweet amorous tussles soon dissipated the constraint and turned it into nameless licence. Ardent kisses repressed trembling sighs, lisped pet names alternated with broken sounds wrenched out of our bliss. It was not until the growing light of the dawn spread through our little window over our dear little bed that our eyelids, inflamed by ardour, dropped and we fell asleep intimately intertwined, melted into one. Morpheus conducted me into the realm of uneasy dreams. I kept seeing and loving what I had just left. In this way we were found by the servant, who came to announce our departure at five o'clock. Hesitantly and tremblingly we dressed, each one in his little corner. Soon we were sitting in the carriage that was taking us to ancient Heilbronn along the familiar road. By ten o'clock we were there. A stroll to the old church, a solid breakfast afterwards, and we were off again up hill down dale along the sweet Neckar, which I shall surely see again only with difficulty, towards Ludwigsburg. Our horses, two pedestrian short-tails, two old acquaintances with which I used to make many a trip to Mannheim, refused to go farther two hours outside Ludwigsburg. The coachman turned wild, thrashed and lashed the poor old nags so that as an old horse lover it stabbed through to my very marrow; finally I took pity on them and gave him a dressing down. Luckily another coachman came along; he was stopped and the other paid and dismissed. In this way we came into Ludwigsburg around eight o'clock. My young spouse, for that is how she was now known, stopped at The Bear. I hurried over to see old Uxkull, who expressed polite pleasure at my arrival. Everything was still as it had always been. After a friendly dinner I went wearily to bed.

On the 28th March, the old man welcomed me at his

coffee table at eight o'clock with a cheerful face and his pipe. That's how I particularly like him, with a smoking pipe; that's when he's very cosy and chats and tells stories, as he's so fond of doing—one witty notion follows another; in amazement you're bound to admire his store of knowledge. Such a practical mind, such a clear understanding is surely seldom to be met with to such a degree. The hours flew by.

Boring visits were made until noon. Luckily we met none of our quasi-relatives; Colonel Lippe was waiting for us at home. A splendid man of the world, he's apparently an able officer. He speaks well and has had a scientific education. At midday I met two Counts *Uexküll*,* very nice chaps but neither with any particular brains; one of them is a lieutenant under Lippe, who is still training him, so to speak, and the other acts as forester for Countess Sayn. The Eschnau wine was first-rate. Art, Italia, and scientific discussions lent spice to the table, which was overflowing with steaming dishes. In the afternoon I drove to the prince's personal physician. He himself wasn't home, but his radiant wife and their two pretty daughters received me with endearing affability—we chatted and laughed a lot— then at five they took me to the Schotts's, where I met a most interesting family.

In the evening we played music. The hours went by very swiftly. At eight I slipped off back to the dear old man, who had meanwhile been waiting for me longingly. A dear note from Helene, who had left The Bear to go visit acquaintances, surprised me at dinner. Tomorrow at ten we're to meet. There was a good deal more talk about our trip, we saw some other things that evening, and some more things were discussed. I didn't get to bed till late.

The following day went by very quickly, nicely and interestingly. At ten I leaned out of the window as agreed, looked over to the Eckarts's, and saw my girl's figure passing by for me to follow. The whole morning I had been

* Uexküll-Gyllenband of the Württemberg branch (Ed.).

rummaging about in the books and cases of my cousins, and so found many a gem and jewel for my collection. Then there *she* was, flashing by; quick, after her, downstairs and away— by the well I caught up with her. I had to greet Helene civilly on the street, but our glances said more to me than "My compliments", or "I wish you a fine day". Soon we were outside the gate and in the neighbourhood of the old castle. Scarcely were we alone when our lips sought each other and our kisses were eloquent above and beyond; the walk was heavenly. The dark subterranean path . . . lengthy embraces . . . the little bench in the corner . . . the shower of stones. As we went home Helene told me about two wasps that had stung her. Parting.

At midday old Uxkull was very serious. He spoke a good deal of his deceased wife, of his imminent end, of his physical sufferings, so that I felt really depressed. At three Lippe's arrival luckily gave the conversation a happier turn, for the tears were already standing in the old man's eyes. The carriage was hitched up and we drove to Marbach, Schiller's birthplace. There we found three old Bavarian generals sitting over a glass of beer; the conversation was empty and trivial. As we drove away a very special joy was waiting for me; that is, to my not inconsiderable astonishment I saw the landlord's daughter, Wilhelmine Krauter, on the stairs; I had met her during my campaign in the year '13. Our meeting gave rise to many a joke and pretty witticism. The way back was most charming; the valley from Ludwigsburg to Marbach, the sunset, the air were all ravishing. On the way the witty conversation of Count Lippe, who gave me a number of notes on the Württemberg army, was very interesting. In the evening we were all merrily together, drinking until eleven. The old man was in the happiest of moods.

Today at eight in the morning, after saying good-bye, we got into the carriage and drove to Stuttgart to see the old man's brother, who received me in the friendliest way. Little Marie came to meet me with a scream of joy! "Dear

Uncle! Here at last!" she said, clapping her hands. I took the dear little thing tenderly into my arms and pressed her little rose face to my lips. Everyone in the house was gay. In the afternoon I went outside to hire a coachman. The only one there had gone out. While he was being called I entertained myself with his daughter, a young and pretty girl who seemed to me so pious and well behaved that I found it impossible to avoid the notion that many ladies of my acquaintance should also have such qualities. In the evening I had to relate to the ladies of the house something of my trips to Italy and Sicily, which seemed to them extremely interesting. Before going to bed we had some more discussion with the Councillor concerning our own family genealogy, Württemberg affairs, the influence exercised on the country by the deceased queen, Livonia and Estonia, as well as the modern German *Zeitgeist*, so that eleven o'clock had struck before we parted. Little Maria sleeps near me; her little bed stands at the door. I believe I can even hear her breathing in the next room.

31 March, a little village near Waiblingen

Here we are at last, my darling Helene and I, cosily together as we used to be. We had a heartfelt reunion. At ten o'clock I went as agreed upon to The King of Württemberg, where she was supposed to come from the Court gardeners with whom she had been stopping. We had scarcely looked around us before flying into each other's arms. A stroll beyond the gate freed us from the inquisitive gaping crowds of idle passers-by, who made no bones about incommoding us. The midday hour went by only too swiftly. We had to part. Two seats for Nuremberg were hastily ordered for us on the diligence and a coachman hired who was to take us to Schorndorf, since the post carriage was not to leave until the following day. With the words, "At three I'll fetch you at the street corner", each one went his way. Before lunch my cousin showed me another private collection of paintings, including a dying Socrates by the good Wächter that is a great credit to him. At midday we drank to each other's

health and by three my girl and I were already sitting
pressed to each other in a close embrace in the carriage,
which soon brought us to Waiblingen, three hours away. Here
we left the old rattletrap and hopped off like two little goats
to Schorndorf, revelling in the beauties of nature. Towards
seven we arrived in a small village whose name I forget but
which will always remain unforgettable because of the blissful
night I spent there in the arms of my Helene. The two wide
beds. The amorous tussles. The *quod libet* in the morning . . .

1, 2, 3 April, Nuremberg

Three days of wearisome travelling! If the inns were
good you could at least rest as you should from these jouncing
and clattering carriages, but the inns make it even more
attractive to get into the wagons than to sit around in the
"barracks". Early in the morning of the 6th we dived below
water a few times like ducks in a pond and went off on foot
as far as Schorndorf, where we decided to wait for the post
carriage. The morning was fine; the sun was hot by nine
o'clock. Tired after a two-hour walk we arrived in Schorndorf at The Ox, where we ordered ourselves a *déjeuner à
la fourchette,** though it could just as well have been devoured
with pitchforks, there were such incredibly vast quantities of
it. By ten the diligence had bounced up. A herd of human
vermin popped out of it. The mere thought of it made my
head spin. Luckily I was able to win over the conductor,
and we got seats in the cabriolet *par sa protection*; we were
more than a little happy about it. After six months to be
in a post carriage again, and with a quasi-wife—how odd
our lives are! The company in the carriage didn't concern
us; we were quite sufficient for each other.

Outside Gmünd we passed by the Hohenstaufen, whose
ruins are scarcely visible any longer but which was once a
magnificent castle—the original seat of the emperors of the
German Reich. The region just around Gmünd is rough and
infertile. Outside Aalen, where we arrived during the night,

* A second breakfast popular at that time (Ed.).

the countryside was almost bare. The terrain must have been very elevated. There was a constant change in passengers after that. The night was horrible. The little one fell asleep on my lap exhausted. I saw nothing of Ellwangen. In Dinkelsbühl a pretty young brunette, accompanied by an elderly woman, got into the carriage. The breakfast was delicious. Helene did her toilette in the private parlour of the inn, which made me angry and she, in her turn, touchy. A few glances into the girl's character often give me a glimpse of something I would rather have ignored. But perhaps I was unfair to her. The future will show what she is, and whether she really loves me as much as she says.

We had lunch in Feuchtwangen. Beforehand I went for a long walk by myself. The meal was delicious. You can see pine forests and fir clusters everywhere in this region, especially in the direction of Ansbach; the forests remind you of Russia and Poland. The terrain is all fragmented; you travel up hill and down dale. Shortly outside Ansbach two ladies joined me as travelling companions; luckily they wanted to go only as far as the next station since one of them, an overdressed doll with repulsive features, started right off by saying that she had brought her undigested luncheon out to the carriage as a libation for the highway. I felt so depressed at this that I leaped out and started for Ansbach on foot, arriving there by sunset.

The first thing I did to familiarize myself with the city was to walk around it, looking at the grounds and the main buildings; towards eight I went to the post house, where I was received by Helene, the company, an out-of-tune piano, and soon afterwards a passable supper. By nine we were off again. I took the horse of the gendarme who was escorting us and rode along for five hours in the most magnificent moonlight. At the monastery* I got back into the coach and made myself very comfortable next to Helene until Nuremberg, where we arrived at four o'clock in the morning. The soft beds in The Wild Man at the post welcomed us eagerly,

* The famous Kloster Heilsbronn (Ed.).

our eyelids sank heavily; we woke at nine. We lounged about
in négligé until noon. I had my head shaved in the morning.
Perhaps that'll strengthen my thinning hair. At noon we
went out. We had taken on a funny old odd-job man who
was supposed to show us all the things in Nuremberg worth
seeing. This way we strolled along arm in arm towards the
castle. The tower guard there, a very comical old man, blew
us a few pieces on his alarm trumpet; he would have cut a
fine figure as a caricature of an archangel in the Apocalypse.
In the picture gallery of the old castle, which had once been
inhabited by the count of the castle and later belonged to
the Brandenburg line, we saw a number of first-class old
German pictures; I took a few sketches of them with me. In
the courtyard there stood a six-hundred-year-old tree trunk;
it had been planted over the grave of a Bavarian princess.
Our curator, a very sweet, humorous bachelor fifty to sixty
years old, livened the pictures up greatly with his lecture.
We went from the castle into the fine Bestelmaier shop,
where we looked at a number of pretty Nuremberg products
and also bought some—among others, a chess set, which,
since Helene can play, may be very useful to us.

In the Campe bookshop, where I went to get something
for the trip to Vienna, we made the acquaintance of the
head of the house, who received us with remarkable amiabi-
lity and whom I found to be a very humane and erudite
man. In the St. Lorenz church together with Helene, who
has a great deal of understanding of art and who expressed
a sound judgement on everything there, I admired the fine
construction of the nave and the splendid stained-glass
paintings. A frugal meal of three courses put an end to
the visit. At six we drove to the baths. The postmaster had
had his horses hitched, so we came up with a roll of trumpets
in front of the bathing house, where everyone looked out of
the window at the strange postal extras. We had a hearty
laugh. The baths were divided by a partition. Heavenly
jests, of a Triton and naiad style, made the time fly. The tea
afterwards was delicious. God Somnus took us soon after-

wards into his beneficent arms. Loving kisses conducted us while caressing each other into the sweet work of sleep.

4 April, Nuremberg

Early this morning we went to church. The sermon was very good indeed. We sat next to the postmaster's wife, who gave us a lot of talk that finally bored me. Beforehand we had listened to a Catholic preaching. As a Prince Hohenlohe, who wants to become a bishop, he should have done it better. In the St. Sebaldus church he showed us the holy tomb, a fine work of art in bronze, and a few excellent paintings. In the afternoon we drove out to Fürth, a rather large nest of Jews, where we had coffee and beer in the bosom of the postmaster's family; on the way back this gave me a dreadful colic that was only heightened by the pathetic jokes of young Hüter. The latter, a painter, though of very mediocre talents, took us to his studio, where everything looked like cabbage and turnips. I praised him in the usual way and took along a typical Madonna, which I liked very much. In the evening we played chess and read from Müller. Helene yawned the whole time.

5 April, Nuremberg

In the morning we went around the whole city. The weather was magnificent, the promenade quite long, for it was not until two that we came back for lunch; the soup was already cold. We spent the whole afternoon packing, teasing, and caressing each other.

Here, in a few words, is Helene's biography, taken from her own mouth:

Until her sixth year she had been brought up by her mother as though in a state of nature. In her seventh she lost her father, who had been fonder of her than of any of the other children. She soon went to a girls' school, where with her bright little mind she made rapid progress which evoked the favour of her superiors but also the envy of her fellow pupils. She had to suffer from envy more and more later because she became very pretty. This, as well as the severity of her mother and her older sisters, probably gave her this aversion to everything feminine, a masculinity that ever since that time may have struck deep roots in her mind. In the period of her loveliest blooming, during her confirmation at the age of fifteen, she had the misfortune to be seduced and dishonoured by a young wastrel who made her proposals of marriage. The remorse and the piercing pangs of conscience due to it now give her character such a marked form and bent that, as she often has said to me, it was shaped and solidified from that time on for the rest of her life. She began to hate the entire male sex and became morally—physically she no longer could—a very strict virgin again. After gaiety and a youthful love of life had returned to her, she lived for her duties, her permitted joys, and her ideals, but not for her own views, which did not develop until later and were ultimately to receive their confirmation. To be sure I never was granted the richest perfection in the possession and enjoyment of this girl of mine, for never is a girl more beautiful, glowing, and charming than she is as a virgin, in the very midst of her blossoming.

In her seventeenth year, after she had had a number of suitors, with the whole of the Heidelberg student body vying for her favours while she laughed inwardly and played out her little comedies and intrigues at the expense of the young fools, a letter called her to Munich (her mother had some business interests there). Among strangers, surrounded by temptations of all kinds, and even fought for by the King and the Crown Prince, she remained true to herself and to her principles, took care of her mother's business, and went by herself from Munich to Vienna to an uncle who kept her in his house for three months. Here, too, there was no lack of trials and snares for the young girl, since she had educated herself meanwhile and had become more beautiful than ever; but after she had withstood everything, she had aroused the jealousy of her aunt and had reached the bold decision to leave the house rather than continue as a burden on her uncle. She went back alone to Heidelberg, where she

could not find enough repose either at home or in her whole
way of life. Unhappy because of some setback, she found
herself vegetating in solitude rather than living. Then she
saw me and *had* to start loving again. This sounds very pre-
sumptuous, but that is really how it was and no other way.

Helene is beautiful, young, amiable, of an engaging,
natural, and easy appearance, an enemy of all constraint;
she embraces freedom, justice, and virtue with an ardent
spirit. Exalted above people's talk, beyond the spirit of the
workaday world, she follows the impulse of her spirit, a
pure creation of God and nature. This gives her whole
being something original, something masculine, which is
radiated in everything and makes her misunderstood by
others. Faithful and constant as steel in the fire, spon-
taneously clever and wise, she knows how to bring the
rough and the soft sides of her nature into harmonious
accord, a fine mixture in word and deed. Very well educated,
adorned by talents, averse to vanity and primping, a lover
of domestic bonds and children, full of love for her mother
and brothers and sisters, capable of the wildest flights of
love but at the same time chaste, she remains for me, while
not an enigma, still a unique being, composed of contrasts
and of constant novelty.

6 April, Daswang

Here we sit, the runaway daughter and I, the seduced
and seducer (a second lost son), in this little village, upstairs
in the warm little room and do whatever love and imagination inspire us to. Today, like every day of this splendid trip,
was intoxicating; I was embraced at every step by Helene's
full white arms and her ardent love. By seven the carriage
was already standing in front of the house. It was very
rough as far as Feucht, a market town. The sun was incapable of mastering the clouds. Lovely dark-green pine
forests—very like the Lithuanian regions. A glance like this
into the past and into my old military life hurts me more than
it helps; it made the moment grim and melancholy for me.

We got out several times today and went walking. Helene can be childlike after all and can leap about and play like a kid goat, but I took joyful note as well of her taut attention as I spoke to her of scientific subjects and saw her religious feeling unfolding as I praised the Christian religion. The girl is very dear to me, but I feel very anxious about her future. Yet she has principles; that's a great deal. We lunched in Neumarkt, a little town. The house gables and the whole tone of the town were in contrast with the little towns of southern Bavaria. Bavarian soldiery, good horses and men. Strict discipline. In the afternoon we were drawn by resounding trumpet blasts to a corner of the town where tightrope walkers were delighting a gaping multitude. Little children were being misused in this, and we were filled with anxiety, fear and pity for the children. We let them go through their profitless, neck-breaking arts, then got into the chaise that was awaiting us and after a six-hour drive arrived here by sunset. The character and the look of Upper Bavaria are quite different from Lower Bavaria. The costumes, the style of the buildings, the region, everything has an originality of its own. But by and large I find the people happy, the spirit of the constitution mild, the government wise, and the Bavarians themselves peaceful and good-natured. They are not, it is true, very intelligent, but they have a sort of bonhomie and loyalty that are very appealing. Rough, sensual, harsh, but faithful—such are their qualities. And the people have always maintained their isolation since bygone ages.

7 April, Regensburg

God, what divine nights we spend with each other! I shall never forget them. It was not until morning that we fell asleep. The coachman awoke us early. It was piercingly cold. We ran on ahead a good half hour to get warm, and with the increasing warmth in the carriage we also got livelier. The coachman told us all sorts of merry little anecdotes, which sometimes came off rather heavily but amused us a great deal anyhow. Towards eleven we caught sight of the lovely Danube valley, which stretches out magnificently from the west down to the plain behind Regensburg. The city lies to the right. There are a great many ancient towers. A very old bridge took us across the Danube, which we greeted very affably, and on to the other bank, where we stopped off at The Emperor of Austria inn. We had a magnificent view from the window. The luncheon was delicious. Afterwards we took a little nap; after the nap we went into the city and visited the cathedrals, where we heard some very good music. Later we went out of the gate and took a look at the surroundings of the city. Sunset on the bridge. In the evening we played chess. Tea was bad. There's no wine at all in all Upper Bavaria, and if you see any occasionally in the taverns you just leave it there. Rhine wine is a completely different matter as far as I'm concerned; even in Roman times they used to say: *"vinum Rhenense decus est et Gloria Mensae."*

8 April, Maundy Thursday, Regensburg

We're both making good resolutions, but that's all it comes to. At 9.30 I had a scene with Helene I'll never forget. We'd had a quarrel about a letter I demanded to read. She flew into a rage and threatened to run off. I begged her to. She really did go and left me waiting in the most painful anxiety for five hours. Towards two, after I'd already eaten, she came back, soberly begging me to forgive her after all. At first I put on a look as though I were indignant, and as though after such a catastrophe we would have to part. This impressed her so much that she fell sobbing at my feet and begged me with tears in her eyes only to love her again. For some minutes I played this hard-hearted and unyielding role. Finally I appeared to give in. We were reconciled and sealed our renewed alliance with an *amoroso* on the bed. At four we visited Kepler's[*]

[*] Johannes Kepler, founder of the new astronomy, died in Regensburg in 1630 (Ed.).

tomb and the promenade. Sunk in thought, I spent some time over the bones of the great astronomer who had been the first to discover the laws of gravitation and of the celestial bodies and the movements of the planets, who introduced some concepts into the system of the universe, who was overshadowed by Newton, and who is now misunderstood. Ah, if only there were such a man alive now, one who could permeate himself with Hegel's logic, what a work that would make!

At ten, the Lord in our hearts, we went to church. We were given seats of honour. The sermon was good, though it left me cold. But the organ playing and the singing put me into a devout mood. I nodded to Helene, and we approached the chalice and the Host. Not without emotion we went home, where we embraced in tears. We had made a sensation; our name was enquired. We were somewhat embarrassed. We decided to leave. There was a ship lying nearby on the Danube. We asked where it was going, and when the skipper said Vienna, we arranged for him to take us along. To go home, pack, pay, and leave were the work of but a moment. In half an hour we were in each other's arms sitting on the topside foredeck watching Regensburg slip into the distance and the banks rush by. There were a large number of workmen, I think about sixty. They had a cabin to themselves. In our own there were some students from Tübingen and Erlangen and some Austrians. It was six hours from Regensburg to Pfatter, the village where we spent the night. The Danube was very wide there, the banks flat. With our picturesque travel book in our hand and ensconced on the foredeck, we scarcely noticed the coarse antics of the young workmen, who often became very loud and filthy. Two nuns sitting forward on the little ship attracted us by their serene, devout bearing. My wife, for that was how she passed everywhere, approached them. The acquaintance left little to be desired. The nuns with their little ward, a girl of eight, became dearer and dearer to us. Helene attached herself to the good women with deep feeling.

The sunset was beautiful. But finally it became quite

chilly, so we wrapped the little one up in my grey coat. Shivering, we arrived in the village. The ship cast out its passengers. Yodelling away, the workmen flooded the village, billowing up and down through it in swarms. Everywhere doors were slammed in their faces. Finally we found some space in the post house, where we were delighted to land. The moon had risen. After we had eaten supper and gone to our little room, we leaned out of the window and before going to sleep looked out at majestic nature. The stars twinkled magnificently above us. Embracing blissfully, we went to bed. Before I forget I must copy the following out of an old Regensburg chronicle I got hold of somewhere, written in archaic German; it's very characteristic. It's in a very special, strong, and energetic language. The old Germans did have something in the construction of language and in their images that was unaffectedly natural and that is completely missing in our own modern, overelaborate writers. The very modern ones want to be a 100 per cent German, but it's no longer the way it was with Luther, Melanchthon, etc. This was what I read in this old topographical handbook of 1721 about the national character of the Germans:

The way the old Germans and the inhabitants of Germany used to be can be read in the old chronicles, that they were industrious, upright, honourable, ardent in warfare, mistrustful, and zealous in their faith, easily won over by money, good friends, open enemies, very disposed to eat and drink, and quick-witted in the mechanical arts, excellent students of nature, remarkable amateurs of the most beautiful rarities, very great chemists, so that the discovery of powder, the casting of cannon, the etching of copper, and the printing of paper must be credited to them. But above all they loved freedom, and indeed to such a degree that they would never endure a leader over them, except when war came, whereupon they would choose one among them who excelled the others in bravery and sagacity. Therefore Charlemagne could never tame the rebellious spirit of his oppressed Germans, and so he said of the German soldiers: "A well-ordered army must have an Italian head, Spanish shoulders, and a German breast and heart."

Chapter II

AN AMOROUS EXCURSION ON
THE DANUBE

10 April

Early in the morning, at four, the skipper woke us. Kisses, *quod libet* in the room. We invited the nuns in for coffee. Departure. Everyone looked for a place below-decks in the cabin. Helene made the acquaintance of a woman from Straubing, I of her husband. The woman overflowed in tears as she thought back over her gloomy life. The husband was intelligent and full of erudite conversation. By chance I turned to a young man who outwardly looked like a young workman but whom I later discovered to be an intelligent student and Hegelian. I was delighted. A lengthy conversation that continued as far as Straubing, where we stopped. We all went into the town together, looked at the church, and finally met in The Grape. Breakfast, and farewell to the good Straubingers; Helene's jealousy because of the one nun I paid court to as hard as I could. A reconciliation. Departure in the afternoon.

The half day spent on the Danube from Straubing to Windorf was magnificent. The air was lukewarm, the region majestic. The Bohemian mountains and the Bavarian forests extend in an endless chain along the left bank of the Danube and make a splendid contrast with the built-up and radiant right bank, which though it remains flat never wearies the eye. You see picturesque villages and monasteries appearing on both sides, passing by, disappearing. A multitude of castles look resplendent on the left bank, the haughty

Nattern mountain towering over them. The whole chain of mountains, where one mountain nestles next to the other, accords the gaze a limitless number of beautiful prospects. Near Deggendorf the mountain chain comes down as far as the Danube. The little town is so romantically situated that Helene jubilantly called to me, "Just look, how beautiful that is; this is where I'd like to live and die with you." Towards evening it became even more beautiful if that is possible. Everything was love and life in nature, around us and in us. Even the ship people seemed to enjoy it, for some of them sang edifying songs, others stared in tranquil wonder at the magnificent setting sun. Helene was ecstatic. An emotional meal, of eggs, with the nuns. Much first-rate laughing and joking. A scene at night with the Austrian Policinello,* whom I threatened to kick all the way downstairs. Helene's vexation at not being able to be with me.

11 April

Cool this morning. The Isar River. A pretty valley near Passau. Vilshofen. The Danube narrows here and flows swiftly between two charming chains of hills. The region gets more and more romantic, the mountains more and more jagged, until lovely Passau opens up to the enchanted eye of the traveller. We landed here at nine. The situation of the city is charming beyond all description. We got ready at once and strolled about the place. It was Sunday; everything was all cleaned up, the streets, the main church, and the parade square where the Bavarian army band had assembled in front of the governor's house to play some lovely symphonies and waltzes. Helene was delighted. At twelve we went to the tavern, where we had a fine meal; we also found a piano that amused us enormously. In the afternoon we went to the Danube again and waited for the signal to leave, which, however, wasn't given for a long time, since most of the passengers were still missing. Meanwhile I chatted with an old burgher who told me a great

* Nickname for a policeman, from the Italian (Ed.).

many sensible things about Bavaria. By four we were sitting cosily together again, Helene and I, singing and chatting away about everything under the sun. The nuns had already gone; a pity. The evening was quite warm. We gradually neared the Austrian border. The banks became more and more picturesque and the current more and more powerful. The Danube constantly twists between the high forested mountain chains that run closer and closer together. Far to the right two shattered fortresses rise up that picturesquely dominate the Danube. At Riedel Castle you can see the High Stone in the Danube that divides Bavaria from Austria. Close behind the mountain, in a fertile spot, lies the first little Austrian village, Engelhartszell, well known for its poll tax and its customs duties.

We revived ourselves in a little village inn in the customs building after we had put everything on the ship in safe keeping; we got a tidy room with a balcony overlooking the Danube. We were more than a little happy at having made our escape so well. The young workmen (each one had to pass the cordon with his pack on his back and his passport in his hand) had besieged a tavern, which was finally taken by actual storm. The sight of Austrian blue and green coats made a disagreeable impression on me. The meal and the evening were delicious. The evening and the night in Engelhartszell belong among the few divine moments I have enjoyed in my fluctuating voyage through life. Helene was all love, all ardour. Merry, blissful little jokes brought on the twelfth hour. Coupled, we lay stretched out in the soft bed, that chamber of joys, that tomb of all longing, and with united effort and delight extinguished the flames. It was only from such pleasure that Muhammad's fiery imagination, born in Arabia's burning air, could have taken the idea of paradise that promises his followers eternal bliss. I shudder to the marrow at the thought of how mankind often degrade to the level of a base lure for vulgar lechery the sweetest and most sacred thing on earth, blaspheming it beneath their feet, and flinging this divine sustenance to the dogs. Ah, if only I had always had pleasure such as this!

12 April, Linz

At seven in the morning the maid, all too early, awoke us. It was only with difficulty that we unwound ourselves out of the warm nest that had become an altar to Aphrodite. What a jump! I had to go to the customs and to the police. My first step was to the police station. The police chief enquired very casually after Helene and asked with some emphasis why she hadn't appeared herself. I had to go and call her. The poor girl seemed embarrassed. I suffered for her. But she soon took heart and came along. Everything was arranged. Next the customs official was courted so that our things might pass easily. He was an Italian. I spoke to him in his mother tongue. This seemed to impress him, and he became accommodating; he was careless in looking through our things, and the examination had a happy ending. The ship and our good Heilbronner were to lie at the customs until the following morning. It was a victory for me; I hired a small boat and decided to go on ahead. I suprised Helene, who was waiting for me with longing, with the happy news that everything had been got through all right, and that we were to go on to Linz at once. A frugal breakfast was devoured. M. Salvator was saluted, and off we went, rocked on the dancing waves of the Danube in a skiff the size of two shoes, on our way to today's destination. I'll never forget that voyage. It couldn't have been more original. Our old friend Heilbronner shook his head doubt-fully when he saw us with all our cases getting into the fragile little boat, which needed no more than a push to turn over or fall apart. We nodded our heads to each other in farewell and swift as an arrow the boat flew off. Engel-hartszell soon vanished. Below Hofkirchen, where the mountains close in and make a beautiful, dark river valley that goes on as far as Aschach, the Danube darts ahead so swiftly that no horse at its most heated gallop would have been capable of overtaking us. The Reinach and Marsbach castles, the villages of Obermühl and Untermühl are situated divinely; the region is incomparably beautiful; the picturesque cliffs and the sombre pines that adorn them so colourfully give the whole valley a shiveringly grim air. We enjoyed it all with our eyes and hearts. Helene's little head was pillowed on my shoulder, my right arm embraced her caressingly. Truly, the Danube became our Lethe, for we forgot the past to revel in the sweet present. With the sinking sun the shadows in the valley grew longer. At every moment the silvery serpentine ribbon of the Danube took another twist and we were surprised by another new and unexpected view.

We landed, and I filled my pipe. Meanwhile Helene was plucking cowslips that were blossoming along the slope of a hill in motley abundance. We also sang little songs of joy; in short, everything in and around us was love and pleasure. I was often obliged to think of situations I had read about so often in novels in which a loving couple, escaped from the Argus eyes of strict parents or relatives, sought their salvation in flight; or of the mythological fable of the first ship's voyage. Goethe's little song of the waves rang out as we went on to Aschach in full awareness of the beneficent sensations of the moment; there an unexpected spectacle of nature, grasping all our attention, turned our sweet oblivion into high tension. Even before we came to the little town we should have noticed a broad plain, but we had been looking at each other so intimately, and kissing each other so long, that when we looked up, still thinking we were in the dark valley, we actually gave vent to an outright shout of joy at seeing everything around us changed so suddenly and so strangely.

The narrow Danube valley had just opened up, and the Danube, broadening out and forming several islands covered over by very youthful greenery, lost itself in a lovely plain that was wreathed by a bluish mountain chain in the shape of an amphitheatre. The mountains divided right and left into two arms, and, rounding off and crowning the beautiful landscape, the Steier and Salzburg mountains, covered with glittering snow, rose high up, but as high as the sky, in an endless line and in a grey-blue form that reminded me of the Swiss Alps. This natural scene moved us mightily.

Helene and I, at first dumb with emotion and amazement, embraced tenderly, and with alternating interjections of mounting rapture we sang the praises of this lofty moment of our happiness, the panorama we were surrounded by, and our receptivity to such joys.

Aschach has the look of an Italian town, for its monasteries and churches and flat roofs give it a wholly southern appearance. For another hour it was still light. The setting sun tinted the lovely skies a brilliant colour. At Gnadental, where Calvary Mount seems to raise its grotesque masses of stone out of the torrents of the Danube, the banks become jagged and sharp again. We were surrounded by sacred darkness. It was cool. My girl crouched down on the floor of the skiff between my feet, wrapped up in my grey campaign cloak; so we plashed on as far as Linz, where we arrived about eight. I left the little one in the care of the skipper, went into the city to look for a roof for us, and nearby on the bank I found the tavern, The Eagle. Soon we were upstairs in our little room, which suited us very well indeed. In half an hour a frugal supper was steaming on the table, and in less than twenty minutes our kindred limbs, entwining each other, were throbbing in the warm little bed that in spite of the somewhat unclean neighbourhood soon made us forget this as well as the whole world.

13 April, Linz

In the morning we went downstairs; view of the Danube; intimate letters home. Promenade in and around Linz. Austrian paper money. The pretty situation of the city, the bridge. The spreading young green of the trees. Walk to the church. The Linz helmets. Lunch—a fine Tyrolean wine. A long evening promenade—the beau monde in the streets. We caused a bit of a sensation. Helene especially attracted the glances of the men. Magnificent air, very pretty Linz girls and women. We went to the theatre: *Hedwig, or the Bandits' Bride*, by Körner, very badly given. The public's mediocre taste. Austrian officers bore me. Supper.

14 April

Lend me your pens, oh Goethe, Herder, and you too, Holtei and Gleim, that I may give a worthy description of the most beautiful day of my voyage! Lend me the palette of your fantasy, inspire me, Jean Paul, instruct me, Friedrich Kind, show me, amiable Matthisson,* how I can recount it, that day, that blissful day that is worth 365 of its brothers!

The young day greeted me this morning with a friendly smile. As I woke up, hesitatingly, my first glance fell on the rosy girl whose eyelids were still shut, whose lovely cheeks were covered with the enchanting flush of Aurora. The sight swiftly drew me out of the realm of sleep-drugged dreams into that of a sweet reality. To leap up, to go over to her bed breathing softly, and to draw her into life and my arms with kisses—were these like the children of the moment. Opening her precious eyes, looking at me in tender questioning, winding her warm soft arms around my neck, and wishing me a friendly "Good morning"—all were a sympathetic response to the moment.

The maid, knocking with the coffee at the door, separated us inseparables. I leaped into my dressing gown, she into her négligé, and there we were, sitting very demurely at the coffee table like an old married couple. "But we must pack our things today, darling Helene," I said caressingly, and instantly the obedient girl was on the floor arranging

---

* Johann Gottfried von Herder (1744–1803), philosopher and man of letters; Karl von Holtei (1798–1880), poet, novelist, playwright; Johann Wilhelm Ludwig Gleim (1719–1803), poet; Johann Friedrich Kind (1768–1843), novelist and dramatist; Friedrich von Matthisson (1761–1831), lyric poet, all German (Ed.).

with her delicate fingers the pressed laundry, the clothes, the books, so that looking at her with pleasure and desire I had to fall on her neck and thank her heartily.

"But give me your Diary today, as you promised me long ago. You will give it me, won't you?" And she obediently handed me the pages dictated by love and honesty. I read and read, and had to read more and more attentively, for a great deal of our relationship was becoming crystal clear to me, so many lovely flowers of her rich and sensitive heart were unfolding themselves with clarity in my own being. "You treasure!" I involuntarily cried out, after finishing this friendly kiss of a faithful soul.

Then we really did abandon ourselves to talking, caressing, reminiscing, dreaming of the Spanish castles of a misty future and of all sorts of things at a lively pace, until the maid surprised us once again by coming in with the lunch we had thought still a long way off. Never, as far back as I can recall, did a meal taste so good as it did today. The sweet Tyrolean wine loosened our hearts and tongues, already loosened, still further, and four o'clock arrived before we had any idea of the time. "But Helene, just look out of the window! Isn't the weather delicious? Let's go up there, up, d'you see, up that magnificent Kapellenberg," I cried. "With joy," was the answer. No sooner said than done. In a quarter of an hour we were already at the bridge. At the coffee house to the right we ate some ice cream. The air was cool. I had taken along supplies for a two-hour hike; our hearts were laughing away; Mother Nature was blooming splendidly all around us.

The walk up was a walk to Paradise. The gentle green of budding shade trees playing with the darker shady pines in alternating colours, the majestic view of the Danube below, of the plain, of the city built in terraces, of the titanic snow mountains of the Austrian Tyrol, the clear skies, the winding way, the musical chorus in the shrubbery, the sprouting blossoms on the path—in short, everything, everything aided our most splendid mood. Chatting gaily on edifying topics we clambered up the high and jagged mountain. Though no Parnassus or Olympus, nevertheless it became our mountain of Muses and gods; for with the classical anthology of German literature in my pocket, with our sense of the beautiful in our hearts, and with the excellent wine we had drunk in the bright and friendly tavern up near the church, this became for us the most divine of all divine mountains. Drunk with joy we camped on its sunny slope and laved ourselves in a view such as could hardly be found in Germany. The calendar from Aachen decided that. We read Schlegel's *Elegy on Rome*, Goethe's *Landlust*, Schiller's *Bell*, and some other fitting poems that kindled and inflamed the heavenly fire of enchantment in our souls. Had I only had a spark of Schiller's art in me I should have finished an elegy that evening that would have entranced and charmed gentle poetic souls. My good Helene joined me in my ecstasy with fresh and lively sympathy, thus embellishing the exalted moment of this spiritualized pleasure.

As the sun set I led my girl down towards the valley. Soon we were surrounded by a magical dusk. Everything around us floated in a half-light—and we in ecstasy. Such are the moments that are sealed with eternal signatures and passages of love. Trembling with desire we hastened into a nearby pine grove, which became the canopy for our sweet longings. Never shall I forget this precious spot—and should my destiny ever lead me again through Linz I shall devote to the God of Love and his holy Mother a thanksgiving on that very place, an offering brought out of a faithful heart. Serene but rich in thoughts of beautiful cast, we went home. The blissful day was completed by devout wishes for the duration of our happiness. Yes, kindly Creator of the Universe, only ten such days in the year and I'll close a life contract with Thee for ever!

15 April, Sarbling

If yesterday was marvellous today was no less so, for the trip on the Danube from Linz here was romantic beyond all description. At eleven the boat we had hired was to depart. We soon finished packing. At the police, where a boorish *commissaire* asked Helene all sorts of insidious questions that embarrassed her, I got annoyed; my annoyance was heightened upon coming to the bank, where we could no longer see the boat. It was gone, but it couldn't have gone a long way off so quickly. We found another boat, flung our things into it and with vigorous oar work went after the receding boat! We caught up with it by Neustadt, and grappled with it like real pirates; we had to bargain with the one sailor on it, and finally we settled ourselves in the boat, where we found a Tyrolean girl we knew who favoured us with the most delightful songs. The skipper and his companions were born Salzburgers, all of them splendid chaps.

As far as Stein, a pleasant town where we later had lunch, the right bank of the Danube is flat, but in the distance you can see the enchanting Linz mountains; Spielberg Castle with its crumbling walls, surrounded by high pines, looms up as a beautiful memorial of ancient history. Many communities, smaller and larger, extend along the Danube, among which the little town of Enns stands out to special advantage. The industry in the region is said to prosper to a very considerable degree. Near Neustadt the mountains begin rising again and become wilder and wilder until the bed of the river around Grein gets so narrow that the water often lashes out violently. The cliffs around here are almost vertical; aligned and tangent they often make the most grotesque and haphazard shapes. From here the boat shot off like a whirlwind out on to the dancing waves, surrounded by the most magnificent groups of cliffs, passed the market town of Sturm, and moved towards the whirlpool that raging and storming received us at the island of Wörth, a frightful mass of rock to the left of the Hausstein.

Meanwhile evening fell. The region grew more and more bloodcurdling; the light of the dying day grew paler and duller until we were enveloped by the black and uncanny darkness. Helene and I had sat almost all afternoon on top of the foredeck, sufficient unto ourselves, and the evening gradually surprised us in our intimate caresses. My heroic little girl had overweeningly mocked the perils of the water, which we had, to be sure, eluded without any particular good luck, and so had offended the sprite of the Danube, who might still revenge herself on us for it, as I laid it down to Helene. She laughed at me heartily. But if ever a water nymph dwelt in the depths of the Danube, she would surely have had to have her dwelling place here, for this region stands out above all the others we've passed through for its fearful and beautiful wildness.

We landed late, after eight. A friendly inn on the water's edge received us. We had first-rate beds and after a glance into the dark Danube valley, brightly lit up by the moon, we sank exhausted into our pillows and slept well.

16 April, Tulln

We had scarcely arrived when we had to leave again. My girl and I decided to go on today to Schönbrunn, which is six hours away, and there devote ourselves for a few days to rural life before being surrounded by the rigid obligations of the city and its wearisome inhabitants. The trip here along the Danube was splendid in the morning, but in the afternoon rather monotonous. As far as Krems and the Göttweig monastery, which you can see proudly resplendent on a mountain, the region is extremely romantic. The Danube flows swiftly in countless bends and turns through beautiful picturesque mountains that delight eye and heart. The young greenery, in contrast with the darkness of the pines, rejoices the former, and the beauty of the total view and its enjoyment the latter. Helene had remained below; I had gone up to the foredeck. When I came back I saw at her side, and very nicely courting her, the young Salzburg student we had met the day before. She seemed to be taking pleasure in accepting his attention offered up like incense. I joked about it; we had all sorts of affinities and with my wife's permission I installed my friend as her devoted page; she accepted his services with an indulgent smile.

We had our lunch in Stein, which looks quite Italian. Helene, who takes great pleasure in every child she sees and has to repress sighs of longing whenever she sees one, had a conversation at the table with the couple running the tavern that interested her very much; since they both had had a lot of children and also pitied our barren marriage, in good Austrian fashion they gave us the means to see to it that we had numerous progeny. In this, all sorts of confidences and marital secrets came to light that greatly amused us. At three we boarded the wooden boat again and taking our places in the space below soon took a siesta *a due voce* that lasted until 4.30. The young page proved very gallant vis-à-vis "my wife", tirelessly arranging pillows for her and gazing at her with deep emotion. She might well take his fancy.

At 6.30 we arrived here. A coachman was soon hired to take us to Schönbrunn for ten florins, and the little Steier carriage soon loaded with our things. Parting from the Salzburg Adonis was very painful for my Helene. She gave him a kiss, which to be sure I had no reason to object to, but which was too hearty and too intense.

17 April, Mariahilf, outside Vienna

At the goal of our voyage, but at the same time on the point of parting from Helene, I stand here like a dreamer to whom past, present, and future appear as cast-off cloth, who cannot master his own feelings, to whom the removal of his beloved gives torment, anxiety, and concern, and who as he stands consolingly at her side is himself in need of consolation. I complain and appear to forget that this earthly existence is no more than a shadow play which, with the appearance of the light (Death), returns to the ultimate source of Being. Then seize courage and take what life offers you; find in pain a source of joy, and in joy a foretaste of eternal life; remember that you are nothing, and that only He to Whom you belong is everything, and that He, not you, is the guide of your destiny!

Only one more night of bliss in the arms of your Helene remains to you, you fool. Tomorrow, when she has been taken from you and you are alone in the great alien city, will be time enough for you to mourn your loss and become fond of mourning. Through night and mist, whirled along by two swift horses, we flew through the distance that still separated Tulln and Schönbrunn. Midway we had to get out because of a steep mountain and continue on foot. It was very windy and the footpath full of stones. We stumbled at every moment; but these hardships were endured; there was something adventurous and romantic about them that made us more gay than annoyed. We arrived at a tavern at the last station outside Vienna, where the coachman and we as well drank a little wine and devoured an egg cake.

Towards twelve we finally arrived in Schönbrunn. Everything was silent; not a light could be seen. Where could we stop, where could we spend the night? The fool in the driver's seat, a real numskull, was completely baffled; I, who was less at home than he, went striding in and around Schönbrunn looking for a little nest for us both, but in vain; after some searching back and forth we had to go back to the village, where to my considerable joy I noticed a light still shining in a house. I knocked, a nightcap made its appearance, and when we asked where an inn might be found, indicated a house standing opposite. Full of impatience I knocked there; the gates opened and a dog barking with fury, a real Cerberus, hurled itself at us; then a growling servant gave us the consoling information that he had nothing left for us, but that in the first village outside Vienna we would surely find some place to stay.

We turned around, and our coachman, who even before had not seemed to be in the most jovial of moods, reacted strongly to the house servant's grumpy reception; he used all sorts of disagreeable language. In the village there was more knocking, complaining, begging, asking, until finally a constable pointed out a corner tavern on the left that also opened up after lengthy cursing. A couple of half-naked Jews came out towards us and welcomed us, each one in his own way, with edifying words that brought the blood to my face in rage. But I had to make the best of a bad bargain, otherwise there would have been no place to stay for the night. I spoke to them nicely, the draughty carriage and the horses were taken in; we were shown into the general guest room and given permission to sit down until the waiter and waitress had been awakened. All this took place in the dark; raven black though it was in the room we had just entered, it was quite clear who was living there and what interesting company was there. Our noses and ears were the first to make the acquaintance of the rabble sleeping there. "The Devil!" cried Helene. "What the hell!" I cursed. "Now then, now then, just let the gentleman shut the door and be quiet, otherwise we can't sleep." "Just shut your mouth," I said, "else I'll shut it for you!" "That's the thanks we get for letting him in," gurgled someone else. "The gentleman is making himself as comfortable as though he'd come in at noon." And so on it went.

Fear alone made me hold my nose with one hand and one ear with the other. I should have been delighted to have still a third hand available to hold my other ear, which was forced to become the target of words it gladly would not have heard. I went out to see the waitress, whom the servant had probably, out of respect, not awakened with sufficient energy, and drummed such a tune on her glass pane that it almost shattered. But I could hear only half words muttered by a thick tongue. "But for heaven's sake, the people there are all drunk!" I cried, beside myself with fury. "Don't know nothing about it, your grace," was the yawn from inside. The Beelzebubs there, and the whole tavern, were such that I ordered the hesitant coachman to hitch the horses up again at once so that we could go on into the city. Meanwhile a candle stump had appeared to illuminate the scene of all the people sleeping there on the straw in manifold groups. Helene burst out laughing at the sight, and I had to laugh along in spite of myself. We were very happy to get out of the place.

We passed the boundary of the city without any trouble; there was no examination, which pleased us both very much. At 1.30 we came to The Cross, an inn in the suburbs, where after long-drawn-out knocking and futile appeals we were turned away. A rest house for seafaring people and workmen was still left. This was also looked into, since we couldn't stay in the street. A sullen servant opened up for us and instead of a room showed us a little space on some straw, then placidly went away again. I would have had none of this, but Helene, who had behaved with extraordinary heroism throughout all the hardships of the journey, remained true to herself now too and said she could make herself perfectly comfortable on the straw; it was only natural for me to share her opinion by now.

I made our bed there with humility and patience; we had to share the place with a dozen sleeping burghers who were snoring horribly and also behaving in a rather ill-bred way with each other; the light was blown out, I moved closer to my darling and tried to sleep. But the girl's electrifying proximity turned the straw pallet into a bed of roses for me and delusively conjured up joys that could happen only in a more comfortable resting place. I had already flung my arms around her, and confused zigzagging thoughts chased one another through my inflamed mind; I heard four o'clock strike, then five; I leaped to my feet and went into the open courtyard where the rosiness of dawn was beginning to break through the half-light everywhere. After lingering easily half an hour there in the cool, I felt better, crept back, and caught sight of a sleeping group that made my hair stand on end. Like a beautiful creature from another world by contrast, the darling girl lay stretched out there looking like a Madonna among caricatures. I asked myself, Should I wake her or not? Yes, for later these fellows will gawk at this jewel and smirk in their bestial way about her enchanting position. Up, up, and about, my child, the sun is on the rise! We must away! And so saying I lifted up the sleep-intoxicated girl and took her out of the tavern into the street.

Yesterday's coachman was awakened, and we ventured into the suburb to look for lodgings. Just where are we? I asked the passers-by. In Mariahilf,* they said. "Oh help us, Mary!" I cried out bitterly. "For eight hours we've been like the most wretched nomads and still we have no shelter! Where is there a place to stop near by?" I asked again. "Over there, here, there," they all said; but there was none anywhere. Finally some friendly fellow took pity on us, and in spite of our savage appearance took us in at the post house. At The Three Hooves. The coachman had been cursing horribly and had wanted to throw all our things out on the ground half a dozen times, but I set things right again; he was paid and the bags were brought in. We were altogether happy when we looked at each other again in the room. Helene was gayer than I. She washed me, combed my hair, and busily made war on my blackheads, and she did it all with such pleasure and liveliness that I began to feel well again and blissful.

Meanwhile the coffee appeared. I dressed and decided to go into the city on a reconnaissance. But we agreed that we would still stay together that day. With tender emotion I left my girl. When I came to the canal surrounding the inner city the view of Vienna struck me to such a degree that in spite of myself I was obliged to stand in amazement. The tower of St. Stephen's, a titanic work of the mighty and grim Middle Ages, rose up magnificently above the city, which seemed aligned with it as the focal point. At first I was unable to make out its construction very well from a distance. Curiosity lent wings to my stride. Kärntner Street, which I walked up, was full of life and announced to me the fact that this was a brilliant capital. Well-dressed ladies and gentlemen, glittering carriages; when I came to St.

* German for "Mary's Help" (Ed.).

Stephen's Square and saw this gigantic building with its filigree tower in front of me, I gaped in astonishment. From there I went to the Graben, the main rendezvous of the Viennese beau monde, which was billowing around the shops in noisy little groups.

It was my intention to look for lodgings at once, in order to escape subjection to the expensive life in the hotels that is so injurious to the purse and so *ennuyeux*. There were some good lodgings, I had heard, in Leopoldstadt. I went to look there; all in vain; there were, to be sure, a few places to be had there, but there was nothing for me. They were either too tiny or too big, too shabby or too elegant. Exhausted from all the running around I started back, buying on the way a hat and gloves, which I needed badly, and finally with much questioning I reached At The Three Hooves, where I found Helene sad and in the midst of suppressed tears. "Why are you weeping so, my darling?" I said caressingly. "Oh dear, I'm to leave you and go to relatives who really don't like me. The lovely times we had on the trip—they'll never come back again. And soon I won't see you again either. You're going away from Vienna and leaving me, and I, poor miserable me, will never be able to have a child of yours, which I've been imploring Heaven for so longingly." The moving naïveté of her lamentation drew my sympathy into the realm of melancholy, and for a long time we sat there embracing each other until the charming and accommodating waitress brought in our lunch. Afterwards we had a substantial siesta and when the clock struck 6.30 we set out refreshed and vigorous for the opera, where we wanted to spend the evening. *Camilla** was well put on. Happy and gay we went off to supper.

Now the sweet thing is lying there, looking at hesitant me with inviting eyes.

* Opera by Fernando Paër (1771–1839) (Ed.).

Chapter III

CONFUSIONS IN VIENNA

2 May, Vienna

I've already spent fourteen days in this proud imperial city and I still haven't written down in my Diary a single word about myself or the things I'm surrounded by. I could really fall out with myself, but that's how it is whenever you get your bearings and begin living in a capital city and finding your way about. Where can I begin? With myself, or with Vienna? I think to myself: everyone knows best. And so, my dear Monsieur Boris, be so kind as to march on.

My first concern was to equip myself for a city—that is, to buy a round hat and pair of boots—then to bring my sweet Helene to her uncle, to report to Clary, and to look for private lodgings. It took only three hours to take care of everything. My toilette was soon done, and my girl was taken with her things to her uncle at the war building, where I took a tender farewell of her. I sent Clary a little note, and she at once convoked me to the Joseph II statue and welcomed me most warmly. And I finally rented charming rooms on a courtyard in the Kärntner Street, No. 1138 at Madame Remnez's, for forty florins—brisk and businesslike, as an old soldier should be. At M. Hennig's, where I was given a most affable reception, I found letters from home, from Heidelberg, and also from Dresden waiting for me. My aunt reproached me for having gone on to Vienna instead of to her and complained that my servant Peter was being a nuisance. An answer suitable to the somewhat impudent content of this letter was composed and sent.

The first three days I was very busy just seeing, hearing, taking things in, and generally looking around. Towards the evening of the fourth, to my considerable astonishment, Helene stepped in and flung herself around my neck with the words: "At last I've found you, after such a search! I thought I'd lost you!" I asked her how she'd found her way to me, and whether her uncle might have thrown her out. Then I heard, to my considerable pain, that her aunt had refused to accept her and that her uncle had placed her with a tailor by the name of Pohl, and had given her hard words and a little money instead of gentle treatment and loving care. I boiled with rage. She soothed me. We sat there in this way until it was dark. Sadly engaged with my own thoughts, I accompanied her home. From then on I visited her at the Pohls', who took her to themselves in a very friendly way; but she was in a very difficult situation. This couldn't go on for long; the coarse company of the apprentices offended her sensibilities. Her uncle got a passport and a hundred florins for her and instructed her to go back to her mother. I took her one morning in a fiacre out to the country, where I rented a pretty and friendly little room with some kind-hearted peasants, where she could live for herself, for nature, and for me in serenity, repose, and contentment. Fresh milk, a pretty garden, Schönbrunn near by, and warm-hearted service are making her stay there as agreeable as possible. I go out every day, sometimes every other day. Then it's always a festival of hearts. The food is brought to us from a nearby inn.

Since then I've also seen Clary once a day, often twice. But my heart is strangely torn, as though split, between Helene and Clary, who both love me boundlessly and both of whom I love in quite different ways. Helene knew about my friendship with Clary. And the latter now learned for the first time what I'd been up to in Heidelberg, how I'd been unfaithful to her. My confession shattered, enraged her. I hoped in vain to lead her back to calmness by words of love. The image of an interesting and endearing rival in love was too painful for her and too vividly before her eyes for the furies of jealousy not to have scourged her heart. Meanwhile I promised her fidelity of soul and explained my entire relationship with Helene until, after a great deal of effort, I finally managed to calm her down again after she had been ill for several days because of the quarrel. I begged for a more intimate relationship, in order to test her. To my astonishment she refused. I yielded to her stern will.

Irony of fate. Our meetings have had something tense about them ever since. Many letters have been written. Thus, one day went by after another. Frankly speaking, there were moments when I wanted to be far away from both of them, in order finally to escape from the painful situation, which was quite alien to me. All this running about, shopping, taking care of things, paying for everything, getting medicine, all this annoyance and waiting will soon be the death of me. I hope it will all take a different turn. Yet in all this, my situation has something so original and piquant about it that I really can't describe it properly, and so I often must laugh at my own activities which seem quite alien to myself.

22 May

The last three weeks of my sojourn here belong to the most painful of my life. Here, in a few words, is what has happened.

My money, which had been dwindling more and more because of Helene's expenditures, was at an end. Too proud to borrow, I had built all my hopes on a small draft, which I was about to send off or cash, when I got a letter from my aunt saying that my servant Peter had contracted some debts to her on my account, and had inconvenienced her very much, with all my many things and cases. Such reproaches from my mother's beloved sister because of a miserable one hundred florins, which for the moment were vital to me, aroused all my sensitivity. I sent the draft to her with the request to be kind enough to send me whatever remained after she had deducted what I owed. Meanwhile Helene's little household fell on me entirely. The small amount of money her uncle had given her was gone and, after all, she still had to go on living.

An excursion to Laxenburg and Baden, which we had undertaken for a few days to dissipate our worries and cares and which was most picturesque, was to worsen our already critical condition still further because of its consequences. The morning was cool; we had dressed very lightly and, unaware of the storm that was coming up, we had thrown ourselves with no particular anxiety into a basket carriage that took us back home at a brisk pace. Meanwhile the storm overtook us; we were soaked through. It grew very cold; we arrived shivering. I wrapped my little one up in the cover coat, put her to bed, and begged her to take care of her health, since she was probably to become a mother. Soon I was on my way back to Vienna, where business awaited me. I had a lot to do that day. I went to bed exhausted.

The next day I had a scene with Clary about confidence that upset her and me so that I came home half conscious; a new fright awaited me there. A note written very urgently from Meidling in obscure language foretold a catastrophe that was bound to fall on both of us. My last two gulden helped me get a fiacre that took me to Meidling at a flat gallop. I found Helene in the most horrible cramps and convulsions; her face was swollen. But she recognized me and—oh, the power of love—she soon felt better. The pains dwindled away and I soon recognized her beloved features and her brightness again. For five hours she had hovered between life and death. The doctor had been there and told her the illness was due to birth pangs mingled with a rheumatic poison moving around in her stomach. I picked her up in my arms and put her into the carriage, and I put her to bed at my place, where I nursed her until 10.30.

Meanwhile I felt a slight sickness in my own body. I got a sore throat, headache; I had no money to consult a doctor; visiting Helene daily and nursing her, ill, languid, with no strength left to plan or do anything, I shrank in my anxiety and need into a half shadow. It was a frightful time I shall never forget. I not only have a clear idea of marriage now, with its cares and joys, but the whole marriage relationship is no longer an enigma for me, since I've led a quasi-married life; and when the real one comes along in the future I shall be up to it and more or less familiar with all it offers and denies one. I was quite skilful as a nurse. I could read everything in Helene's eyes. I also observed that my zeal in waiting on her did her a lot of good. The idea that she might be a mother made her blissful. She lives in the future and dreams of maternal happiness and the joys of children, so when she paints these pictures with her characteristic liveliness tears of emotion often come into my eyes. Every time I had to go to town it seemed to me that my better half was staying on at her side. And my steps became quick and hasty as I approached my precious, much beloved Meidling.

But again and again my heart would swell in anxiety whenever I had to visit Clary, who like Héloïse would press her love upon me in swooning rhapsodies. However much I considered it my duty to manifest a response to this old love of mine, I still loved her spirit and respected and treasured her with all my strength, but it was always a sort of agony and sense of duty rather than my heart that led me to her. What torment! Her letters were full of grim melancholy and a depth of feeling that can be understood only by someone capable of appreciating it. Often, at home, as I lie stretched out on my sofa contemplating my present condition, repose from my worries as a lover and husband illuminates my future and past with the critical gaze of reason; I leap to my feet in spite of myself and condemn my boundless weakness of character and make myself the bitterest reproaches for being able to lead such a pointless and self-destructive life. But then habit, with its sweet and soothing accompaniments, and the affection I feel for both women slips back into my heart with such seductiveness that sister reason has to say good-bye and I have to say to myself, "Things really are for the best this way." It is then, when I am seized and mauled by the demon of unrest, that I would love to go up the tower of St. Stephen's or the Mölker Bastei, where I could commune and argue with myself and my destiny in the open.

I had had a completely different conception of my stay in Vienna, from a scientific point of view too. I had proposed to make Hammer's acquaintance, visit him very often, listen to astronomical seminars in the academy, and collect interesting statistical data on Vienna and the Austrian states. But all that has more or less evaporated. Reduced to my womanizing, I find I have only a few free moments left for paying superficial consideration and attention to and noting the most important things. I read a little about Vienna in an historical work. I also survey everything around me with the eyes of criticism, but I lack, after all, the characteristically fresh interest of a traveller given over only to his reflections. In general, I observe to my own vexation that my interests, which I should most gladly direct to the state and to my own future activity, are taking on an ideal tendency that doesn't seem to me to have the slightest practical utility. Will the empirical side, the pleasure in what is useful, grow with the years or will an indifference to earthly things always be my constant escort?

Others in my place would have made a point of having the treasures of the palaces, the museums, and the art collections opened up in order to gather material for all sorts of useful reflections; they would have gone to parades, manœuvres, public festivities, the Prater festivals, and public institutions to study the spirit of the people in this way and the national character through a physiological, political, or other sort of glass. They would have set out for themselves a daily occupation of self-education or of satisfying their thirst for knowledge through libraries or exchanges with interesting people. But nothing of this will do for me and my metaphysical mind, which turns aside from all these trivialities as they manifest themselves in those eternal delusions, time and space, that are the idols of the average man, stamped though they are with the brand of utter worthlessness. My mind keeps me permanently in the zones and regions of abstraction and makes everything else so repugnant to me.

As a soldier I was quite alien to myself, as a student less so; now as a successful lover still more so again; perhaps I'll find myself and my inner destiny. Then I'll cling to the kernel of life, which so far has always slipped out of my grasp like a glistening eel, so that nothing in the world will ever wrest it away from me. In every respect Vienna has been a very important place of sojourn for me, since it was here that I put my ego to the test of reason and reflection and spent many a lonely evening with thoughts that led to happy results. I should be only too glad to see Hungary, but I shall not be able to. I often had the intention of going to the Belvedere Palace, but I found no time for that either. To make up for it I often go to the theatre. I recently saw Schiller's *Maria Stuart* played by Loewe.* My whole being dissolved in raptures at the perfections of both the poet and the players, who linked hands in harmony. I would have been very happy to see Schroeder,† who gave an excellent performance as Elizabeth in Grillparzer's *Sappho*, but it was not to be.

In general, I don't enjoy Vienna very much. My whole being and all my time are divided between the two women. On occasion, as I saunter in the evening to the canal and meditate on my peculiar star, on the strange entanglements and manifold crisscrosses of my destiny, I'm impelled to believe that I have been chosen for an eternally restless and

* Ludwig Loewe (1795–1871), famous actor at Vienna's Hofburg theatre (Ed.). † Sophie Schroeder (1781–1868), tragedienne at Hamburg and Vienna (Ed.).

constantly changing life. Sometimes I compare myself with a wormy apple which, brought to early maturity by an insect's poisonous bite, attains its earthly goal in complete measure; then I dream of philosophical happiness and serenity for my restless spirit that after years of roving back and forth attained a robust intensity that would never have been achieved in favourable circumstances.

What pleasure it must be to find oneself in everything that one was, is, and will be, and to be able to arrive at a categorical conclusion with respect to the natural necessity of one's earthly purpose. It will, I hope, still come to that. If I am in time and space, then that which I am must also shape itself in time and space; so patience and endurance, Boris, the struggle within you will one day give you a splendid victory. I must still work and think strenuously. Therefore, Göttingen for practical sciences, and for the ideal sciences half a year's sojourn in Berlin under Hegel's tutelage.

28 May, Vienna

Parting from Clary yesterday was heart-rending. I see only now what I mean to her. It was with effort that she could still stand up. Tears long stored up seemed to cloud her eyes, yet she was unable to weep. The pain was stronger than she herself; I could see that, until she took hold of herself and stumbled out of the room. One last glimpse of a brimming soul in which could be heard, "Forget me not, beloved," and my lover had vanished, perhaps for ever. Troubled and sad I slipped back home to pack. My things were soon in order; I played a few more of my favourite tunes on my little piano, which I'm going to miss very much. At nine I went to see the good Hennigs. Their sympathy for my fate could be seen in everything. That night I slept very little. The singularity of my situation wrenched me out of sleep into the labyrinth of the future. Mixed sweet and horrible images churned up my fantasy. I didn't fall asleep until morning.

The coachman awakened me. In half an hour I was ready.

Helene was awaiting me in The Lamb. We said an affectionate farewell to Vienna, then went arm in arm to the boundary line; Helene had an old permit that could no longer be used. We had hoped we would be able to get through, but an accursed Argus of a concierge held us up with a demand for the cards. I could, to be sure, show my own, but the Devil alone knew how the poor girl was to be helped through. For the moment we had to delay making conversation until the pass I had given the coachman finally appeared and saved us both. At Brigittenau, near the long bridge, we became acquainted with our travelling companions; they consisted of a faded, arrogantly boring Viennese and his hunchback wife who were journeying to Prague just to take their straw heads to some other place in Austria, the fatherland of morons.

The acquaintance was soon begun. There were two guitars on hand. Differences were overcome by music. A sort of pseudo-alliance came into being, based on a happy-go-lucky conviviality, that was bound to end with our separation in Prague. Charades were played, as well as the game of Geography, and songs sung; the weather was fine, the coachman made a merry clatter with his whip, the horses charged swiftly and easily ahead with the heavily laden rattletrap. So the time went by very quickly. For quite a distance we could still see the tower of St. Stephen's; the mountains on the other side of the Danube accompanied us for a while. The lunch was passable. Conversation with an Austrian invalid. Boring afternoon. Lodgings for the night in Hollabrunn.

29 May, Iglau

A pretty little town. A sudden change of air; rain and wind. The strange costumes of the women. A general view of Moravia—the Bohemian mountains, the situation of Znaim. A language of Slavonic origin; when it's spoken distinctly I can understand almost everything the people say. Marital scenes and little jokes in the carriage. The trivialities of the couple from Vienna. But we get on well together.

30 May, German Brod

A hare hunt; the poacher. The quantities of pheasants and hares. Convivial games and music in the carriage. A silly luncheon. A lecture. Love.

31 May, Bohemian Brod

The plump waitress. All four of us sleep in one room. Pretty country all day; the peasants' pub. I waltz with Helene. A splendid evening and a still lovelier night.

1 June, Czaslaw

A Bohemian spot. A boring morning. Frightful weather. Lunch in the post house. Billiards. An intimate conversation about past and future. A scandal about pistols and fireworks.

2 June

Arrival in Prague. A stroll. We had to spend two nights between Iglau and Prague. Both places were terrible, but we were happy and contented. We certainly made up the most heterogeneous carriage quartet that ever existed: Helene, the sweet, fiery, tender, sensitive, witty, beautiful, and sweet-natured being; Mme Schmidt, her neighbour, a spiteful, short-spoken, coarse, rough, stupid, and twisted woman; Boris, a thoughtful one, taking in the world with the eyes of a philosopher, a cold, serene, reserved, and warm-hearted friend of the Good; M. Schmidt, an average man who looks at the world with the eyes of the senses, violent, sanctimonious, ostentatious, and all on the whole a secret enemy of the non-Ego. What a contrast! Nevertheless there was peace and harmony among us all. We carried this to the point that we all four once slept in one room without embarrassing each other. During the day we generally played cards, sang, laughed, chatted. In the evenings we played chess. At night we chatted in a neighbourly way about different things. We led a life that even the angels in Paradise might envy if they were of the earth. The women were always on the lookout for each other. And Helene, even when she was teased on a touchy subject, always gave in good-naturedly. She really is like a mimosa, and she turned things aside so that everything ended with jokes and laughter.

I often see her deep in thought, twice with tears in her eyes too; this must be because of our imminent parting. It's quite out of the question for her to be putting it on. But who can know women? Which of them can love disinterestedly? But if that is the case here, as I firmly believe it is, it is the unprecedented devotion of an even rarer girl, who deserves to be treated in a way no married woman could demand. Whatever happens, I've never had such a psychological lesson. In any case, I thank the Creator for this rare encounter. The months of close living will always remain deeply etched lines in the pattern of my life.

The rest of the trip was like the beginning. On the last day the weather was excellent. Our night's lodgings outside of Prague were splendid. Bohemia, the whole look of the country, was of great interest for me since I had known it before. I couldn't pay much attention to details, since I was too busy with Helene. The picture of my imminent reunion with my family in Dresden is now the focal point of my thoughts. This is an important epoch of my life, which will have a decisive effect on everything waiting for me.

2 June, Prague

Earlier, I went off at once to the post, but the post carriage had already left; now I shall have to wait until Tuesday. The Three Linden Trees took us in. Bath. Brass bathtubs. Erotic fantasies in a Roman manner. Lunch in the tavern. In the evening, the theatre; rather shabby.

3 June

Today the dear sweet girl really did weep. She sees the necessity for our parting. Tuesday morning we part. I go

to meet my fate, she goes to her relatives beyond Dietz.
How sorry I am for the girl, how tender is my affection for
her! It would be futile for me to attempt to describe it. I
shall never forget our walk today. We had had lunch on
Färber Island, with a Bohemian band delighting us. The
pyramidal poplar arched over our heads in a broad and
lofty canopy. The cool fresh air was delicious. Our neighbours came for dessert. We drove around to Schützen Island.
The man at first bored me with all sorts of worn-out anecdotes, later with his billiard playing; his wife did the same
to Helene, until finally we separated, to our considerable joy.

We strolled along towards the Old Town, went up
Hradschin Mountain, visited the cathedrals, where there
are wonderful old works of German art, and finally we went
up into the tower. Prague with all its lovely surroundings
lay at our feet, cut through by the Moldau, like a steaming
dish of red crabs. The mountains of Saxony and Switzerland
towered high in blue lines along the horizon. The air was
heavenly. Emotion and astonishment held our enthralled
tongues paralysed. It was with difficulty that we wrenched
ourselves loose from the beautiful tableau. By sunset we
were in the charming garden behind the castle. Loving
couples, leaping fountains, and Helios's parting rays lighting
up the fragrant flowers and shrubs radiated enchantment
all around us. It was dark before we returned home. A little
ditty on the engaging guitar accompanied us to our bed.

4 June

Today I bought a copy of Homer. We're reading the
Odyssey with indescribable pleasure. The translation by Voss
is very good. Helene is alive to beauty and seems to understand the life of the ancient Greeks. As for me, the ancient
bard warms my heart.

6 June

I feel a drive, an urge to go to Dresden and finally embrace
my family there, but I'm still chained to Prague by the

fetters of another love. Oh habit, most mighty mistress and guide of mankind, have you so enveloped me that at the mere thought of having to leave Helene I shrink back? But there's nothing to be done about it. My departure is decided. The day after tomorrow I'm off. She is to go to Eger and Frankfort, and I to my own dear ones, who are surely impatiently waiting for me already. Yet we have spent blissful days of intimate dalliance here. There's not a region of this ancient Roman city that we haven't visited. Walks to the Wimmer gardens and the Canal gardens. Sentimentality in the evenings. Ancient Homer! You inflame my fantasy! With all our souls we've been following the ingenious, godlike Odysseus on his wanderings, suffering and rejoicing with him. Today my Helene displayed the most concentrated attention. It's unbelievable what slumbering talents lie hidden within this girl; if only they could all be wakened! I still have a great many hopes for the future, which she proposes to devote only to me and to perfecting herself. My half-year association with her has transformed me.

Chapter IV

INTERLUDE IN DRESDEN

7 June

Our bags are already packed. Tears in our eyes; the fateful hour is approaching. But she's very much in control of herself. I've taken care of her future as well as I can for the moment; anything else that's needed will soon be found. It was high time and necessary for us to part, before some unfortunate discrepancy crops up to tragically unmask the hitherto successfully executed pseudo-marriage. Last night we were still very gay. We went to Farber Island; more delicious than ever. A lovely gleam shimmered around its charming outlines. In the evening we went to *The False Prima Donna*, which amused me vastly. We were still very cheerful together. So tonight—a pain shoots through my heart when I think of it—is our last together. I'll revel once again in the heavenly possession of this precious creature; in her arms I'll forget my existence and the imminent parting. I'll embrace the future and the past in Muhammad's moment of paradisaical voluptuousness.

9 June, Prague to Dresden

Monday afternoon, having paid the bill, which was quite big, put our names down at the post, and taken leave of the city, little Helene and I, our night jackets under my arm, went out from the gate on foot. We went by the sand gate alongside the city with a big detour by way of the Margareten, where we refreshed ourselves with some beer, cheese, bread, and butter. There was a magnificent sunset; we walked steadily along the highway towards the station, which, however, we never did reach since it took us too long. We stayed overnight in Herrendorf, but we never got any rest. For in the public rooms a peasant wedding was being celebrated that let itself be heard far and wide, including in the little room in a sort of wing that after much pleading had been cleared for us; the most horrible cacophony and caterwauling. The aroma from the nearby water closet was so awful that I found it impossible to repress my nose's rightful indignation, though I smoked two full pipes in order to purge the air somewhat.

For the last time I was to rest alongside my girl. The thought seized me with all the agonizing vividness that can overcome a sensitive heart. She was combing her beautiful, chestnut-brown, waist-long hair. I sat by her side, observing her. The coarse merrymaking of the carousing Bohemians beneath, the peaceful serenity of nature outside; the bright rays of the full moon vied with the cloudy light of our little night lamp and spread a magical half-light through this peasant room full of agricultural tools. All this aroused in my soul a grim mood mingled with melancholy. I took the sweet child in my arms. Tears were flickering in her eyelashes. "When shall we ever sit so tenderly, so close to each other again?" she sobbed, hardly audible. With difficulty I repressed a heavy sigh; my head fell backwards on to the pillow; a piercing pain overcame me. I felt the power of sweet habit, gentle longing; the imminent picture of our parting hovered agonizingly before my eyes. Finally, after a long-drawn-out embrace, our eyes closed. During the night we awoke several times because of the noise and the scenes below. By five o'clock I was already awake. Swiftly I drew my darling out of the arms of her half-sleep. Refreshed by the coolness of the morning and greeted by the lengthening rays of the sun, we strolled down to our destination, the station, where we intended to part. By seven we were in Predigluck. The inn on the Heerstrasse gave us a friendly reception. Our empty stomachs found the meal excellent. I drew my weeping darling to my troubled but longing heart and flung myself on the bed, which became an altar for our parting love. Once again we tasted of the chalice of blissful pleasure.

Soon afterwards there appeared the diligence, which reminded me painfully of the sombre moment of parting. I tore myself away from my darling, bent and sunk in grief. "Hold me tight!" she cried once again, so that a pain shot through my very marrow. "Take care of yourself and your child!" I cried out to her, and there I was, as God had ordered, out of the door and into the carriage, where for a long time I was unable to recover myself. At first the passengers stared at me in questioning amazement; I must have looked very wild and distressed because they asked me whether I was ill. The fresh air and the jolting of the carriage finally brought me to my senses. Sombre and turned in on my own thoughts, which were following my darling on her way to Karlsbad, I reached the Lehlaan station, where a glass of Melniker revived me. The company, especially the conductor, was very cheerful. I could not be, yet I took part in the conversation and by the time we came to Laun, which I recognized again from 1813 and where our good Kutuzov died,* I was calm again.

The little town is wonderfully situated. I took a walk for an hour and a half in the mountains, where the post carriage drove more slowly. Later I was overcome by sleep, which did not leave me until we got to Töplitz at four o'clock in the morning. The sight of these familiar old battlefields aroused altogether peculiar feelings in me; I fell to thinking of the confusion of the past and compared it with the present. I thought of how, just six years ago, a tidy little cuirassier officer, I came through these passes with the regiment and how we heard the skirmishing of the small-arms fire of the French vanguard and rejoiced at it; how Protassov formed us by squadrons *en échec*, and how we approached the enemy on the way to Kulm. How we were greeted by a shower of cannon shell, how the day ended,

* This is an error of the author since Kutuzov died at Bunzlau (Ed.).

and how the next day we took Vandamme captive, and how the whole corps surrendered to us unconditionally in a state of rout. I thought of the camp near Töplitz, of the celebration we made in honour of the monarch, of the wild life, and of the present, so peaceful and more meaningful. If I draw a parallel between then and now, I must exult over the times gone by and rejoice over the better present, and feel freer and better!

With such feelings I arrived at the station. The first thing my questing, assessing eyes fell on was the monument cast in black that the King of Prussia had had erected in honour of his fallen officers. I stood in front of it for a long time plunged in thought; my neighbour from the post carriage aroused me from my dreams, which were devoted to the nothingness of all earthly existence, in order to invite me for a stroll to Mount Nollendorf. I said yes at once, and we followed our noses straight up the mountain. A philosophical walk. The gentleman displayed gifts and intellect. A lovely view from on top, of Bohemia and the mountains. The diligence was to leave at one. Lunch in Peterswald. Heat. Passes. Thoughts of Helene. A view of Dresden. I scarcely had caught sight of the towers when my heart began pounding madly. I could no longer sit still in the carriage. I felt as though I had to leap out and fall into the arms of my family. At half past seven we arrived. Customs held me up for a long time. I stopped at The Rose. The servant was sent to find out where my family were staying. Meanwhile, I took a bath, where I was surprised by Peter.

8–14 June, Dresden

That same evening I saw the Prince, my grandfather; our joy was unfeigned. I saw Mlle Eckart again, the old servant, the pugs, all my old acquaintances after two and a half years; the furniture and the arrangement of the rooms were still the same. But I found the Prince very changed; grief seemed to be devouring him, for the soul of the whole house, my dear grandmother of blessed memory, was missing. The following day I was lodged in The Anchor. I was to live there at his expense. That suited me very well indeed. At two in the afternoon from then on I always appeared for lunch; in the forenoon I was to come only around half past nine, to greet the old man in bed. I was to turn up in the evenings at six and then again at nine for vespers. This was how regularly the visiting hours were laid down; they were punctually kept, too.

I spent the rest of the day walking, writing, and reading. In this way the time passed, one day like another, until two letters—one from Vienna, the other from Hof—wrenched me out of my indifference. Both gave me a great deal of pleasure, especially the second; Helene's pain over our parting, her wealth of soul poured out over the precious sheets with such warmth and tenderness. Clary seemed more composed; her spirit rose above the moment and like an eagle hovered aloft in the higher altitudes, to me like the ideal of the loveliest femininity. I answered both of them immediately. I wrote a letter to Helene's mother; I owed her that much consolation. How it was taken, and what effect it had, I am very curious to learn.

Dresden's surroundings are peculiar to it and are very lovely. Today I was on the Easter Meadow and in the Brühl Terrace. Everything beckoned to me radiantly. Heaven and earth, trees and people all seemed so friendly, so bright. Prince Repnin* has left an eternal memory here among the people, but it is accursed, and rightly so. He behaved quite abominably; he did his best to inflame the poor oppressed Saxons against the Russians. Both he and they were successful. Woe to them—Nemesis will surely seize them one day.

I have a little piano in my room that gives me a lot of pleasure; though a little tin box, it produces chords that sound more ideal harmony in my soul than on the piano

* Prince Nikolay Vassilyewitsch Repnin, Governor of Saxony in 1813 (Ed.).

itself. I'm also very happy with my books. Whenever I look at my old notebooks and think of what I've written down and heard, and of how little progress I've really made in science, and of how far I still am from true wisdom, I feel despair. The opera house is magnificent; Marconi's *Jean de Paris* was very edifying. Though not classical, the music was beautiful. The composer's élan was really splendid, and the subject very fetching. Yesterday I saw *Don Garzio, Doctor of his Honour*, by Calderón. The ensemble wasn't bad; the production passable. Withal, however, the subject was not suitable for our stage. The tragedy left an unpleasant depression with me. In general I prefer to read tragedies, except for the classical ones such as Schiller's *Don Carlos, Wallenstein*, or Goethe's *Tasso*, which I prefer to see, since they can thereby exercise their full effect.

13 June

Since the day before yesterday I've been plagued again by the demons of jealousy and dejection at the same time. Really, what a strange contrast in my inner being! I don't understand it. Mlle Charpentier, in whose witty company I spent some very absorbing hours and whom I've already revisited, yesterday revealed to me, however cleverly she tries to conceal it, only too distinctly the weakness and vanity of her sex. Her affected though somewhat old-fashioned make-up and all sorts of movements and remarks amused me mightily, though at the time I saw through them immediately.

The Eckarts are aiming at a match! Ha ha!

17 June, a walk into Saxon Switzerland

Correspondence in the afternoon; a letter to Mama. Afterwards I went down into the garden of the winter building, from there to the great wheel, and finally up the little tower, from where I had a heavenly view of Dresden and its surroundings, as well as a glimpse of Saxon Switzerland.

19 June

Yesterday I rose with the larks. The morning was magnificent. Involuntarily I broke into the melody of the Swiss family: "Oh how wonderful, oh how lovely!" Everything around me was celebrating a rebirth after beneficent repose. I had my morning contemplation on the Rasenberg, in the favourite spot of my blessed grandmother; I plucked a bouquet and walked in the fields. Graul was waiting there for me. Soon afterwards, I put my little pack on my back and we started walking not to Pirna but to Pillnitz, because I wanted to begin where I should have stopped according to what grandfather had wanted. There we said good-bye to each other. Like an overloaded mule I went straight on towards the Porschberg, from which you can see Dresden and the entire Elbe valley. Lunch in Lohmen at two. A nap. At 3.30 I set out; I went through a fine forest to the Bastei; an astonishing sight. The Elbe valley at my feet, three mountains looking up to heaven like three giants in front of me. A school-teacher with eighteen children, all blooming, healthy, and full of zest; it's real bliss to see the coming generation in its ripening strength.

Rathen, in the evening

I arrived very tired, boarded a little boat, and had myself taken by two nice young chaps to the Königsnase and then back again. This cliff had a very strange shape. It looked exactly like the profile of the unhappy Ludwig.* I stood in front of it for a long time and reflected on the destinies of peoples and monarchs; the revolution with all its atrocities passed before my imagination. Darkness had enveloped me when I got to the tavern. An egg cake and black peasants' bread accompanied my exhausted body to bed.

Bad Schandau, in the morning

The trip here was heavenly. As travelling companions there were two peasant women with whom I had a most

* Probably Louis XVI; Ludwig in the original German (Ed.).

charming conversation. They told me all sorts of stories about the last war and complained bitterly about the Russians, who in my time had behaved here most barbarously. If you only knew, I said to myself, that you have one of those invaders sitting by your side right now you'd speak more gently. But I let them chatter on.

Bad Schandau is situated very invitingly on the Elbe, whose waters bathe the walls of the city. The baths lie up ahead, in the valley. Before settling in I took a look at everything. The whole layout pleased me enormously. I decided to rest here for a few days and to make my trips from here. There was, to be sure, no company here, but solitude is something I require just now. I have so much business to get through with myself that I need no one around. No bathing place in the world can be so lonely and abandoned as this most charmingly situated little place. The only ones taking the baths are an invalid lieutenant and myself, though there are a great many people travelling through.

20 June, Bad Schandau

For a few days now I've been living in enchanting solitude. I take strolls every day, in the morning and evening; I also take the baths, which are doing me a great deal of good. The water tastes of iron; it looks reddish in the tub. Among the Schandauers who come over here a lot I've found some very nice people, among others a pastor in whom I instantly discerned a scholar; our conversations, which generally deal with pedagogy, often turn very lively. The landlord's little daughter is round as a butterball and wears a high apron; she's caught the waiter's eye and behaves very prettily in the garden whenever she goes out. I smoke a peaceful pipe with my invalid Hennig and chat with him about bygone days of war. Today some burghers turned up again. The jabbering finally became very disagreeable. The Saxon is, after all, something of a fool, even though he can chat and jest quite elegantly. I would trust myself to pick out a Saxon among other Germans at once, he's so different from his neighbours and countrymen in his looks. Pedantry, gossipiness, and gaucherie are the badges of his coat of arms. On the other hand, he makes up for it by profundity, zeal, fidelity, and other praiseworthy qualities.

3 July, a walk to Tharant

I'd hardly come back from my walk to Saxon Switzerland when I decided at once, since my family had not yet arrived, to go to the mountains again; this time I selected the opposite direction and went towards the west, through the magnificent plain of Plauen, which I already knew from my army years, towards welcoming Tharant. On the way I was overtaken by rain, but the bad weather soon dissipated and the sun came out of the clouds once again.

Towards noon the dark valley full of shade trees revealed itself, and I caught sight on the left of Tharant's lovely ruins, with the peaceful little city at their feet. Going straight to the bathing house I ordered a place at the table and went out until lunchtime to the sun temple, where I had a beautiful view of Tharant. Very soon my stomach lured me back into the dining room. As I passed by, a wonderful voice reached my ear. I asked the waiter who the girl might be who was singing so beautifully. "A Mademoiselle Krause from Dresden," he said, "who comes here for the baths. Her father is a physician and an amateur musician." "Announce me," I said. After all, I thought, as a foreigner and under the pretext of the informality of the baths you can make her acquaintance. Upstairs I found a musical triumvirate cosily gathered around the piano: the father, who did the accompaniment; the singer, with an interesting face; and an attentive listener, a Baron Ende, a scientist at the local forestry school, which has about 100 men in it. I was received very civilly; I asked them please to go on, and then I heard a bravura aria that gave proof of the tremendous scope of a voice that seemed to me extraordinarily rich and clear; I was completely enchanted. Unfortunately we were summoned to the table only too soon. I took a place opposite little Mara, whom I entertained as best I could. The girl has an indescribably penetrating gaze; on occasion it encountered my own with such challenging coldness that I became really quite dizzy. The father is bringing her up systematically as an artist and actress; he lets her run around all day long with all sorts of men and students. Keeping in mind this principle of the necessity and utlty of an emancipated education to harden her and make her impervious to the shafts of love, he is sending her next year to Italy by herself. Her naïveté, which made her address everyone, man and woman, in familiar terms, contrasted with her sixteen years and with the pretty, coquettish little Paris skirt, which was à jour until practically at her knee; it seemed an affectation to me.

Over the dessert there was some philosophizing. Schelling and Hegel were put on the carpet; my vis-à-vis displayed a great deal of erudition. The coffee made the conversation still livelier. At five o'clock I was to take part in a little musicale. Beforehand I went up on the ruins and looked around at the little city and the students. Before the appointed time I made the acquaintance of a professor who told me something of the situation of the local academy and of the sciences that were cultivated here, as well as of the way they were dealt with. The tone of the students seemed to me more than free. At 5.30 I was with the doctor. The piano was tuned, the little room filled up, and lo! there came into the room several interesting creatures with the sweetest faces. A number of classical things were played. Old Krause acted rather pedantic the whole time. The beautiful girl sang like a goddess. In this way the evening passed, until a few elderly ladies gave the signal for leaving. One of them, Mme Nostitz, who had two remarkably beautiful daughters, of whom the elder had completely enwrapped me with all the charms of her sweetness, turned to talk to me, and taking advantage of the moment I made so bold as to ask her for permission to escort her home. It was a long way, but it seemed short to me, for I was wonderfully entertained. The girls were clever and spoke well. With the promise to come again soon I took leave of them.

4 July, my family arrives

The premonition I had this morning was right. They're there, my heart's beloved! What bliss, what happiness! Restless, as though something were urging me on, I leaped early in the morning from my bed. I was dressed in a flash, paid the bill in a flash, and as though I were being drawn by some power to Dresden I made the three-and-a-half-hour trip in barely three hours. I was welcomed at the door of my house by Peter, who gave me the intoxicating news that the family had arrived the day before. I rushed off to see Grandfather, and from him rushed up to Alex in his room. But his room was closed; I had to go down to see Mother. My heart almost burst; tears welled up in my eyes. The door opened and through it I caught sight of the well-known figure of the best mother in the world; I sank speechless at her feet. Weeping for joy I embraced her knees. Julie, my deeply beloved and kindred soul, also came in, glowing with love! The scene was shattering; the embraces were worth a lifetime.

It was not until later that I saw my stern father. When I was allowed in to see him, he ordered me to be silent, as I was overcome by emotion and begged him, with heartfelt tears, for his forgiveness and his friendship; but I was well aware of what he was feeling and how powerful his emotions were at the sight of his eldest son. It was natural for him to repress them, and he left the room. I intended to be quite natural and to show myself to him just as I was, come what may. I was well content with that, since I knew only too well that he loved me, and how much he loved me. To Mother and to my sister I expressed myself fully. I found Alexander very changed. His looks had lost something; perhaps his inner being had gained all the more. The morning went by like a lovely dream. At midday we gathered together at the Prince's, who didn't let slip the opportunity to bring out his little jokes, phrases, and arresting familiarities, which struck my family, and especially Julie, who didn't know him, as extremely odd. In the afternoon I got a heart-rending letter from Helene in Frankfort; bereft of everything she's in the direst misery. As quickly as I possibly could I wrote to her and sent her money to comfort her as much as possible. Her plight gave me bitter grief.

6 July

They want to leave tomorrow, for Karlsbad. That's far too soon for this loving child's and brother's heart. I'm going with Alexander, as Mama wishes, through the Saxon mountains and the Harz mountains to Göttingen, where we are to arrive by the middle of September. Our road leads us by Würzburg and Frankfort. Homburg is three hours from there. I'm to see her again; my heart is pounding. Will I find her in good spirits and worthy of me? If it is as I wish, I'll take her along to Kassel, where she can spend the winter near me.

9 July

The others have left. The parting was painful. Can it be that I'll see them again this year? As they left Father embraced me. This sign of his paternal favour made me feel wonderful. The day after tomorrow we're to start off on our journey. I'm longing for it.

11 July, journey to Göttingen—Tharant

Grandfather's farewell was lukewarm. Mlle Eckart wept; the faithful soul loves us because of our blessed grandmother, whom she sees in us. All the servants, with tears in their eyes, wished me health and happiness. Peter, whom I'll be dismissing to please my parents, was supposed to accompany us. Our packs were ready. He carried them out to the edge of the city. Farewell, dear Anchor, dear Dresden!

Thank you for all the happy hours I spent within your walls!
At the mill we caught up with Peter. We had one more
drink, to a happy reunion, then I dismissed the faithful
fellow, who had served me honourably for ten years. When
we saw each other alone and helped each other place his pack
on his shoulders, we silently pressed our hands together.
And then, in the name of God, we went off towards our
destination. At eight we arrived in Tharant. We flung
ourselves exhausted into bed. In the evening: the ruin, a
frugal meal, bedbugs.

12 July, Freiberg

We got here completely drenched. The umbrella I took
along did yeoman service. The march today lasted four
hours. We were walking through a rough, wild territory.
Alexander made the time pass by telling me stories of the
life at home. He also treated me to some accounts of his
years of service, his turbulent adventures in Poland, etc.,
and led my imagination back to the long-since-forgotten
regions where once my wandering soldier's feet had tarried.
In this way we came to Grillenburg. A frightful road as far
as Freiberg. The marketplace here. Arrival at The Star;
luncheon at the table d'hôte. Limpetlike friendliness on the
part of the gesticulating, voluble actuary, Helliger. An
excursion with him. He showed me the town hall, the place
where the first mineral lode was found, the sculptured head
and the place of execution of the robber-prince Kunz von
Kaufingen, and then took me to visit his family. A siesta
at home. Letters. Supper. Intimate conversations.

13 July, Freiberg

Frightful weather. There must be some special process
going on in the upper atmosphere. The media of cold and
heat are engaged in an open feud this year; the changes in
temperature are great and so sharp that we are bound to
think that some meteorological revolutions, arising out of
the displacement of the poles, are taking place up there. After

the most frightful heat we ever had in Dresden, a cold wave
followed that made your teeth chatter.

In the morning I paid my visit to the rector of the university, Lampadius, an intelligent fellow who told me a great
deal about the structure of minerals and also pronounced
some excellent judgments concerning physics. He gave me
some advice about how to go about seeing some of the
geological sights here in Freiberg. I also visited Gerlach's
brother, a book dealer. I had a most interesting, Freemason
kind of conversation with him. From there I went with
Alex and Mme Henkel to the museum. Piano playing. But
a Prussian minister of state fell foul of us and drove us away.
Luncheon in The Star. Afterwards we drove to the mine. A
philosophical moment down there in the dark depths.
Splendid paraphernalia and machinery to pump out the
water. A storm frustrated our visit to the amalgamating
works. I spent the evening with old Gerlach. He babbled
all sorts of things to me about the Masonic orders and, as I
noted at once, spoke only to hear his own voice and to give
the much-travelled half-instructed brother and master from
Russia a high opinion of his own Masonic insights, in which,
however, he succeeded only partially. Among other things
he called Freemasonry the religion of men, the activities
of the lodges a mere farce, and the basic principles of the
order *pure* morality—with the objective of maintaining
everything in man that was reasonable. All this seemed
very charming to me. So we parted, he very satisfied with
me and extraordinarily so with himself, I the richer by one
more experience of Freemasonry. There was a lot of talk
today about the comet, which was supposed to have brought
about the rainstorm and the frightful heat. What fantastic
nonsense!

14 July
Until about nine o'clock it poured as though from
buckets. We had hired a small gig as far as Chemnitz. The
clouds hung so low that we couldn't see a thing around us.

We crouched down behind in the old carriage with the umbrella spread out in front of us like a shield; we went that way as far as Lobkowitz, where we finally caught up with the diligence and got two places in the extra coach wagon between the boxes and cases. This drove us mad with annoyance; we felt like puppets wired between boards, we were sitting so tightly. On the way we took aboard a poor blind woman, whom the coachman, however, soon drove off again, probably because she wasn't pretty enough for him. We didn't get to know the other people in the post carriage until we got to Zwickau, where we got seats in the carriage. There was one lieutenant there, a very nice chap who was travelling to his sister's wedding. The other passengers were of no consequence, except a student from Erlangen who displayed a great deal of erudition and with whom I had an excellent conversation. But stop! I had almost forgotten my pretty neighbour and her brother; I won her heart by offering her my umbrella to go to see the Schönburg prince's castle. Managed to pay court to her in the carriage.

15 July

We had forgotten to order seats in the post carriage, so today we were stuck in the extra coach again. We made the time pass very well by gossiping and chattering as far as Reichenbach, where we had lunch. Alex tells things with the same liveliness I used to have myself, but which I've completely lost now because I think much more. We always fall out whenever I counterpose my philosophical view of life to his own less correct one. Outside Reichenbach we met several families emigrating from the Pfalz on their way to Warsaw. Statistically I'm quite unable to solve the problem. With all the wars, can the number of people have grown so enormously in Germany that they're being expatriated from every region, exchanging certainty for uncertainty? Is it some dissatisfaction with the strict and oppressive measures of the governments or a real shortage that forces the people to it? Plauen, which we passed towards three and which Saxony purchased from the Reuss family, has a splendid situation. The region around here is wooded and has exactly the same stamp as nearby Bohemia. The fat merchant's wife in the carriage. Jokes. We made a lot of fun of her. Her sensitivity. Arrival at the Bavarian border. Customs and passports. In the morning, towards six, we're to arrive in Hof.

16 July

Memories of Helene. A visit to the doctor. A stroll. Diary. A scene with Alex. Yes, this I must illuminate a little more. I had gone to the post to pay the fare for our seats to Bayreuth. When I came back I was supposed to give him what was left of the money. A deficit of one florin turned up. He made a remark about it in a vexed tone; I snapped at him at once, very annoyed. A lively argument came about, which ended with insulting remarks. I dropped a word concerning the necessity for us to separate; it was endorsed at once and so we decided to part as soon as possible. He paid me 50 per cent for my trip to Göttingen and made another remark about the impossibility of our studying together. The incident was to be kept from our parents or disguised, and so we prepared to part.

When blood was running more quietly and reflection had once again mastered my impetuousness, I reproached myself for my hot-headedness and animation, since I can, after all, be quite composed and cold-blooded. Luckily for both of us an incident took place that brought us together again. That is, towards ten a gentleman who I had already heard was lodging with us in the same inn stepped into the room, and imagine my astonishment when I recognized my friend Holst, from Livonia, coming towards me with open arms. I was overjoyed. We sat down for a chat at the table, filled our pipes, and told each other what had been happening to both of us until then. He was coming from Karlsbad, where he had been taking the baths for his health, and was going to Switzerland by way of Heidelberg, where he

intended to visit some of his countrymen. As a fiancé,
escorting a Mlle Essen from Riga, he once again seemed to
me quite commonplace. I congratulated him heartily on
this forthcoming union. Then I told him of my wanderings.
Everything seemed to be of interest to him. Thus the time
flew by until mealtime, when we decided over a glass of
wine to do the trip together as far as Würzburg. Alex, who
makes friends easily, thought this quite agreeable and so we
stayed together and made peace by shaking hands.

Holst is a pedagogue in heart and soul; he has magnificent
schemes for his life and for his career. His spirit rises up
with noble élan to the divine, which seems to imbue him
completely. In order to put the seal on his education he is
going to see Pestalozzi* in Yverdon. His notions about
educating the youth of Livonia and Estonia and reforming
our pedantically routine schooling are very laudable; but
he lacks the means to carry them out.

Departure from Hof. Cramped; philosophical conversations in the carriage; boring company. Supper in a tavern.
Fine trout. Arrival in Bayreuth. I went to see Jean Paul.
He's in the country. Lunch in the village. Pretty countryside
as far as Bamberg. Helene's name in the register. Surprise.
A stroll. A beautiful bishop's palace. I enquired about
Helene, casually, and heard only nice things. Warm beer
at a tavern in the evening. Then a philosophical conversation, which bored Alex.

17 July

Early departure. Silence. Holst asleep. Fine country as
far as Würzburg. Arrival. I raced after Helene's trail.
In The Eagle I finally heard good news. She is said to have
turned up everywhere, quietly and demurely. Alex is staying
here. Holst is going on to Heidelberg.

* The learned Heinrich Pestalozzi (1746–1827) directed an academic
centre at Yverdon from 1804 to 1825 (Ed.).

Chapter V

A HOUSE FOR HELENE

18 July, Aschaffenburg

Alone and sunk in my own thoughts I got into my return
chaise in the morning. The coachman drove whistling over
the lovely bridge on the Main. The day seemed bent on
turning very hot. We had been rolling along for two hours
when we caught up with what looked like a travelling workman. The coachman offered him a seat; the chap with the
pack accepted. We settled down peacefully together; I
instantly recognized a gentleman traveller. After an exchange
of the initial banalities we drew closer to each other. I
learned that he was a lieutenant in the Hessian guards and a
baron. I had known of the family from Silesia. As soldiers
we greeted each other with even greater fellowship. There
were a great many points of contact between us, and a well-
laid acquaintance was soon made. He told me a great deal
about his service and about Hesse itself, which was very
interesting to me. We had lunch in a village tavern. Here
over a glass of wine the conversation turned to love and
women, and this added one more engaging feature. In a
word, tormented by the pangs of love and by unsympathetic
relatives opposed to his marriage, he had undertaken this
excursion as a distraction and was just now on the point
of going back. This was just about the same as it was with
me, with the difference that my prospects were cheerful
and his were gloomy. We trustingly exchanged confidences
and, with a promise to stand by each other whenever necessary, continued our journey. In the village I had also made
the acquaintance of an ex-Napoleonist who was journeying

back home with a very beautiful wife from Hungary. Monsieur Frenchman was not bad, but his wife was charming. She was very pregnant and absolutely enchanting. The evening was wonderful. For about an hour we went for a stroll. The air was balmy. Our souls expanded; conversing intimately, we made our way into the city I knew so well. In joyful haste I saluted the Neckar. At the farm I enquired after Helene. Good news.

19 July, Gonzenheim, near Homburg

In the morning at 5.30 my skiff was ready, with the skipper in it. I gulped down my coffee. One more hearty handshake for my lieutenant and I was off, down to the shore and into the boat. The trip was rather boring, since the banks of the Main are flat, nor was the company interesting. I amused myself smoking and steering, and so towards eleven we came to Hanau. We went out on the shore, since we had a contrary wind and the boatmen wanted to rest. Meanwhile I made a sortie into Hanau. Argument with the officer of gendarmes and the skipper. The gig. The heat. Frankfort. Coffee in a little village. Arrival in Gonzenheim, a village half an hour out of Homburg. It was my plan to bury myself incognito in order to operate from here. My disguise, in which I meant to surprise Helene, had already been taken care of; a friendly peasant woman had taken me in very kindly. Towards eight in the evening, when it was already getting dark, I decided to go into the city to launch my espionage. The fellow in question wasn't there. I took my package and set out rapidly; I was soon in front of Hangar's house, where she was supposed to be living. My heart was pounding audibly. I took hold of myself, pulled the bell, and was already standing inside the entry before I had thought of what I was going to say. An elderly female and a younger one appeared in front of me; I stammered out something or other about delivering a package and about Helene Hahn; they said she was staying with Pastor Hahn in Gonzenheim, but if I would be so good as to step inside and refresh myself. . . .

But I had had enough of their faces. A quick compliment and *whoosh!* outside, in furious leaps and bounds through Homburg, on the highway, and in one stretch over to Gonzenheim in front of the pastor's house. With the words to myself, "If only you'd known in the beginning that she was only three steps from you!" I finally arrived. Now, stepping cautiously, I crept around the house. A ray of light from the lower window and two shadows moving against a lit-up wall heightened my curiosity to the extreme. I mounted a ladder leaning against the house opposite and was inspecting from above the interior of the room where I could see two masculine figures, but no Helene, when a house dog I hadn't noticed betrayed the eavesdropper. The Cerberus forced me to stop being a night crawler, and finally I went to the door and announced to the people inside intentions of which I was quite unsure myself. At the door the pastor, with a candle in his hand, and his son received me with a questioning look. Disguising my voice and pulling my cap down over my eyes I made much of holding out my package. Then I heard my darling Helene's sweet voice trilling down from above, "Is it something for me? Yes? Oh dear, I'll be right down." With a good-evening, be back soon again, I slammed the door in the face of the people downstairs and was out in the open air, giving myself a breathing spell.

In another second I would have betrayed myself by some rash action. Should I go back again and reveal myself, or go off to Homburg and hang about there a few more days, undiscovered, waiting for her? The second seemed to be more advisable. Yet I had to see her once again before being recognized. So I went back outside the house, stationed myself at the windowsill, and watched her busily kissing my portrait. I could no longer restrain myself; I bounded into the house and into her arms, forgetting all other concerns. She fainted. I lifted her on to the chair. My kisses aroused her. We calmed down. Astonishment and embarrassment of the pastor's household. We were no longer in the least embarrassed, and chattered on until eleven at night.

20 July

Morning coffee in the bower. Closer acquaintance with the family. Helene as a housekeeper and nurse. Lunch with the ageing landlady of the tavern. At four my girl appeared at my window all dressed up. An intimate stroll. Caught by the rain, we hurried back. Helene told me what a bad time she'd been having in the house. Supper, then a blissful parting. An appointment to discuss her removal as soon as possible from the house, which is tiny, decrepit, and practically tumbling down; it's more like a cow barn than a pastor's house.

21 July, Gonzenheim

Heavens, how happy I am! What is greater than love! My Helene's has transported me into the realm of the eternal bliss of the blessed spirits. I've just come from her. Her kisses are still burning on my lips. Nor is there any feeling or any love that could be compared with hers. In the morning I found her dressed lightly in the yard among the cows and goats she was milking. I thought her indescribably enchanting in this domestic and rustic occupation. Involuntarily *Luise* by Voss* came to mind. We had coffee in company. In the evening a walk to the well. Stormy weather, followed by a fine evening. Our enthusiastic reunion. Appointments for the future. A decision: to take Helene along to Kassel.

22 July

A long walk with Helene. A reunion at the well. We go into the town. In the afternoon the whole house fell into the greatest disorder, since some building had to be started. Chess and a stroll. I took leave of the family and of Helene.

* Idyllic story of the Heidelberg poet Johann Heinrich Voss (1751–1826) (Ed.).

The trip to Frankfort. Stormy weather. Arrival at The Lion.

27 July, Frankfort

She's here at last! I'm very happy she's with me and away from that house. Towards ten Alex and I were going to our room when the servant told us on the stairs that a lady had been there wanting to speak to me; I could find her at The Swan. I bounded over there and knocked; a well-known voice said to come in—it was she! Our reunion was heartfelt. We chatted until midnight about our various affairs. Then she pushed me out of the door. I walked thoughtfully home, bound to her once again. In the morning I visited Helene and the Renners. Lunch with her. Alex made her acquaintance. Rather a stiff conversation. She made a good impression on him. Arrangements for the journey.

29 July, Vilbel

Already I'm in possession of my rose-coloured girl again. Already, after a long-drawn-out, an eternally long-drawn-out eight weeks I have enjoyed those sweet gifts that Amor has presented so copiously to us mortals. In vain had men and circumstances sought to separate me from her. She is mine once again. Her whole being was aflame.

Meanwhile I had rented two seats in the post carriage and a chaise as far as the first station, where we were to get aboard. I went ahead on foot. At the gate I got in, after pausing on the way to buy a copy of Virgil, and then all went by in a fast trot as far as here. A pleasant room was cleared for us, but we didn't let ourselves be shut up at all; we preferred fresh air to sitting around in the room and went off to the meadow, where we lay down beneath magnificent fruit trees and spent one of the loveliest intimate evenings I'd ever had. The air was balmy, the region charming. Everything we said to each other was so gripping and of such consequence that we returned home as though intoxicated by happiness and joy. There are some holy days in one's life; I account today one of them. A duet at the dinner table. A heavenly night!

30 July, Kassel, in the evening

So here we are, after so many boring days of travel, finally at our destination. Luckily the diligence was comfortable. But the company was beneath comment, except for an ex-academician who seemed to remember me from Heidelberg but whom I pretended not to know at all. Towards the end a number of extra carriages were hitched on to our post carriage that were full of rabble with whom you couldn't exchange a single reasonable word. Soon we were at the gates of Kassel. We had hardly got out when we made our way to The English Arms, where we have a nice room on the second story and are being waited on by very nice servants. We took a bath at once. That was very good for our weary limbs. The supper was heavenly.

1 August

In the morning I got into a more than slight difficulty because of my passport. I had arrived as M. von Güldenband. There was a small argument with the police captain. I settled the whole affair by a visit to Chief of Police Mangers, who took away my passport under a promise of silence, but to make up for it gave me a residence card in the name of Güldenband. At five o'clock we set out for Wilhelmshöhe. The afternoon was magnificent. The situation of this really princely castle and gardens astounded me. I was obliged to confess frankly to Helene that I had never seen anything of the kind that was lovelier. Physically Helene wasn't up to the strain. We arrived exhausted at the inn. Tonight will doubtless turn out a little more tranquil.

2 August

In the afternoon we went to the meadow near Au; very charming; it has the prettiest trees and a picturesque fishpond with swans on it. We had taken the Virgil along.

The witty poet and his descriptions, especially of the burning of Troy, stirred us considerably. An expensive tavern. A splendid evening. Home to a supper spiced with jokes.

3 August

We decided to ride to Göttingen. At six o'clock I tore myself out of a deep sleep. My passport turned up. Rode a mare; a miserable nag. Lunch in Minden. Fulda valley; the town has a very pretty situation. The Hanover boundary line. Red uniforms. A boring stretch to Dransfeld. I joined up with a student who told me how things were in Göttingen. A fast trot as far as the Göttingen plain. I tied up my horse. No letters at the post. I moved into The Crown. A student tavern. Before evening I took a good look at everything. Meyendorff gave me information on the academic life. I investigated everything properly. Difficulties about my passport and credentials. At the police station four times. Very annoying. Carousing with the students.

4 August

Impossible to find a suitable place for Helene anywhere. Heat. Lunch in The Blue Jug. My horse collapsed of fatigue. I rode cross-country to Dransfeld. A dangerous detour to Minden. The tired horse fell down twice. In Minden I tried to rent a country house. A surprise arrival in the evening. I found Helene reading. Supper: an eel; Morpheus.

7 August

Mme Siebrecht offered us her country house. We went there, looked it over, and soon came to terms. In the afternoon I read Helene Goethe's *Tasso* aloud. Walk to the country house. Helene surprised and delighted. An intimate evening. Tomorrow we move there.

8 August, in our "Sans Souci" at Kassel

After much roaming a place to rest at last. What a wonderful feeling it is to be able to say to yourself: Here you are, standing on your own acres! The rent is twelve thalers a month. For a pretty house with a garden it's not too much at all. We've settled ourselves in very charmingly. Our meals are made by Mme Rodemann, also for twelve thalers. We've got a maid for two and a third, a very respectable person. I've also taken care of our mental and spiritual nourishment; there is many a gem in the books we order from the circulating library. And what does a man want after all? What is so-called happiness in life but peace and serenity inside oneself and outside? That's what I've finally achieved, for a couple of months. To seek nature and to peruse her great book I merely go into my garden, where with deep pleasure I carry on a conversation with flowers, trees, and bees about God's omnipotence. To seek communion with the human reality I take my Helene on my lap, chat, talk to and caress her awhile, rejoicing in love. To seek myself, I discover myself again in thoughts. Who would dare vie with me in happiness? Only last night, stretched out on soft pillows, we dallied with each other. Looking on through clear windows Luna smiled kindly down on Amor's antics. A host of joys and love-gods swarmed around us. My girl was blazing with ardour.

[From the Russian]

What I am about to write must not come to the eyes of my girl. Moreover, I haven't written Russian for quite some time now. I look with pleasure at the old familiar letters, at the beloved script of my dear homeland.

In six weeks I'm going to Göttingen. She would like to live near by, but that can't be done; it's too dangerous. I intend to leave her here under the care of some old woman. She must perfect herself in the sciences. Let her gradually be weaned of me. Also, it's advantageous for me to leave her for a time. For I lose my health when I live with her. Here, there, sometimes at night, sometimes during the day— with time even a Hercules would collapse. And to tell the truth, with time it gets boring, interminable, to live with only one woman. The old demon is beginning to make me restless again. But it's sad to leave her so alone, without help. She's in love with me as though I were Christ. Only through me does she breathe and burn with all her heart. Let us see what God wills!

The theatre in Kassel is passable, the museum not bad; the library is said to be beautiful. The castle now being built is going to have a splendid layout and is supposed to become one of the handsomest prince's castles in Germany, as the architect himself assured me a few days ago. What always makes me feel so good about Kassel is that you can see the horizon everywhere ringed by mountains. The new city is very pretty, and the Frederick Square with its two watchtowers very nice. The banks of the Fulda are ugly, as is the old city, where the filth and disorder strike out in all directions no matter what the police do. I don't know very much about the life of the inhabitants otherwise, though I've made some observations about the pedantic and parochial side of their lives. The women here are uniformly not bad. There are lots of brunettes. I've also seen a great many beautiful children. The police are very strict; the system of surveillance is worse here than anywhere else; there are innumerable regulations. The coal here is the source of an important branch of commerce; the agriculture is blessed; the land is fertile. There is much fruit, especially apples and pears, which are very tasty. The government is accepted, though the opposition is not small. The Jews are endlessly oppressed. The artisans are well-to-do, since in spite of the poverty there's also a good deal of luxury.

I've never been as pleased as I am here; the life I lead is so comfortable and marvellous, it's hard to imagine. I've hardly ever been so tranquil, healthy, and gay as I've been here, and yet in spite of everything I don't feel entirely at home in this little Eldorado of ours. I have no idea why. The eating, the drinking, going to bed, getting up again, taking walks, reading and playing chess, chatting, kissing and caressing, the dalliance, the work, and so on have never been done with so much leisure, with so much comfort and pleasantness; yet I feel as though I have to get away. It's been three weeks now that we've met again and are together; they've gone by like so many days, rich in delicious pleasures of domesticity and friendship. Nevertheless it seems to me that Kassel is no more than an interim station. Could it be the feeling of being deprived of all my things, which are lying in Göttingen? Or is it the surroundings, the people, that make me feel so alien and chilly here?

We get up earlier than usual; our morning toilette is soon done, Helene's silken, chestnut-brown hair is soon combed, braided, arranged. My light summer suit is soon put on, the steaming coffee draws us invitingly over to the sofa; my little pipe is just the thing. At eleven we're reading, at twelve we're at the piano, at one we're at lunch, where we do ourselves well. In the afternoon there are campaigns and battles on the chessboard; then Virgil or some other classic unites us again, and our cosy little seat at the garden hedge comes to mind. The evening is so beautiful it warrants an excursion to the nearby mountains and fields, especially the Wilhelmshöhe; if the evening is overcast then there's a convivial tea, some games or music. A frugal supper of potatoes and cooked fruits ends the day. But night and Brother Fantasus beckon us to our double bed. That's how it is, day in, day out, in healing monotony.

And who could have failed to see the nice little house on the right of the highway, near the princely garden? But if you've never been inside, please, do come in! I'll lead you into my dearest own. Granite steps will lead you into our beehive; Italian windows, almost as wide and almost as high as the room, catch the light in great abundance. The anteroom, as nice as it is clean, shows you two doors. The left one leads into the divan room, in which there are soft pillows for your comfort and convenience, magnificent tapestries that will transport you to the land of the Alps, engaging drawings, and a little piano close by the window

whose tonal delights await you. The whole room is a rect-
angle, and from the window on the left you have a view of
the Wilhelmshöhe, from the one on the right you can look
opposite to the charming garden with its tapestries of
flowers, lawns, and fruit trees. If you turn left from the cor-
ridor, you'll be welcomed by our agreeable study; there
you'll see, on the left, in one corner, the antique little stove,
in the other our desk surrounded by books and writing
things; and, near by, the cosy sofa with a round tea-table
in front of it, and two pictures, hanging over it. A light
softened by the blinds falls on the yellow-tapestried room;
comfort and serenity have chosen for themselves a secret nook.
This door on the left leads into the third and last section.
This is the dwelling place of amourettes and fantasies,
the real "Sans Souci", the sojourn of delicious hours and
splendid dreams. A little paradise called, in a word, the bedroom: a half-darkness lies over bed and furniture; the former
is for two, large enough for the antics of ever-changing love.

10 August

Helene won't be having children, as I see; she too is in
despair about it.

12 August

I lead such a cheerful and satisfied life in our rural "Sans
Souci" that I have decided to call it that from now on.
Helene, to whom I suggested it, liked it too. We divide our
time between what is agreeable and what is useful. We do a
solid amount of reading and working. I try to exercise as
beneficial an effect as possible on Helene's spirit and mind,
and to draw her attention to the qualities a woman must
have if she is to lay claim to culture. She's formed the best
resolutions for the winter, when we shall have to live
separately. Her limpid mind and her industry can soon raise
her above the shortcomings of her previous education. Music
and drawing give her pleasure; I mean to retain her an
instructor, so that in this too I shall have no reason to

reproach myself. All the hints I give her fall on fertile soil, and with time they will doubtless bear fine fruits.

13 August

I shall put down here in a few words everything I've collected in the way of notes on Hessen-Kassel but haven't ventured to enter into the Diary.

This rather rough country of the ancient Catti has about 1,300,000 inhabitants, governed by a capricious, stingy, but otherwise very able despot. This extraordinarily rich prince* is not ashamed to oppress his people and to cut them off from any chance of attaining a moderate prosperity, even though he has a private treasury of 45 million thalers. Not content with having produced eighteen children by a mistress and thus having introduced confusion into his family, he daily offends morals and justice by favouring things no private person ought to permit. The Crown Prince† is a worthy adjunct of the father and imitates him, yet the two live in constant hostility. During the country's Westphalian period the court of Jérôme was supposed to have been brilliant, and there was a great deal of money in the country. Now everything is dead. The merchant estate complains especially. The soldiery are very badly paid and stand out because of their braids, which look frightful. The present prince has done a great deal for the embellishment of Kassel and its surroundings; that must be said of him, but perhaps that would be the only praise one could give him. Of all the Germans the national character of the Hessians seems to me the deepest and most reserved. There is a lot of education in the country. The land is fertile, the peasants industrious. Kassel is a pretty little backwater of 14,000 inhabitants.

15 August, "Sans Souci"

Occasionally one finds oneself in situations that simply

---

* Wilhelm IX of Hesse, who ruled from 1785 to 1821 (Ed.).
† Crown Prince Wilhelm II (1821–1847) (Ed.).

cannot be described. That's what I'm in now. Without money or clothing (since my trunk is still in Göttingen, and all I have is two and a half thalers and a coat) I'm playing the role here of a grand seigneur. The promenaders greet us as M. and Mme Güldenband. How is it that, all at once and completely against my will, I've acquired celebrity that crushes me to the ground? Because the Prince deigned one evening to overhear me at a musical entertainment and has told the story further. I'm beside myself. And it can have terrible consequences. I can withdraw as much as I wish, but there is always someone around our house to catch sight of the mysterious strangers. If the Chief of Police keeps quiet and my family learn nothing of it, that will suit me very well. I really must roar with laughter when I think of having attracted the attention of all Kassel with two pairs of trousers and an Italian cavatina!

16 August

If the consciousness and the knowledge of complete happiness in the present will serve as proof of domestic satisfaction and of love, then I am as happy in Helene's tranquil possession, here in this rural solitude of mine, as any man can be. Yet from time to time there is this endless longing in my breast for change and wandering; my gaze is so restricted, and my soul always yearns for the other side of the mountain. No lengthy repose on one spot; always the quest for what lies beyond. Then what is fate? What is happiness?

19 August

Now, following my twenty-sixth birthday, and before closing my Diary, I wish to say one more hasty word to myself. My parents have come to Ems; Alexander, who's taking the baths there, doubtless finds this very welcome. I'd very much like to be with them, but that's impossible because of my purse and circumstances. For another four to six weeks Helene and I are going to stay on here in our seclusion. Then it's off to Göttingen and from there, God willing, back to Russia. How all that will take place I have no idea, nor do I want to have any, since ruminating about it would be merely a waste of time and also evoke futile worries that, in any case, will come of their own accord. The beautiful relationship we have is developing into an enduring one full of consequences, since these intimacies and this deep penetration into each other's character is linking us together with a firmer bond. The days, filled with reading, music, gardening, strolling about, and household chores, flow by like a still, limpid rivulet between flower-decked meadows. I feel very well indeed; in addition I have much opportunity and leisure to meditate on myself and my destiny. Moreover, the regular way we live contributes a great deal to our bodily health. Today I thought a great deal and for a long time about myself and my fate. I'm no longer young; I am a grown man. Another few years and it'll be downhill all the way. The mature man stands there glancing back at his youth with one eye and at his old age with the other. Oh God, where has the time gone! The three years I'll soon have spent abroad have flashed by me far too swiftly.

30 September

Alex has come back from Ems. It was more than a slight surprise. He settled himself in with us and the day before yesterday went off to Göttingen, where he's arranging his affairs; he came back last night. Today I had to reprimand him for having treated Helene somewhat offhandedly; she complained and I quite civilly asked Alex to leave. He moved into The Court of England inn, where I shall see him often. In a week we're going over the Harz mountains to Göttingen. Helene is staying here. Everything is taken care of. I'm leaving her almost all my money. Autumn is advancing on us with rapid strides. The parting is going to be painful.

EPILOGUE

At this point the Diary breaks off, and even some notes Boris made later fail to give us a clue to the further fortunes of Helene. At some time, soon after the last pages of the Diary were written, there must have been a parting—painful, of course, for both, though surely more so for Helene. Perhaps she knew her Boris, and so knew what was bound to happen; perhaps she never believed in a happy ending and slowly had to learn to return to a disenchanted world. The figure of Helene, while appearing to us exalted by the love of her impetuous admirer, nevertheless remains remarkably pallid and shadowy in detail. Lovers are, as a rule, mediocre portraitists; whenever they attempt to portray the object of their love they are really portraying only their own feelings, that is to say, themselves.

If we did not know that there really existed a middle-class Heidelberg girl by the name of Helene, we might think that the writer of the Diary had invented her. With the help of their imagination poets allow a figure to appear, play a role, and to vanish once again into the wings the moment their scene is over. But Helene was no figment of fancy. She lived, she was young, pretty, in love, sad, happy, worshipped—and abandoned. That is all we know of her.

Our parting with Helene is final, but more has come down to us of the later life and fortunes of Boris. If all thirty volumes of his Diaries had been preserved the nineteenth century might have found its own Casanova. Like his predecessor, the celebrated Chevaliér de Seingalt, Boris Uxkull too was always on his way to the "great adventure". It did not have to be love, inevitably; war, politics, philosophy, the arts, distant lands, and alien peoples also enthralled him for a time, although not for so long or so intensely as his encounters with the fair sex.

War simultaneously intoxicated and repelled Boris, as a cavalry ensign and later as a lieutenant. With the hot-headedness of youth he longed to wrest from philosophy his own answers to the riddles of life. His interest in the concerns of his era brought him, as it did so many independent minds, into conflict with the all-powerful Chancellor Metternich, the guardian of everything in that era. The friendship of the young Baltic baron with Franz von Baader, the brilliant philosopher and intrepid reformer, seemed suspect to Metternich's secret agents. Like Baader, Uxkull himself acquired the aroma of a "liberal" and a "demagogue", and so was put on the black list of Metternich's secret police. Reports written on Metternich's orders by Prussian police spies concerning a trip of both "suspicious subjects", Baader and Uxkull, from Munich to Riga can still be read in the Secret State Archives in Berlin.

But his excursion into politics had no serious consequences for Uxkull. His Russian citizenship, his wealth, and his social position shielded him from Metternich's dungeons. Boris was always able to withdraw to his native Estonia whenever one of his escapades proved too dangerous or he himself grew weary of his restless life.

After his stay in Heidelberg Boris—as described by Karl Rosenkranz in his 1844 biography of Hegel—led "a magnicent wanderer's life. At one point he would be beneath the ruins of Ephesus, then in the snowy wastes of Sweden, then in Paris, then in Rome; wherever he went he was accompanied by a copy of Hegel's *Logic*. His entertaining letters to Hegel, especially from St. Petersburg and Paris, conveyed to the philosopher a well-rounded portrait of current history and vignettes from the social stratosphere. . . . Hegel was always on terms of friendship with Uxkull, who invited him to visit him in Estonia, and in many entanglements also tried to aid him with advice, which was accepted by

Uxkull with gratitude and with success." Although adventures of the mind were capable of enthralling Uxkull, still
it was passion that remained the axis of his heart.

Quite often alarming rumours about life led by the young
lord and heir to the Fickel estate would come to his home—
some acquaintance might have seen him at the theatre or
in a restaurant with an "unknown lady" in Zürich or Milan
or Vienna—yet Boris never had anything more to fear than
a mild rebuke from his relatives, and their concern that he
might contract an "unsuitable marriage".

Nor was this concern without foundation. Upon deciding
to enter upon marriage at the age of fifty, Boris did, in
fact, marry a minister's twenty-year-old daughter, Klara
Walter.

Even before this, however, Boris's life at home in Estonia
had not gone on wholly untouched by scandal. The cause
of this was a natural daughter, Julie, whose mother is
thought to have been an Italian nun. Boris is supposed to
have abducted her from a nunnery in Florence and to have
lived with her for a time in Zürich. There she is supposed
to have given birth to Julie.

Twenty years later Boris took Julie home with him to
Fickel, with the intention of having her legitimized as his
daughter. In doing this he had grossly offended the unwritten
laws of his milieu and had evoked its enmity, though he
suffered less from this, to be sure, than his daughter. Julie,
a girl of great charm, took refuge from vexations and from
the allusions to the "shame of her birth" in a marriage with
a man she did not love, a distant cousin of Boris's, a Baron
Uxkull-Gyllenband. She secured a divorce after only a
few years and then married a Swiss physician. Boris was
always on his daughter's side and took generous care of her,
but he was unable to protect her from malicious tongues.

But is there anything else we know of Julie's mother? She
is supposed to have been called Beatrice and to have been
remarkably beautiful. Boris never disclosed her real name,
and he was just as reserved about her later fate as he was

about that of Helene. A family tradition tells us that Beatrice married an Italian and lived on for many years in the Swiss Ticino, without ever seeing her daughter or Boris again. Julie was born in June 1821; hence Boris must have known her mother in the spring or summer of 1820, only a few months after the end of his great love affair with Helene.

Boris was twenty-six years old when he separated from Helene. His contemporaries described him as a "handsome, elegant man, with great blue eyes, a large but finely shaped nose, and a somewhat too mocking line around his mouth". His bearing and manners are said to have been "distinguished, and his dress as slapdash as an artist's".

Like many poets, painters and intellectuals before him, Boris too was drawn to Italy again and again. As early as the summer of 1815—that is, before he met Helene—he had, as he says himself, travelled through Italy "with Goethe in his hand", and then, after parting from Helene, he was filled once again with an itch to move about and with a longing for the South. Heidelberg without the great Hegel, who was now teaching in Berlin, could no longer attract him, and so, at the beginning of 1820, he packed his bags and stepped into the Florence coach. It was there that Beatrice—or whatever her name may have been—the "nun of Florence", must have managed to kindle a new passion in the heart that only a short while before had been blazing ardently for Helene.

Men like Boris, as Casanova put it so tellingly, love "women to the point of madness, but their freedom still more". A reputation for superficiality, faithlessness, and frivolity is naturally not spared those who live according to this motto; nor are they spared the reproaches of those who in this world not only hold power and respect but also allocate them. But surely we shall never find a great adventurer who is not ready to pay this price with joy!

A BRIEF SUMMARY
OF HISTORICAL EVENTS*

1801
Alexander I becomes Tsar of Russia.

1804
Napoleon Bonaparte becomes Emperor of France.

1805
Third Coalition war: Great Britain, Russia, Austria, and Sweden combine in order to restore European equilibrium; Prussia remains neutral.
At Austerlitz Napoleon defeats the combined Russian and Austrian armies.

1806
The Confederation of the Rhine.

1806
France goes to war against Prussia and Russia, defeats the Prussians at Jena and Auerstedt.

1807
France defeats the Russians at Friedland.
The Treaty of Tilsit.

1809
France goes to war against Austria.

* Dates are given in accordance with the Russian (Julian) calendar; dates according to the Western (Gregorian) calendar are given in brackets.

1812

Russia's refusal to take part in the continental blockade of Great Britain provokes the displeasure of Napoleon, now at the summit of his power. The Grand Army is assembled, consisting essentially of German, Italian, and Austrian mercenaries and of French troops, totalling 600,000 men, confronted by 260,000 Russians.

10 June [22 June] French troops cross the Memel (Nyemen).
5 August [17 August] The Battle of Smolensk; the city, in flames, is left to the French.
26 August [7 September] The Battle of Borodino, on the Moskva; an orderly retreat of the Russians to the other side of Moscow. Napoleon occupies Moscow, with only 100,000 men left.
3–8 September [15–20 September] Moscow is burned; Napoleon's peace offer is rejected by Alexander I.
7 October [19 October] Napoleon retreats, first towards Kaluga in the southwest, where the road is barred to him, then towards Smolensk in the west.
15 November [27 November] The Berezina is crossed.
23 November [5 December] Napoleon abandons his army, now shrunken to 50,000 men, and flees towards Paris.
18 December [30 December] The Convention of Tauroggen, between General York and General Diebitsch.

1813

German War of Liberation.

16 February [28 February] An alliance is agreed to at Kalisch between Russia and Prussia, whose armies assemble in Silesia.
5 March [17 March] Frederick William III's appeal "To my people".
15 March [27 March] Dresden is occupied by Russians and Prussians.
20 April [2 May] The Battle of Lützen; Dresden is reconquered.
8–9 May [20–21 May] Napoleon wins the Battle of Bautzen. The Allies fall back towards Silesia.
25 May [4 June] Cease-fire until 10 August; at Prague negotiations are mediated by Metternich, whose suggestions are rejected by Napoleon.
31 July [12 August] Austria declares war on France.

11 August [23 August] The Battle of Grossbeeren.

14 August [26 August] Blücher defeats Macdonald at the Battle of the Katzbach.

15 August [27 August] An attack on Dresden, held by Napoleon, fails.

18 August [30 August] In the Battles of Kulm and Nollendorf the French under Vandamme are defeated; 10,000 prisoners are taken, including Vandamme.

4–7 October [16–19 October] The Battle of the Nations, at Leipzig. Napoleon retreats over the Rhine; the Confederation of the Rhine dissolves.

18 November [1 December] The Allies resolve to continue the war.

1814

The campaign is carried into France.

20 December [1 January] Blücher encamps at Kaub; the main army crosses the Rhine at Basel in order to reach the plateau of Langres.

6 February [18 February] In a number of battles Napoleon thrusts the Allies back as far as Troyes.

15 February [27 February] The Battle of Bar-sur-Aube.

26 February [10 March] The Battle of Laon.

9 March [21 March] The Battle of Arcis-sur-Aube.

18 March [30 March] The Battle of Paris; entry of the Allies.

18 May [30 May] The First Treaty of Paris.

1814–1815

The Congress of Vienna.

INDEX

OF THE MORE IMPORTANT PEOPLE MENTIONED IN
THE DIARY